THE MILL CREEK

The Mill Creek

An Unnatural History of an Urban Stream

Stanley Hedeen

Blue Heron Press
Cincinnati

Blue Heron Press
The Rivers Unlimited Mill Creek Restoration Project
2 Centennial Plaza, Suite 610
805 Central Avenue
Cincinnati, Ohio 45202

ISBN 0-9643436-0-6

Printed with soy-based ink on recycled paper.

To Mike Fremont,
champion of Ohio's streams

An Apostrophe to Mill Creek

Thou rude little stream, so modest in mein,
  And flowing so quietly by,
No white pebbled floor or rock mantled shore,
  Nor cliffs mounting rugged and high...

Yet dearer to me than Niagara,
  Or all the grand rivers of earth,
For a spot I descry, thy waters near by,
  Marked out as the place of my birth...

'Twas there in the glades, and deep forest shades,
  My happiest moments were spent
Unburdened with care, and free as the air,
  A rustic young monarch I went...

When summer had come in verdure and bloom,
  With other young truants I ran
Along thy green banks, with many wild pranks,
  And oft in thy waters we swam...

With the hook and the line, unheeding the sign,
  We angled thy waters for bass,
Yet ever content, if homeward we went,
  With shiners enough for a mess...

But Oh! fleeting time, with ruthless design,
  Hath wrought many changes since then.
His magical wand hath swept the woodland
  And furrowed the faces of men...

—John G. Olden, 1885

Foreword

TO THOSE OF US who know the Mill Creek as a foul-smelling, waste-laden stream flowing through a concrete trench, this book contains some surprises. One of the important achievements of Stan Hedeen's book is that it helps us to imagine the Mill Creek as it once was—and as it could be again. Another is that it reminds us of the crucial contributions the Mill Creek has made to the growth and development of Greater Cincinnati. It is possible to think of the degradation of the creek as the price that Cincinnati chose to pay for prosperity. A more truthful analogy: the sacrifice of the Mill Creek was not a payment, but a loan, one that is now coming due. But more on that in a moment.

Two hundred years ago, the creek was a valuable source of water supply for homes, agriculture, flour and timber mills, and business and industry. The aquifer within the Mill Creek floodplain provided safe drinking water for numerous communities. The fertile floodplain provided rich soils for farming and the Mill Creek stream corridor provided an abundance and diversity of plants and wildlife. The forest canopy was so dense, Dr. Hedeen says, that a squirrel could travel the entire length and breadth of the 166-square mile watershed and never touch the ground. Early settlers enjoyed swimming, canoeing and fishing in the Mill Creek. They lived in one of the most beautiful valleys in the world and they reaped all the benefits of clean water and a healthy riverine ecosystem.

The Mill Creek: An Unnatural History of an Urban Stream also describes more than two hundred years of human misuse and abuse of an invaluable natural resource. This history of the creek documents, for the first time, how changes to the quality of the natural environment occur over time and how ignorant, careless and irresponsible human behavior can destroy and diminish the very resources that people rely on to sustain them. Sadly, today the Mill Creek is one of the most severely polluted and physically degraded streams in the United States.

The Mill Creek today presents a whole host of problems to people who live and work near it or in its watershed. To describe the creek is to write a catalogue of environmental horrors. Landfills, garbage dumps and orphan accumulations of toxic waste line the stream's banks (two Superfund sites are located in the drainage basin). The creek is constantly polluted by raw sewage from combined sewer overflows. After decades of residential and industrial pollution, very little of the once diverse biological population remains; what few fish species survive in the creek are grossly contaminated. In spite of a vast investment by the U.S. Army Corps of Engineers, flash flooding is still a problem. Except for a few public parks, the aesthetically blighted, virtually deforested valley is devoid of green space and recreational opportunities.

Historically many people contributed to the pollution of the Mill Creek unwittingly; they simply didn't know any better. Others may have thought that polluting the creek was a necessary trade-off to ensure economic development and prosperity. Now we know that we can't afford to write off our natural resources. We know that we have severe environmental problems today because in the past we did not take into account the costs of pollution, the depletion of our natural resources, and the destruction of our ecology. We know that natural resources are the base of our economy and that the health of the economy and the environment are indivisible.

We know that to develop a sustainable future, we must conserve healthy ecosystems, reclaim and restore degraded resources, prevent and reduce pollution, and assiduously comply with and enforce environmental regulations. Achieving sustainability will also require the involvement of all sectors of society in decision-making, environmental justice, environmental education, enhanced public understanding of the importance of environmental quality, and a heightened respect for the rights of future generations to survive and thrive.

We know that rivers and streams are irreplaceable natural resources and that they are extremely valuable assets for urban areas. We know that cleaning up the Mill Creek will yield a great deal more than the obvious—and important— environmental benefits. It will open new opportunities for job training and employment. It will enhance property values. It will make possible the revitalization of neighborhoods and communities. It will provide for recreation, parks, and greenways. It will create a renewed sense of civic pride throughout the Mill Creek valley. It will substantially improve the overall quality of life for Greater Cincinnati.

Nationally, there is new federal attention to urban streams and a concerted emphasis on watershed and ecosystem approaches to solving water quality and quantity problems. The catastrophic flooding of the Mississippi River during the summer months of 1993 taught us the need for a holistic, comprehensive, ecosystem-based approach to watershed management.

Federal agencies like the Corps of Engineers that traditionally used engineering solutions, including channelization, to reduce flood damage, now recognize that non-structural methods that work in harmony with the natural ecology can be more efficient and cost-effective. There is a new understanding that flood control projects must be environmentally beneficial and multi-objective in scope, providing greenways, parks and recreational resources, wildlife habitat, and community improvements.

Although ecological restoration of damaged natural environments is an emerging field, work is advancing rapidly around the country, providing case studies and models for the work that lies ahead on the Mill Creek. Today we have the benefit of learning from others around the United States who have been working to reclaim their water resources, including the Anacostia, Kissimmee, Charles, St. Johns, Chicago, Cuyahoga, Los Angeles, Sacramento, Willamette, Columbia, Little Miami and other rivers.

Since Dr. Hedeen finished writing this book in September 1993, several significant events have occurred which bring new hope, focus, resources and energy to tackle the myriad of environmental challenges and opportunities found in the Mill Creek watershed. First, we are developing political consensus. A Mill Creek Watershed Steering Committee has been created and is providing a forum for representatives of the thirty-four political jurisdictions located in the watershed to come together—for the first time—to talk about Mill Creek.

The Watershed Steering Committee also includes representatives from business and industry, from nonprofit groups, and from local, state and federal government agencies, including the National Park Service's Division of Rivers, Trails and Conservation Assistance. The steering committee is seeking an intergovernmental agreement among affected political jurisdictions to establish a permanent watershed council. The Watershed Steering Committee recognizes the need to develop a strategic plan of action, to enhance public accountability and effectiveness through the creation of annual work plans and progress evaluations, and to actively solicit meaningful public input and involvement in the planning and implementation of future projects.

Second, we are beginning to address one of the biggest sources of pollution to the Mill Creek: combined sewer overflows. Like many older cities, Cincinnati's sewer system was designed to carry stormwater in addition to sanitary and industrial sewage. Continuing development in the Mill Creek drainage basin has resulted in too much flow for the system to handle, and every time it rains the combined sewers overflow, discharging untreated industrial and domestic waste into the Mill Creek and its tributaries at 158 locations in the watershed.

The combined sewer overflows (or CSOs) have been and continue to be a major source of water pollution and a potential health threat. Under new and enlightened leadership, the Cincinnati-Hamilton County Metropolitan Sewer District is developing a detailed correction plan for CSO problems. Remediation of the Mill Creek watershed's CSOs will be a critical component of any future comprehensive watershed restoration strategy.

Third, we have launched a major educational initiative to address the widespread lack of public understanding and awareness which has permitted the destruction of the Mill Creek. In January 1994, a new community-based organization was formed, Rivers Unlimited Mill Creek Restoration Project (RUMCRP).

RUMCRP is working to build an informed and responsible public and to gain support and enthusiasm for environmental improvements. We are working to reconnect people with the creek psychologically and to help them see it as a natural resource worth reclaiming. We are providing teacher training and creating an environmental education program for students that encourages imagination, fosters creativity, and helps make the intellectual connections between human behavior and environmental conditions.

The board and staff of the Mill Creek Restoration Project believe we must work towards economically sound ecological restoration of the Mill Creek watershed, a working concept first developed by the Pacific Rivers Council. Because of the severity of the Mill Creek's problems, we must concentrate on ecological restoration and regeneration, and by doing so, create job training, employment, and community revitalization opportunities.

We believe people everywhere should be able to enjoy a healthy environment and that inner city, lower income neighborhoods have borne a disproportionate share of the environmental problems for too long. We believe that children need healthy green places for their physical and mental growth and development and that too many generations have grown up with only asphalt and pollution surrounding them.

We believe restoration and regeneration of the Mill Creek riverine system is now feasible and prudent, from both an environmental and economic standpoint, and that to accomplish it will require gumption and the political will of all those living and working in the Mill Creek valley. Reclaiming this resource will take twenty or more years. That's why we believe it is critical to educate students today who will become community leaders tomorrow.

Rivers Unlimited Mill Creek Restoration Project is proud to publish this history of the Mill Creek. For those of us who live and work in the Greater Cincinnati area, this book can be the starting point for future action and discussion about the Mill Creek. Beyond those geographic boundaries, it is a foundation for understanding the broader issues of the environmental consequences of human behavior. Now it is our profound duty to act on what we know.

Robin Corathers, Executive Director
Rivers Unlimited Mill Creek Restoration Project
November 1994

Contents

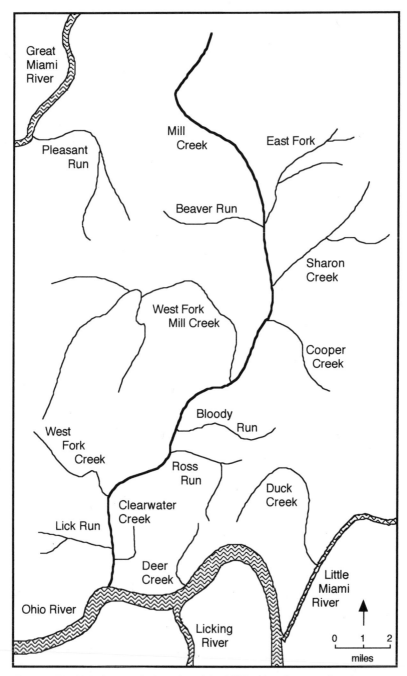

Figure 1. The Main Stem and tributaries of the Mill Creek and surrounding rivers.

Introduction

AS CREEKS GO, the Mill Creek in southwestern Ohio is a rather large one. The twenty-eight mile long stream is fed by several major tributaries. It drains approximately thirty-five square miles of Butler County and one hundred and thirty square miles of Hamilton County (Figs. 1 and 2). From its source at seven hundred eighty feet above sea level, the creek falls almost twelve feet per mile to its mouth on the Ohio River, four hundred forty-four feet above sea level.

Although these are impressive numbers for a creek, they don't come close to the parameters of a river. So why produce a book-length study on the history of the Mill Creek? A provincial answer is because the Mill Creek's role in the development of the Cincinnati area is second only to that played by the Ohio River. A broader answer is because the creek's myriad problems are typical of those experienced by urban streams across the United States, such as the Los Angeles River, the Chicago River, the Cuyahoga River in Cleveland, the Schuylkill in Philadelphia, and Rock Creek in the nation's capital. Metropolitan waterways everywhere suffer from the afflictions of sedimentation, industrial wastes, sewage, channelization, and impoundment. The history of the Mill Creek is the shared history of the nation's urban streams.

Like most historical studies, this one deals with its subject matter chronologically. Part One covers the early settlement of the Mill Creek Valley and the resulting environmental problems. Part Two is concerned with the spread of industry and water pollution in the stream basin. Part Three deals with the increase of population and sewage in the Mill Creek watershed. Finally, Part Four examines the role of the U.S. Army Corps of Engineers in the valley and

1

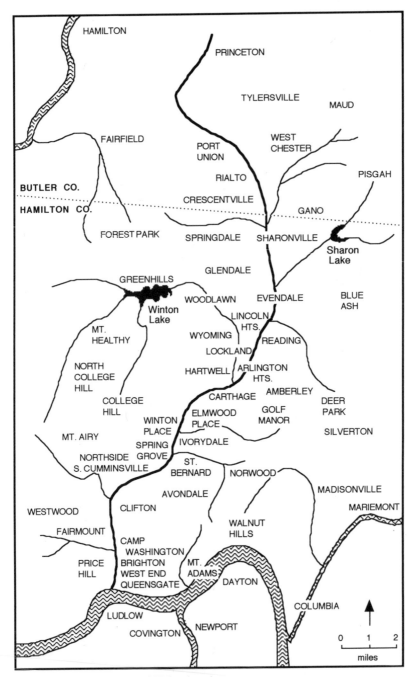

Figure 2. Place names in the Mill Creek region.

ends with a vision for the Mill Creek's restoration.

Abraham Lincoln succinctly reviewed a book by noting that "People who like this sort of thing will find this the sort of thing they like." I trust that you will find enjoyment and enlightenment in the following pages, although the subject matter is often not very pleasant to contemplate. More importantly, I hope that this story of the Mill Creek's past degradation and future restoration will motivate you to join others in understanding and reclaiming the stream running past your own neighborhood.

The author would like to acknowledge the creative work of Kathy Hedeen, who prepared the graphics in the book. I also thank Drew Diehl, Mike Fremont, and Tim Hedeen for their suggestions for improving the text. I owe a great deal of gratitude to Pat Leach, Ryan McClay, and Verna Wall of Xavier University's Biology Department, and to the helpful library staff at The Cincinnati Historical Society, and the Rare Books Room of The Public Library of Cincinnati and Hamilton County. Finally, credit should be given to Lucie Usher for design and typography and to Robin and Don Corathers for their invaluable contributions to the preparation and publication of this book.

Stanley Hedeen,
Xavier University,
on the banks of Ross Run

PART ONE

Settling the Valley,
Unsettling the Creek

Wild Turkey
Male.

Turkeys were abundant in the Mill Creek Valley when settlers arrived in the late eighteenth century. (John J. Audubon lithograph from the collection of The Public Library of Cincinnati and Hamilton County)

CHAPTER ONE

Maketewa and the Miami Purchase

[The Mill Creek's] been a lot of different colors—yellows and greens. It's never the color of water. And it's hard to explain what it smells like.
      —Debbie Wietmarschen of Reading, Ohio, April 8, 1984[1]

[I have] no artificial colors, irritating fragrances, formaldehyde preservatives, stripping alcohols or harmful chemicals. Because what nature created with care, only nature can care for. I am the best of nature. [Signed] Mill Creek Shampoo.
      —*The Cincinnati Enquirer* advertising supplement, March 9, 1986

Isn't Mill Creek a lovely name for a shampoo? Yes it is, unless you live in Cincinnati, home of Procter and Gamble Co. Late last year, P&G acquired Richardson-Vicks Inc., which makes, among other things, a shampoo called Mill Creek. To people in other cities, Mill Creek has the sound of pastoral purity. But Cincinnati actually has a Mill Creek, and it's anything but pure....
As for Mill Creek shampoo, the [P&G] spokeswoman concedes, "I'm not sure I would want to wash my hair in something with that name."
      —*The Wall Street Journal*, p. 25, April 11, 1986

FOR THE CINCINNATI market, the product could have been relabeled Maketewa, the creek's now-forgotten Indian name. Maketewa was well known to the native inhabitants, whose trails to Kentucky hunting grounds to the south and major Indian villages to the north paralleled the stream. According to legend, Maketewa's broad valley was the location of a great battle involving almost four thousand Indians. Early settlers in present Hartwell are said to have found bones and weapons thickly scattered over the battlefield site.[2]

Although earlier European and American explorers and trappers had wandered through the area, Thomas Bullitt and his party may have been the first non-Indians to use the Maketewa Valley trails. In mid-1773, Bullitt led a group of aspiring land surveyors up the valley toward Old Town, a large Shawnee village near present Xenia. There they gained the permission (or toleration) of the Indians to survey town sites in Kentucky. Bullitt and his party then returned

7

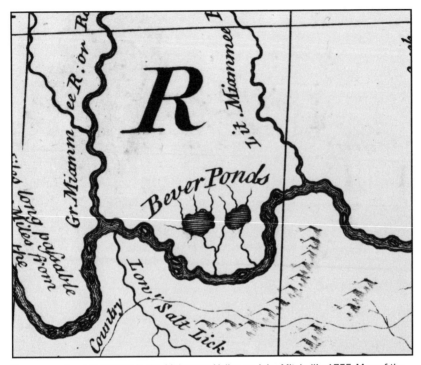

Beaver ponds were located in the Maketewa Valley on John Mitchell's 1755 *Map of the British and French Dominions in North America*. (From the collection of The Cincinnati Historical Society. B-94-252)

to the Ohio River and floated downriver to plat several Kentucky settlements.[3]

Pioneer villages proliferated in Kentucky in the 1770s. The Indians' resentment against this invasion of their hunting grounds soon caused the Maketewa Valley trails to become warpaths. Continued Indian attacks on the Kentucky settlements were answered in 1779 when Col. John Bowman led an expedition of volunteers up the Maketewa and Little Miami Valleys to Old Town, which they attacked and burned.

During the next year there occurred the earliest known Indian-pioneer confrontation in the Maketewa basin. On April 11, 1780, five hundred men from a large fleet bound for western Kentucky chased a hundred and fifty Indians up the Maketewa Valley from their Ohio River campsite. In August 1780 and November 1782, in retaliation for continued Indian raids on Kentucky settlements, George Rogers Clark led expeditions of volunteers north via the Maketewa Valley to attack Shawnee villages in Ohio. The 1782 expedition of more than a thousand Kentuckians included such notable figures as Simon Kenton and Daniel Boone.[4]

These conflicts took place in the natural setting first described by British explorer Christopher Gist in his journal entry of February 17, 1751:

> [The land is] well timbered with large Walnut, Ash, Sugar Trees, Cherry Trees &c, it is well watered with a great Number of little Streams or Rivulets, and full of beautiful natural Meadows, covered with wild Rye, blue Grass and Clover, and abounds with Turkeys, Deer, Elks and most Sorts of Game.

Gist also noted that "The Ohio and all the large Branches are said to be full of fine Fish of several Kinds." Several of these watercourses are shown on a 1755 map by John Mitchell, a map that also includes "Bever Ponds" in the Maketewa basin. Maketewa itself first appears on Thomas Hutchins' 1778 map as a "Creek 10 Yards Wide."[5]

Christopher Gist summed up his 1751 description of the area as follows: "In short it wants Nothing but Cultivation to make it a most delightfull Country." Thirty-five years later, Benjamin Stites came to the same enthusiastic conclusion as he rode through the southwestern Ohio land. Stites had come down the Ohio River in 1786 on a trading expedition from Pennsylvania. Upon landing in Washington, Kentucky, he was asked to lead a party in pursuit of Indians who had recently ridden away with stolen horses. Stites' posse of Kentuckians crossed the Ohio and traveled up the Little Miami Valley as far as the site of present Xenia, where they abandoned the chase. They then crossed westward to the Great Miami Valley and followed it south to the site of the present city of Hamilton. From there the party rode east into the Maketewa Valley, which they followed down to the Ohio.[6]

During the course of this journey, Stites noted that the fertile land described by Gist was easily accessible via the Maketewa and Miami Valleys. Stites returned to his native New Jersey determined to interest someone in a plan for settlement of the land between the two Miamis. Soon he met John Cleves Symmes, a congressman from New Jersey who had already shown interest in western colonization. Stites convinced Symmes to see the Ohio country himself in 1787.[7]

Upon returning from his Ohio tour, Symmes contracted with the U.S. Treasury Board for his Miami Purchase (Fig. 3). The boundaries of the Purchase were the Great Miami on the west, the Ohio on the south, and an eastern boundary line running northeast from a point on the Ohio twenty miles east of the Great Miami. The northern boundary was an east-west line drawn from the eastern boundary to the Great Miami, so as to encompass one million acres. The tract included the entire Maketewa watershed.[8]

In order to raise funds for his acquisition, Symmes began to sell land warrants even before he made his initial payment to the Treasury. Fittingly, Benjamin Stites obtained the first warrant on December 17, 1787, and on the same day contracted with Symmes for twenty thousand acres. The contract referred to Maketewa as the Mill Stream: "Captain Benjamin Stites enters ten thousand acres and the fractions on the Ohio and little Miami and... ten thousand acres on equal lines or Sections at the Mill Stream falling in to the Ohio between the little and great Miami." In an undated supplement to this contract, the stream became a creek: "The last ten thousand acres is to be taken in the following manner two Sections at the mouth of Mill Creek & the residue to begin four miles from the Ohio up mill creek."[9]

The Indian name "Maketewa" could not have meant "Mill Stream" or "Mill Creek," since Indians had no water mills. Settlers, on the other hand, desired grist mill and saw mill sites, as Symmes was well aware. His January 8, 1788 New Jersey newspaper advertisement for Miami Purchase land buyers emphasized that the tract supported "Every kind of grain and... finest timber of every kind known in the middle states.... Millstones and grindstones are found in some of the hills." The designation of Maketewa as Mill Creek represented a subtle commercial message in Symmes' overall advertising campaign.[10]

Notices such as the above achieved their intended results in the East. Enough land warrants were sold by July, 1788, to enable Symmes to start out for Ohio with a party of easterners. Near the end of August, the group paused in Limestone, Kentucky, to wait for provisions and a company of soldiers to accompany them to the Purchase. Symmes sent surveyors ahead from Limestone to more fully plat the Purchase lands. A group of settlers led by Benjamin Stites, who had likewise come west to Limestone, accompanied a survey crew as far as the Little Miami Valley. On November 18, 1788, at a site on the Ohio about a mile below the mouth of the Little Miami, Stites and his party began clearing ground for Columbia, the first settlement in the Purchase.[11]

The second settlement in the Purchase was established a few weeks later at Losantiville, literally "the town opposite the mouth of the Licking River." The site had been bought from Symmes in January, 1788, by Matthias Denman of New Jersey, who subsequently formed a partnership with Robert Patterson and John Filson of Kentucky. Israel Ludlow, another resident of New Jersey and chief surveyor of the Miami Purchase, became the third partner in the land venture after Filson disappeared during an exploratory trip to the Great Miami. Patterson, Ludlow, and a party of settlers sailing from Limestone arrived in Losantiville on December 28, 1788. They broke up their boats, carried the lumber to higher ground, and built their first cabins.[12]

Symmes and his party finally embarked from Limestone on January 29, 1789. The Ohio River was "several feet higher than had been known since the white people had introduced themselves into Kentucky." The party found all but one house at Columbia to be awash in the floodwaters, while downstream at Losantiville all the homes were clear of the flood. As they passed the flooded mouth of the Mill Creek and continued downriver, it became obvious that the townsite proposed by Symmes at the mouth of the Great Miami would be underwater. They landed instead on February 2 at the most northerly bend of the Ohio River in the Purchase. There Symmes decided to plat the village that he

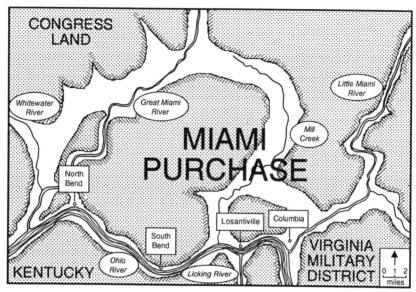

Figure 3. Southwestern Ohio in 1789 (with valleys shown in white).

called North Bend. Later in the spring of 1789, he platted South Bend near the most southerly point of land in the Purchase, on the Ohio about halfway between Losantiville and North Bend.[13]

Four settlements had been made on the Ohio between the Miamis in less than six months (Fig. 3). River transportation between them was possible, but the difficulty of rowing upstream made an overland path preferable. The major ford on the route was over the Mill Creek at about the site of the present Gest Street bridge. However, if this "first crossing" was flooded, a traveler was obliged to go some miles up the stream in order to ford it. In a 1789 letter from Symmes to Jonathan Dayton, the absentee New Jersey owner of the land through which the stream discharged into the Ohio, Symmes suggested that Dayton send out "some persons to settle each side of the creeks mouth," for "here in a few years will be a valuable ferry." Dayton liked the idea of a ferry, and asked Symmes to establish one in 1789 "on the best terms you can, for three years, upon condition however that it shall revert to me at the expiration of that time." But a Mill Creek ferry wasn't inaugurated until the early 1800s, long after the establishment of Ohio River ferries connecting Kentucky with the Miami Purchase.[14]

The first Ohio River ferry was launched in 1790 at the site of Losantiville, probably because the army in 1789 had chosen to build Fort Washington on the east side of that town, high above the floodway. In January, 1790, Northwest Territory Governor Arthur St. Clair visited Fort Washington, made it his headquarters, changed the name of Losantiville to Cincinnati, organized the

Fort Washington was built at Losantiville in 1789. (From the collection of The Public Library of Cincinnati and Hamilton County)

Purchase into Hamilton County, and made Cincinnati the county seat. Most new immigrants to the area chose to stay in Cincinnati under the protection of the fort, and only a few brave pioneers moved into the interior of the Purchase. The earliest settler of record in the Mill Creek Valley was James Cunningham, who in 1789 cleared and occupied his tract in what is now Evendale. Indian hostilities, however, forced him and his family to return to Cincinnati in 1790.[15]

Due to the antagonism of the Indians, most early settlements in the interior of the Purchase included blockhouses into which attacked settlers could retreat. These fortifications were known as "stations," with small numbers of army regulars sometimes stationed at them. In April, 1790, Symmes wrote Dayton: "We have established three new stations some distance up in the country, one is twelve miles Up the Big Miami, the second is five miles up Mill creek & the third is nine miles back in the Country from Columbia."[16]

The Mill Creek station in what is now Northside was erected by Israel Ludlow in March, 1790, close to the "second crossing" of the stream. A nearby blockhouse erected by Joseph McHenry was probably built during the same year. In 1792, Jacob White constructed a station at the "third crossing" of the Mill Creek at the north end of present Carthage. Additional stations were built near the stream during the 1792-1794 period: Griffin's in present Carthage, Vorhees' in present Lockland, Runyon's in present Sharonville, Tucker's and Pleasant Valley in present Woodlawn (Fig. 4). The nearby Mill Creek provided these stations with stone and clay for construction, and a reliable source of water. The stream also provided a site for dunking guilty parties when ordered by improvised courts of law at the stations.[17]

Despite the defense supplied by the stations, Indian raids into the Purchase continued and punitive military campaigns were mounted. On September 30, 1790, General Josiah Harmar set out from Fort Washington with a force of 1,450 men (Fig. 4). They camped the first night on the branch of Mill Creek that is now known as Ross Run, named after an early settler in St. Bernard. The next night's campsite was on the Mill Creek tributary that was later named Sharon Creek, because it flowed through the town of Sharon, or Sharonville. From there, the army crossed into the Little Miami Valley and continued northward until it encountered, and was defeated by, an Indian war party.[18]

The failure of Harmar's campaign emboldened the Indians to increase their attacks on the pioneer settlements. In his June 19, 1791 letter to Dayton, Symmes complained that much land remained to be sold, "yet so greatly troublesome have the Indians been since the last fall's expedition as to arrest that business altogether, for lands at any distance from the Ohio." Symmes prayed for the success of the upcoming campaign being planned by General Arthur St. Clair.[19]

On August 7, 1791, St. Clair moved his command from Fort Washington up the Mill Creek Valley to Ludlow's Station in order to procure better food for his army's thousand head of cattle (Fig. 4). Following a period of training, St. Clair's force of 2,700 men left Ludlow's Station in September and marched northward to their November 4 vanquishment on the banks of the Wabash River. Survivors of St. Clair's routed army quickly retreated toward Cincinnati. Many of the men paused for a full night's sleep at Ludlow's Station, assuming that Indian pursuers would not venture so close to Fort Washington. Orderly William Wiseman later related how his killing of one of the station's cattle for fresh beef inadvertently caused the immediate resumption of the retreat down the Mill Creek:

> When it was within two or three yards, I fired at it, and it fell. Just at the same moment, it happened that a burning log, from a heap in our neighborhood, fell from its place on the foot of a sleeping soldier, and awakening him with the cry of pain, "O Lord! O, Lord!" This created a universal panic, and all believed that the Indians were upon us, sure enough. The officers from the block-house, and the various neighboring parties, could be heard jumping, one after another, into the creek, to make their way into Cincinnati.

The failure of St. Clair's campaign caused Symmes to expect "that the late defeat will entirely discourage all others coming to the Purchase from Jersey for a long time. Indeed it seems that we are never to have matters right—what from the two succeeding defeats of our army."[20]

In 1792, President George Washington appointed General Anthony Wayne to replace the disgraced St. Clair as commander of the western army. Wayne and his well-drilled troops arrived in Cincinnati on May 5, 1793. Finding Fort

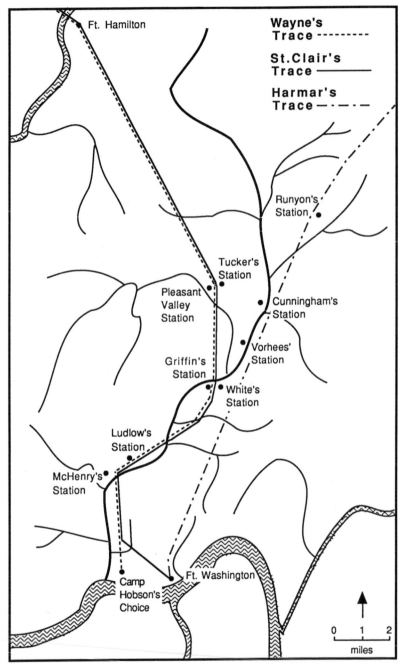

Wayne's Trace --------

St.Clair's Trace ————

Harmar's Trace —·—·—

Ft. Hamilton

Runyon's Station

Tucker's Station

Pleasant Valley Station

Cunningham's Station

Vorhees' Station

Griffin's Station

White's Station

Ludlow's Station

McHenry's Station

Camp Hobson's Choice

Ft. Washington

0 1 2
miles

Figure 4. Pioneer stations, army installations, and military roads of the Mill Creek region in 1793.

Washington too small to accommodate his force, Wayne established Hobson's Choice, a camp just west of Cincinnati near the mouth of the Mill Creek (Fig. 4). There he thoroughly trained the army in the techniques of Indian-fighting. Finally, on October 7, Wayne broke camp and followed the Mill Creek past Ludlow's Station to the first night's bivouac. The following day the army of three thousand men passed White's and Tucker's Stations on the way to the second night's encampment at Fort Hamilton on the Great Miami River. From there Wayne proceeded slowly, building forts as the army went north.[21]

As Wayne's forces cautiously advanced, Indian attacks continued behind them in the Purchase. On October 18, a party of about thirty Indians attacked White's Station and the nearby cabins on both banks of the Mill Creek. The Indians shot Andrew Goble and two children of Mrs. Moses Pryor, and also would have killed Mrs. Pryor and her remaining child had they not escaped through the waist-deep waters of the creek to the blockhouse. Some of the Indians killed in the skirmish were unceremoniously buried on the north bank of the Mill Creek, their bodies partially covered with stalks, weeds, and earth.[22]

During the following spring, on April 25, 1794, a party of Indians ambushed a company of four horsemen involved in troop supply for Wayne's army. The attack took place on the road between Ludlow's and White's Stations, at a ford over a small Mill Creek tributary where the horsemen had stopped to water their animals. Of the two men killed, one was scalped and left lying in the stream. This event caused John Ludlow, Israel's brother, to subsequently refer to the stream as Bloody Run, a name that it retains to this day.[23]

General Anthony Wayne's August 20, 1794 defeat of the Indians at the Battle of Fallen Timbers and the signing of the treaty of peace at Greenville on August 3, 1795, finally brought an end to Indian attacks in the Purchase. Families abandoned the Ohio River villages for the interior, which was now safe for settlement. In his August 6, 1795 letter to Dayton, Symmes observed that North Bend "is reduced more than one-half in its numbers of inhabitants since I left it to go to Jersey in February, 1793. The people have spread themselves into all parts of the purchase... and the cabins are of late deserted by dozens in a street." The aboriginal inhabitants of the Maketewa Valley had been displaced at last, an exodus summarized fifty years later by William Davis Gallagher in his poem "The Spotted Fawn":

> By Maketewa's flowery marge
>   The Spotted Fawn had birth,
> And grew, as fair an Indian girl
>   As ever blessed the earth;
> She was the red chief's only child,
>   And sought by many a brave,
> But to the gallant young White Cloud
>   Her plighted troth she gave.

Oh, the Spotted Fawn!
Oh, the Spotted Fawn!
The light and life of the forest shades
With the red chief's child is gone...

From Maketewa's flowery marge
    Her bridal song arose;
None dreaming, on that festal night,
    Of near encircling foes;
But through the forest, stealthily,
    The white men came in wrath;
And fiery deaths before them sped,
    And blood was in their path.

Oh, the Spotted Fawn!
Oh, the Spotted Fawn!
The light and life of the forest shades
With the red chief's child is gone.[24]

CHAPTER TWO

Inhabitants and Immigrants

By stagnant Mill creek's muddy marge
  The spotted frog had birth,
And grew as fair and fat a frog
  As ever hopped on earth;
She was the frog chief's only child,
  And sought by many a frog;
But only upon one she smiled,
  From that old rotted log.

  Oh, the spotted frog!
  Oh, the spotted frog!
The light and life of Mill creek's mud
Was the lovely spotted frog!...

From muddy Mill creek's stagnant marge
  Her bridal song arose,
None dreaming, as they hopped about,
  Of near encircling foes;
But cruel boys in search of sport,
  To Mill creek came that day,
And at the frogs with sticks and stones
  Began to blaze away!

  Oh, the spotted frog!
  Oh, the spotted frog!
The light and life of Mill creek's mud
Was the lovely spotted frog!

—Lewis J. Cist[1]

"THE SPOTTED FROG" was written by Lewis Cist in 1845 within a month after the publication of William David Gallagher's "The Spotted Fawn." In Cist's parody, as in Gallagher's poem, an original inhabitant of the Mill Creek's shoreline was eulogized. The four-inch-long spotted frog (now known

The spotted, or leopard, frog lived along the lower Mill Creek's marshy margin. (From the collection of The Public Library of Cincinnati and Hamilton County)

as the leopard frog) once populated the lower creek's marshy margins, a habitat that it still occupies in other parts of Hamilton County. Other frogs that children collected from the Mill Creek probably included the one-inch cricket frog, the four-inch green frog, and the eight-inch bullfrog, all still common at other locations in the region.[2]

The larger frogs preyed on their smaller relatives, as did various reptiles, birds, mammals, and fish. Turtles were plentiful in the same pools where children collected frogs. These shelled reptiles probably included the snapping and painted turtles, as well as the rarer map turtle, a species that once inhabited Bloody Run near its mouth on Mill Creek. Frog-eating garter, northern water, and queen snakes still live along clean portions of the Mill Creek's tributaries.[3]

The great blue heron, a very efficient frog-catcher, once hunted the stream in present Northside. Black-crowned and yellow-crowned night herons also have been recorded stalking in the creek. The raccoon, an omnivorous mammal with a taste for frog legs, was chased by John Olden along the Mill Creek's banks through "tanglewood, marshes and brake." This pursuit occurred in the early 1800s when Olden fished the stream for bass, probably northern smallmouth, the bass species recorded from the creek by Milton Trautman in *The Fishes of Ohio*.[4]

Unlike the frog-eating smallmouth bass, most of the other thirty-nine fishes catalogued by Trautman from the Mill Creek feed exclusively on invertebrates, smaller animals without backbones. Stream invertebrates also sustain amphibious salamanders, five species of which may still be found in clean sections of the Mill Creek and its tributaries. The raccoon, frogs, turtles, snakes, and herons listed above likewise consume aquatic invertebrates, as do shore-dwelling birds. The author has watched the spotted sandpiper and the Louisiana waterthrush probing for food in unpolluted areas of the creek. A black rail, one of the rarest American birds, was observed along the lower Mill Creek in about 1865 by Charles Dury.[5]

Dury, a collector of beetles, joined the above animals in taking insects from the stream, but no one has amassed a complete collection of the Mill Creek's myriad invertebrate species. An appreciation of the diversity of these animals might be gained by examining a 1969-1971 United States Environmental Protection Agency census from nearby Shayler Run. This unpolluted stream, located twenty miles east of the Mill Creek in the Little Miami watershed, was found to support seven worm species, six molluscs, six crustaceans, and ninety-four insects. The latter included thirty-five midge and mosquito larvae, fourteen beetle adults and larvae, ten caddisfly larvae, eight true bug adults and nymphs, eight dragonfly and damselfly nymphs, seven mayfly nymphs, three cranefly larvae, three soldierfly larvae, one blackfly larva, one horsefly larva, one mothfly larva, one stonefly nymph, one dobsonfly larva, and one springtail.[6]

Because Shayler Run's drainage area is smaller than that of the Mill Creek,

The great blue heron was a common visitor to the Mill Creek. (John J. Audubon lithograph from the collection of The Public Library of Cincinnati and Hamilton County)

additional invertebrates typical of broader and deeper stream environments have been recorded from the creek. An 1842 excursion to the Mill Creek by the Cincinnati-based Western Academy of Natural Sciences collected shells of several species of snails. The Academy sponsored a second field trip to the Mill Creek in 1846 in order to show its rich shell assemblage to the visiting Englishman Charles Lyell, the founder of modern geology. A "very large & fine" specimen of *Unio alabus,* a species of clam, was taken from the stream and exhibited at the Academy meeting of February 14, 1848.[7]

By probing the sand deposits of the Mill Creek, Charles Dury in 1878 gathered 147 individuals of a beetle species, *Omophron robustum,* that previously had been represented by a single specimen taken at Lake Superior. He supplied nearly every collection in the United States and several in Europe with specimens from his large sample. Dury continued to capture beetles and other animals from the Cincinnati area, and in 1914 became president of the Cincinnati Society of Natural History, now the Cincinnati Museum of Natural History. Many of the 75,000 beetles in the museum's collection were taken by Dury from the Mill Creek and its valley between 1877 and 1931, the year of his death.[8]

All of the animals mentioned thus far are ultimately dependent on photosynthetic plants that capture energy from sunlight. This energy is passed along the creek's food chains, going first to plant-consuming invertebrates, fish, turtles, birds, and mammals. Avian herbivores include ducks that "were very numerous in the creek" in 1805, and still visited it "during their migrations in great flocks" in the 1860s. Mammalian vegetarians include the beaver that once occupied bank dens on the Mill Creek and lodged in dammed ponds on smaller tributaries. These animals often left the water to feed on the bark and twigs of trees that lined the creek.[9]

Beavers are like most woodland stream-dwelling herbivores in that they gain more of their food energy from surrounding trees than from aquatic vegetation. Tree material enters the stream as leaves, twigs, bark, flowers, fruits, seeds, and other plant parts. These sink and become colonized by fungi, bacteria, and "shredders"—insect larvae that feed on both the plant debris and the microbes growing on it. Shredders include various caddisfly larvae, stonefly nymphs, and cranefly larvae. Another group of invertebrates known as "collectors" feed on the fine particulate organic matter that results from the action of the microbes and shredders. Among the collectors are midge larvae, blackfly larvae, and mayfly nymphs.[10]

A few herbivorous invertebrates are "grazers" that feed on the algal coating of the rocks and stones in the stream. These include some stonefly nymphs, snails, and beetle larvae. Grazers are rare in shaded woodland streams where algal photosynthesis may account for 1 percent or less of total energy supply, the other 99 percent being imported from the forested watershed.[11]

The shredders, collectors, and grazers are in turn eaten by predatory

Beavers that lived on the Mill Creek and its tributaries fed on the bark and twigs of streambank trees. (John J. Audubon lithograph from the collection of The Public Library of Cincinnati and Hamilton County)

invertebrates and vertebrates. Like the aquatic herbivores that make up a portion of their diets, these carnivores do not depend solely on the stream community as their food source; they also feed heavily on terrestrial invertebrates that are washed or blown into the stream from the surrounding woodland. Thus, a closer look at the Mill Creek watershed's forest is warranted, since it once provided most of the food for the creek's animals.[12]

The Mill Creek and its valley were entirely covered by a deciduous forest canopy when Symmes' men surveyed the area in 1788. In the southern portion of the watershed, dense woodland caused Symmes to become lost for two days as he attempted to go from North Bend to Ludlow's Station in October, 1790. Colonel Winthrop Sargent, an adjutant-general on the staff of General St. Clair, noted in his September 6, 1791 diary entry that "the troops marched from Ludlow's Station for the Miami; the distance, about eighteen miles; a road to be cut the whole way through considerable woods...." This unbroken forest enveloped not only the western portion of the Mill Creek basin through which St. Clair's army advanced, but it also overlaid the eastern area of the watershed known to early settlers as "the woods," due to the large size and number of trees that covered the land.[13]

According to Symmes' narrative of the two days he was missing in the forest, "the weather was very dark & rainy all the while, and yet I escaped the Indians, tho the wolves had nearly devoured me in the night as I could make no fire." The gray wolf was a despised woodland carnivore, as was the much rarer mountain lion. In 1797, the Hamilton County Commissioners began budgeting $200 a year to pay bounties for the pelts of wolves and wild cats. The county paid out $166.75 in 1800 for seventy-five wolves and one wild cat, species unknown. In spite of such an annual harvest by bounty hunters, "the wolves' long howl could still be heard" during the early 1800s in the Mill Creek Valley.[14]

Other forest mammals provided meat for the first Cincinnati settlers who "hunted on Mill Creek, four or five miles from the town." In the early town marketplace, a quarter of black bear cost twenty-seven cents and a similar amount of venison cost twenty-five cents. Woodland birds such as wild turkeys and passenger pigeons also were killed and sold.

Both species nested in the Mill Creek Valley, and large flocks of migrating pigeons often paused in the area during the early 1800s. Samuel Cary, a pioneer resident of present College Hill, later remembered the spectacle created by the abundant birds:

> Flocks of unnumbered millions of pigeons, which by their numbers darkened the sky, and by their movements produced a roaring like the waves of the sea, were often seen. Day and night the air was black with them. Occasionally a flock would alight in the woods in such numbers as to break large branches from the trees.[15]

A visitor to a Cincinnati market in 1815 noted among the things for sale were "wild animals that have been taken in the woods; cages of red-birds and parroquets." These birds, the cardinal and Carolina parakeet, were common in the forest surrounding the city. On May 18, 1819, westbound naturalists noted in the bottomlands just below Cincinnati that "the fruit of the sycamore is the favourite food of the paroquet, and large flocks of these gaily-plumed birds constantly enliven the gloomy forests." Edward Mansfield observed the parakeet "at Ludlow station in great flocks," perhaps because of the availability of sycamores or "buttonwoods" that flourished along the sides of the Mill Creek. A view from the western slope of the creek's valley revealed that "It was a very beautiful stream, and its serpentine course could be traced... by the white trunks and branches of the buttonwood trees which grew upon its banks."[16]

Animals that prefer open areas were, of course, scarce in the forested Mill Creek watershed. The robin, for example, "was a rare bird, seen only at intervals, and always alone. He seemed, indeed, unsettled, undomesticated, and like other emigrants perplexed and undetermined as to where he should locate."[17]

Unlike the robin, perplexed human pioneers received good advice concerning where to settle in the Miami Purchase. The English writer Francis Baily, an early visitor to the Purchase, told his readers that "If any one... would wish to fix his residence amongst the first inhabitants, he ought to choose out a spot where he can fix a mill, as this is a thing indispensable in a young country; he ought to build both a grist-mill and a saw-mill as soon as he has built himself a house." The flour, meal, and lumber produced by these mills could either be used by the settler or exchanged for other commodities as needed.[18]

James Cunningham undoubtedly had mills in mind when, on May 26,

Large flocks of Carolina parakeets gathered along the Mill Creek. (John J. Audubon lithograph from the collection of The Public Library of Cincinnati and Hamilton County)

1789, he entered land warrant No. 382 in the register's office at North Bend. He reserved section 28, T. 4, R. 1 in present Evendale, through the length of which runs the Mill Creek. In the summer of 1789, Cunningham became the first settler of record to clear a lot and build a house in the Mill Creek watershed. Before he could construct his mills, however, Indian incursions during the winter of 1789 caused Cunningham and his family to abandon their unfortified settlement. Cunningham relocated to Cincinnati, purchased a city lot, erected a cabin, and worked as a government teamster. The reduction of Indian hostilities in the autumn of 1793 allowed Cunningham to return permanently to his Mill Creek settlement, where he subsequently built both a saw mill and a grist mill.[19]

Additional mills on the creek were constructed in the 1790s downstream from Cunningham's settlement. Minny and Abraham Vorhees erected a saw mill south of their father's station in present Lockland. In present Carthage, Jacob White built a saw and grist mill by his station, and James Caldwell constructed one near Griffin's Station. Symmes built his house in North Bend from lumber sawed at Caldwell's mill and hauled over the present North Bend Road leading west from Carthage.[20]

Israel Ludlow built either a saw mill or a grist mill east of his station in present Northside. Cincinnati historian Arthur G. King suggests that the Mill Creek was named on the basis of Ludlow's mill, which may have been constructed in 1791. This date, however, postdates by four years Symmes' use of the name "Mill Stream" in his 1787 contract with Stites.[21]

Grummon's mill in present Fairmount was the southernmost one on the creek in the 1790s. Cincinnatians carried their grain by horseback to this mill, which was located two miles from town. Several years later, James McCash recalled a memorable trip home from the mill with his sack of meal:

> My bag slid off, and I was in a pretty fix. There was no human being nearer than an old fellow named Harkless, who lived in Wade's woods, and there was no path opened to his cabin that I knew of. So I first sat down and cried, and then mounted the mare and returned to the mill, and got the miller to put the meal on the beast for me.

James was five or six years old at the time, when "Hands were scarce, and boys were expected to do what I cannot get boys to do now for me."[22]

More mills were put up in the early 1800s on tributaries to the Main Stem of the Mill Creek. On West Fork, Ezekiel Hutchinson built a saw mill below the present Mt. Airy Forest. On the West Fork Mill Creek, the McFeely brothers constructed a grist mill at a site now flooded by Winton Lake, and Jediah Hill erected a saw mill north of present Mt. Healthy. The still-existing covered bridge next to the latter site also was built by Jediah Hill, using timber he gathered along the creek and sawed in his mill.[23]

In 1809, a traveler from Lebanon to Cincinnati observed that the "Mill creek is a fine stream, on which are several mills; and the bottoms thro' which

Trees provided pioneers with timber for their homes, such as this log cabin built in 1795 near Ludlow's Station in Northside. (From the collection of The Public Library of Cincinnati and Hamilton County)

it flows are of a very rich soil." Nutrient-rich soil and accessibility to mills are important qualities of choice farmland. Other characteristics of a prime agricultural territory are relative flatness, adequate groundwater, a bedrock level deep enough to permit cultivation, and easily reachable markets. The area bordering the length of the Mill Creek exhibits all of these features, and so it became the first land in southwestern Ohio to be extensively farmed.[24]

By 1817, a ride out from Cincinnati to the headwaters of the Mill Creek revealed the following sights to English visitor John Palmer:

> We passed through a thickly, but lately settled country, frame and log-houses, and cabins, and fine farms of corn, wheat, rye, and oats, on both sides of the road, many just redeemed from nature; the smoke of the fires, made in burning the trees and underwood rising around us, and large fields of naked trunks and branches of the girdled trees, met the eye at every turn of the road.[25]

The process of girdling trees was described by another British traveler:

> Among the most laborious occupations of the settler is... cutting down the trees. Some of these are so gigantic, that the labour of chopping them down would be immense. He therefore cuts off the bark in a belt about four or five inches wide, and this is called girdling. The tree dies, and the year after, when it is dry, it is set on fire, and continues to burn slowly until gradually consumed.[26]

Although most of the timber was burned away, some was saved for use in fencing, heating, and construction. The saw mills on the banks of the Mill Creek converted the pioneers' lumber into posts, beams, sheathing, flooring, and boards for doors and partitions. A second building material, brick, later was produced along the Mill Creek shores from the clay deposits of annual floods. On his trip through the Mill Creek Valley in 1817, John Palmer noted that "substantial brick farmhouses" had replaced wooden dwellings in the earliest-settled agricultural areas.[27]

Timothy Flint's memories of the winter of 1815-1816 in Cincinnati provide a vivid description of the changes occurring in the area during the early nineteenth century. By "making remoter journeys from the town, beside the rivulets, and in the little bottoms," Flint was able to summarize the progression of settlement in the Mill Creek Valley:

> Nothing can be more beautiful than these little bottoms, upon which these emigrants, if I may say so, deposite their household goods. Springs burst forth in the intervals between the high and low grounds. The trees and shrubs are of the most beautiful kind. The brilliant red-bird is seen flitting among the shrubs, or, perched on a tree, seems welcoming, in her mellow notes, the emigrant to his abode. Flocks of parroquets are glittering among the trees, and grey squirrels are skipping from branch to branch. In the midst of these primeval scenes, the patient and laborious father fixes his family. In a few weeks they have reared a comfortable cabin, and other out buildings. Pass this place in two years, and you will see extensive fields of corn and wheat; a young and thrifty orchard, fruit-trees of all kinds, the guaranty of present abundant subsistence, and of future luxury. Pass it in ten years, and the log cabins will have disappeared. The shrubs and forest trees will be gone. The Arcadian aspect of humble and retired abundance and comfort, will have given place to a brick house, with accompaniments like those that attend the same kind of house, in the older countries.[28]

Passenger pigeons became extinct when large stands of timber were destroyed. (John J. Audubon lithograph from the collection of The Public Library of Cincinnati and Hamilton County)

CHAPTER THREE

Deforestation and Death

The fiat went forth from the spoilers—
The myrmidon sons of men—
That the forest, the warder of rivers,
  Should pass from the valley and glen...
And the murmuring groves on the ridges
  Heard in the morning still
The ax-blows resounding, repeating
  The rumble and roar of the mill.
The vast forest mourned to the brooklets:
  "Beloved, the hour has come.
The Day God will drink at thy spring-pools,
  And the voice of thy music be dumb"...
The birds flew far and were silent,
  The west wind sobbed in pain,
And bore in the eve her teardrops
  To the barley blooms on the plain.

—Lillian H. Shuey[1]

THE WAVE of clearing and settlement moved up the Mill Creek Valley from its mouth where, in 1822, one visitor reported that "all of the land in the immediate neighbourhood of Cincinnati is without a tree upon it." By 1842, the English traveler and author Charles Dickens was able to portray the lower Mill Creek Valley as "richly cultivated, and luxuriant in its promise of an abundant harvest." For Henry Teetor, a local historian writing in 1882, the migration into the Mill Creek basin took on religious significance:

> The wave set in motion by an Infinite hand for an infinite purpose rolled on, while upon its crest sat civilization sanctified by Christianity. It waved a magical wand, and a wilderness became an Eden. The waste of woods, within three generations, has become a populous and powerful realm.[2]

This expression of the principle of Manifest Destiny was also being realized in the upper portion of the valley. In 1836, the northernmost mill ever to

29

By 1881, the woodland in Hamilton County's Mill Creek Township had been reduced to 15 percent of its original coverage. (Postcard from the collection of The Public Library of Cincinnati and Hamilton County)

be erected on the Mill Creek was built by Isaac Davis on the headwaters near Princeton. And on the East Fork, a Mr. Avey operated a grist mill near West Chester. Barley, corn, and wheat were grown in large quantities on Butler County lands by 1882, and the acreage was steadily increasing. In 1916, deciduous forest ecologist Lucy Braun wrote that "Nothing of the original vegetation of this part remains" in the upper Mill Creek Valley. "It is all farm land."[3]

As the choice agricultural lowlands became thickly settled, upland timber was felled in order to establish croplands on the plateaus between the Mill Creek tributaries. Uncleared hillside forests between the uplands and the lowlands were used as woodland pastures for cattle, sheep, and swine. The hogs fed by constantly overturning the soil, thereby exposing the tree roots and, subsequently, destroying the timber. Close pasturing by cattle and sheep proved equally destructive in many cases.[4]

Even trees on very steep slopes did not escape destruction. Maple, beech, and hickory were cut for firewood, and poplar and walnut were harvested for lumber. The leather industries of Cincinnati created a large demand for tanbark, and so the oak timber within a seventy-five to one hundred-mile radius of the city was "ruthlessly slaughtered." By 1881, deforestation had reduced the woodland in Hamilton County's Mill Creek Township to 15 percent of its original coverage.[5]

Forest mammals such as the black bear, gray wolf, and mountain lion disappeared from the Mill Creek watershed. Some sylvan birds also were extirpated: turkey, ruffed grouse, passenger pigeon, and Carolina parakeet. These species initially declined because of hunting pressure, and finally succumbed as a consequence of loss of woodland habitat. For example, Charles Dury regularly shot squabs at a passenger pigeon nesting area in a woods bordering the Mill Creek during the mid-1800s. But when this forest disappeared after 1875, so did the pigeons.[6]

The passenger pigeon became extinct in the Mill Creek watershed, as well as in the world, when a captive female died in 1914 at the Cincinnati Zoo. The Carolina parakeet likewise became extinct, locally and perhaps globally, when a captive male died in 1918 at the same zoo. Both species needed large, continuous areas of deciduous forest for their gregarious feeding and nesting habits. With the great North American eastern woodland cut back to small pockets during the nineteenth century, these birds had no more chance of surviving than, literally, fish out of water.[7]

And what of the fish in the water? Two of the species that once lived in the Mill Creek are now in danger of statewide extinction. One, the river chub, inhabits streams with stony bottoms and little or no aquatic vegetation; it feeds on aquatic insect larvae beneath and around boulders and stones, and builds large nests of pebbles or small gravel. The other endangered species, the eastern sand darter, lives and breeds in the sandy areas of streams. It feeds by burying itself in the sand with only its eyes exposed, and then dashing out to catch passing invertebrate prey. The disappearance of both chub and darter from the

The black bear was one of several forest mammals that disappeared when their woodland was eliminated. (John J. Audubon lithograph from the collection of The Public Library of Cincinnati and Hamilton County)

Mill Creek basin was probably caused by bottom-smothering stream sedimentation resulting from the destruction of the watershed's forest cover.[8]

Several studies have found that an undisturbed forest will experience a soil erosion rate of less than fifty tons per square mile per year, while a cleared forestland may have an erosion rate of more than five hundred tons per square mile per year, depending on the climate, slope, and soil type. The increase in sediment yield is due to the elimination of tree roots that hold the soil in place. An excellent investigation of the Potomac River basin above Washington, D.C. clearly showed the effect of tree cover on the sedimentation of streams. The researchers found that, for a given sub-basin, the smaller the forested area, the larger the sediment yield. A second relationship also was illustrated by the study: the greater the cultivated area, the greater the sediment yield.[9]

As the Mill Creek basin was settled, the clearing of the woodland exposed the soil, and the subsequent plowing of cropland stirred the soil up into greater contact with the eroding agents of rainfall and snowmelt. The resulting increase in erosion sediments reaching the Mill Creek adversely affected the stream's fish populations. The river chub and the sand darter probably disappeared from the creek when their stony and sandy bottom habitats were silted over by erosion sediments. Or the fish may have been extirpated because of other effects of sediment: causing asphyxiation by clogging gills, obscuring mating activities that rely on sight, and destroying eggs in spawning areas. The latter circumstance brought about a complete kill of developing king salmon in another Mill Creek, a tributary of the Sacramento River in California. There the smothering action of erosion sediments caused poor oxygen delivery to the eggs and inadequate cleansing of metabolic waste products from the embryos.[10]

Increased sediment deposits also adversely impact stream invertebrate populations. As the Mill Creek's streambed was silted over, the variety and abundance of bottom-dwelling animals decreased. This reduction in the number of invertebrate prey resulted in the decrease of such vertebrate predators as fish, salamanders, turtles, and shorebirds.[11]

In sum, the clearing of forestland and the cultivation of cropland increased the sediment load and reduced the animal community in the Mill Creek. These same human activities also increased the intensity of other physical parameters: temperature, sunlight, nutrients, floods, and droughts. As will be seen next, the elevated levels of these factors caused a further reduction in the diversity of life in the creek.

Thomas G. Lea, the discoverer of the Mill Creek Valley's indigenous Lea's Oak, collected several species of plants from the creek's bottomlands during the years 1834-1844. His herbarium specimens definitely indicate the presence of fields and the absence of woods alongside the lower Mill Creek. This is consistent with written evidence that the first areas cleared for agriculture were the "intervals," flood-prone lands whose soil is continuously replenished by annual inundations.[12]

A pioneer Price Hill farmstead. Clearing and plowing increased the erosion of the soil into the Mill Creek. (From the collection of The Cincinnati Historical Society. B-94-243)

In 1882, Henry Teetor mourned the loss of the streamside forest that once shaded the creek: "Before the woods upon its margin bowed to the axe of the pioneer, how cool and inviting its banks." Woodland removal that increases summer shoreline temperatures also elevates summer streamwater temperatures by four to thirteen degrees Fahrenheit. Water temperature affects many stream factors, such as chemical concentrations and reactions, dissolved oxygen levels, metabolic rates of animals, and cues for life cycle events. Elevated temperatures in the Mill Creek possibly caused the elimination of some thermally sensitive invertebrates and fish.[13]

The higher summer water temperatures of the unshaded Mill Creek were caused by greater solar input. A growth in aquatic vegetation also resulted from the greater exposure to sunlight, aided by increasing amounts of plant nutrients reaching the creek. These nutrients, primarily phosphorus and nitrogen, flowed to the creek as part of the erosion sediments from the surrounding cleared and cropped lands. Another source of nutrients was manure from meat and dairy farms in the valley. The disposal of this natural fertilizer amazed a British immigrant to the Cincinnati area in the mid-nineteenth century: "It will seem strange to English farmers, but it is true, that vast quantities of barn-yard manure have been 'dumped' into the rivers to get it out of the way."[14]

The greater input of sunlight and nutrients caused an increase of algae and rooted plants in the creek, a change that is documented by specimens in Lea's

Removal of shoreline trees elevated the summer streamwater temperatures. (Postcard from the collection of The Public Library of Cincinnati and Hamilton County)

herbarium collection. At the same time, the decline of the watershed's forest cover caused a decrease in the amount of tree detritus reaching the stream. The energy supply for the Mill Creek's animals now came more from aquatic plants and less from terrestrial plants than it had previously.[15]

Major shifts in invertebrate and fish species compositions have been found during studies of woodland streams undergoing losses of shade, increases of nutrients, and decreases of detrital inputs. Once-rare invertebrate grazers that feed on algae and submerged plants increase in number, while formerly abundant aquatic shredders and collectors who feed on terrestrial plant debris decrease. Fish that previously fed almost exclusively on shredders or collectors are forced to select a broader range of food types; species unable to change their food habits disappear from the streams.[16]

The Mill Creek undoubtedly underwent these shifts in invertebrate and fish faunas during the clearing of its watershed. Many of the other thirty-eight fishes recorded from the stream joined the river chub and the sand darter as species extirpated from the Mill Creek basin. The rosyface shiner, for example, was commonly taken from the Main Stem during the nineteenth century, and the brook silversides was collected from Bloody Run. Neither species has been collected from the Mill Creek or its branches during this century, although they still occur in other, less disturbed Ohio streams. These fishes may have disappeared because of invertebrate population changes caused by an increased growth of aquatic plants and a decreased inflow of tree detritus. Or, they may have been extirpated due to the physical results of deforestation: increased sedimentation, elevated water temperature, or altered flow regime. The latter result of land modification remains to be discussed.[17]

The clearing of woodland eliminates the tree roots and litter that normally allow forest soil to retard and moderate water runoff. Deforested watersheds, therefore, endure higher floods of shorter duration and low flow periods of greater length. As early as 1790, Noah Webster noted that:

> The amazing difference in the state of a cultivated and uncultivated surface of earth, iz demonstrated by the number of small streems of water, which are dried up by clearing away forests. The quantity of water, falling upon the surface, may be the same; but when land is cuvered with trees and leevs, it retains the water; when it iz cleered, the water runs off suddenly into the large streems.[18]

As rain and snowmelt more quickly drained off the cleared Mill Creek watershed in floods, less water was left behind to keep the creek running during periods when precipitation was at relatively low levels. During the nineteenth century, many perennial springs that supplied the Mill Creek "have, since the removal of the back-lying forest, become but 'wet-weather springs,' absolutely dry in late summer," according to one observer. But the dried-up springs and streams were not due only to deforestation. Where swamp woods were cleared, the lands were also ditched and tiled in order to lower the water table by increasing the rapidity of runoff. For example, in the swampy region

Deforestation caused higher floods and longer droughts in the Mill Creek channel. (From the collection of The Cincinnati Historical Society. B-94-249)

southeast of Hamilton that "formed the head source of Mill Creek... ditches were dug, and the country drained, enhancing its value tenfold." The combined effects of forest elimination and field drainage systems caused the Mill Creek to experience flood peaks and low flow periods that were more severe as well as more frequent.[19]

Fluctuating water levels are a natural part of stream hydrology, and so aquatic organisms are adapted physically and behaviorally to changing flow regimes. But under conditions of extreme dewatering, as may occur during dry seasons in a modified watershed, portions of a stream community may be lost entirely. In the case of fish, low flow events may prohibit seasonal movements, prevent adults from spawning, and interfere with egg or fry development. Severe low flow periods probably were responsible for the decline and disappearance of at least a few of the Mill Creek's fish species.[20]

High flow events are not as likely to adversely impact fish, but they certainly inconvenience people. The earliest mention of flooding in the Mill Creek is found in the Cincinnati newspaper *Liberty Hall,* on March 12, 1805. During the following year, Caldwell's mill in present Carthage was swept away by a flood of such suddenness that the owner had to escape from the moving wreckage "by a bold and successful leap for the bank."[21]

An 1808 flood caused the breakup of the first bridge built over the Mill Creek. A Mr. Parker had constructed the floating span across the mouth of the creek in 1806. Efforts to erect a bridge at this point had begun eight years earlier when Symmes pledged $100 to construct a span "either of stone or wood, on pillars or bents, so high as to be level with the top of the adjacent banks." Other pledges included $70 from Israel Ludlow, $40 each from William Henry Harrison and Cornelius R. Sedam, and lesser amounts from several other subscribers. The proposal for an elevated bridge failed for want of sufficient funds.[22]

A later subscription drive for a cheaper span was successful and, in 1806, Parker constructed his floating bridge by using tulip poplars from the adjacent Mill Creek bottomlands. Just before the bridge timbers were swept away in the 1808 flood, the bridgetender stripped the planking from the span. These planks from the Mill Creek's first bridge later formed the floor of Cincinnati's first warehouse.[23]

An elevated, 120-foot long toll bridge was built at the site in 1811, or possibly 1816, by banker Ethan Stone. This bridge was carried off in 1822 by a Mill Creek that had been swollen by a night of heavy rains. The same flood also doubled the width of the lower creek, probably a consequence of the settlers' clearing of shoreline trees whose roots had stabilized the stream's banks.[24]

Ethan Stone replaced his flood-destroyed structure with a longer bridge that was subsequently sold to Hamilton County and made toll free. Displaying no more respect for public property than it had shown for private spans, a flooding Mill Creek in 1832 lifted the county bridge from its piers and carried it

The original Spring Grove Avenue bridge. (From the collection of The Cincinnati Historical Society. B-94-241)

down the Ohio River to an island six miles above Louisville. A steamboat's attempt to tow it back to Cincinnati failed, and so the bridge was instead dismantled, loaded onto a flatboat, brought back to the Mill Creek, and reinstalled in its original position. Upstream on the creek, the Colerain and Hamilton Road bridges, floated off by the same 1832 flood, were also rebuilt.[25]

The higher and more substantial type of wooden span erected later in the nineteenth century was better able to withstand floods, although such a bridge was still vulnerable to human destruction. One Mill Creek span was supposedly burned down "by a man whose horses' feet stuck fast in a hole of the planking, which made him so angry that he vowed never again to be stopped there by the same cause, and therefore he set fire to the bridge before he left the place."[26]

As the number of bridges in the valley increased, travelers no longer had to risk fording the creek, an especially dangerous undertaking during periods of high water. "Many lives were lost in early days, at such times, of those who rode or drove in, ignorant of the depth," according to an 1845 note by John Matson, writing of the ford at the "first crossing" of the Mill Creek. Several drownings also occurred upstream at other fording points. A tombstone at the Reading Public Cemetery records the deaths of Thomas Parnell, his wife, and their two children, "All of whom were Drowned in Crossing Millcreek June 27th, 1838." At the bottom of this stone is inscribed the following verse:

One army of the living God,
   To His command we bow;
Part of the host have crossed the flood,
   And part are crossing now.

Dear Saviour be our constant guide,
   Then when the word is given;
Bid death's cold flood and waves divide,
   And land us safe in Heaven.[27]

CHAPTER FOUR

Strangers Underfoot and a Stream Underfit

The sluggish artery of the Concord meadows steals thus unobserved through the town, without a murmur or a pulse-beat.

—Henry David Thoreau[1]

THOREAU WROTE the above about the Concord River flowing unseen under the bridges in Concord, Massachusetts. It is certainly true that when spans replace fords, the public thereafter ignores the stream underfoot unless it stinks, drowns someone, or overflows its banks. On the other hand, bridges provide nesting and roosting sites for animals who are very much aware of the stream below.

One bridge-inhabiting species is the cliff swallow, a bird that feeds on flying insects emerging from immature stages spent underwater. The swallow originally bred only in large colonies on river and stream bluffs out of the reach of predators. The birds in a colony plastered their bottle-shaped mud nests onto a rock face overlooking the watercourse below. The portions of North America without rocky bluffs were therefore without cliff swallows, at least until humans constructed perpendicular walls on which the birds could build their nests.[2]

In 1804, the garrison of troops originally stationed at Fort Washington crossed the Ohio River to erect and occupy a new riverfront fort in Newport, Kentucky. In 1815, a United States Army major named Oldham noticed a few cliff swallows constructing nests on the walls of the fort building under his charge. It was here on April 20, 1819, that John James Audubon observed a colony of several hundred swallows "busily engaged in repairing the damage done to their nests by the storms of the preceding winter." Emigrants from the fort's increasingly-crowded colony probably constructed the first nests on early bridges erected over the adjacent Licking River and the nearby Mill Creek. The cliff swallow became a member of the Mill Creek's fauna thanks to the suitable nesting sites provided by humans.[3]

A second avian newcomer to the Mill Creek Valley arrived in Cincinnati

39

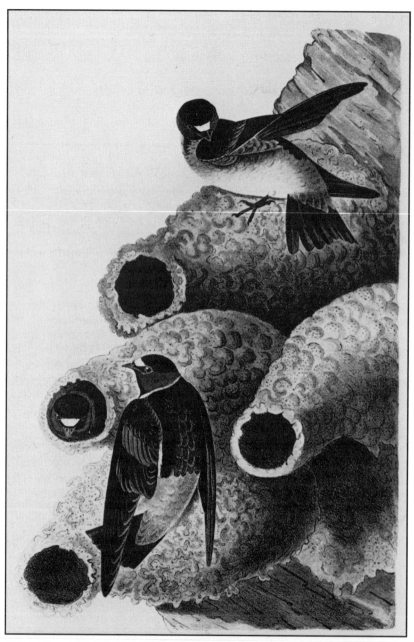

Cliff swallows built their mud nests on the early Mill Creek bridges. (John J. Audubon lithograph from the collection of The Public Library of Cincinnati and Hamilton County)

during the late 1860s or early 1870s. The European house sparrow, unlike the cliff swallow, was deliberately imported at a cost of eight dollars per pair. Eighty pairs from Germany were released by the city with the hope that they would multiply and feed on the insect pests of street trees and park vegetation. The sparrows' early history in the city was reported by Cincinnati naturalist Dr. A. Zipperlein in a note to *Feathered World,* a weekly periodical published in Berlin:

> They accepted the hospitality of the Americans only three days, and then, on that principle according to which every immigrant should shape his conduct, not to depend on others, but only on himself, and stand on his own feet, they deserted their festive boards and the charming parks, and wended their flight to Mill creek—a creek flowing through the western part of the city, whose banks are inhabited by German gardeners and dairymen.... The speech had a familiar tone to them; they saw German gardens, stables, and the old manure heaps, and the possessors of all these treasures, who had seen no German bird in thirty years, perhaps, rejoiced at the arrival of their feathered guests.[4]

The Mill Creek swallows, on the other hand, did not rejoice at the arrival of the foreign birds. The aggressive house sparrows destroyed the swallows' eggs, killed their young, and usurped their nests. By 1878, a colony of sparrows had entirely replaced the colony of several hundred rough-winged and cliff swallows who nested on the Brighton Bridge over the Mill Creek. The native rough-winged swallow continued to nest along the stream in suitable bank burrows, but the cliff swallow disappeared from the creek and from the nearby Miami and Erie Canal. The cliff swallow even disappeared from the sparrowless portions of the Mill Creek Valley, perhaps due to the painting of exterior walls, which made the wood too smooth to hold nests.[5]

Thus because of human intervention, the cliff swallow was both added to and subtracted from the Mill Creek bird fauna during the nineteenth century. As for the fate of the farm-based house sparrow, Dr. Zipperlein continued:

> Their well-known prolific tendencies were not lost in the new climate. A year afterward single pairs came into the city here and there to look about them. The report must have been favorable, for soon they began to colonize themselves in the city.... Since then they have increased by the thousand, they are in every street in the city, where there is always a rich feast.[6]

Other non-native animals besides cliff-nesting swallows and alien sparrows have been recorded along or in the Mill Creek. At least two Indian elephants forded the creek in 1905 during their escape from the Hagenbeck-Wallace Circus at the Carthage Fairgrounds, and two Asiatic goldfish were seen during a biological survey of the stream in 1972. These fish may have been descendants of the first goldfish to live in the public waters of Ohio—escaped garden pond animals that were discovered during 1888 in a canal basin adjacent to the creek.[7]

The introduced species that had the greatest impact in the Mill Creek Valley was the malaria-causing *Plasmodium vivax*. This Old World protozoan parasitized humans and mosquitoes, native insects that spent their larval stages in the overflow pools on the valley floor and their adulthoods within a mile of their sites of emergence. The malarial parasites arrived in the Mill Creek basin in the blood of some early settler or settlers. When the infected human was bitten by an appropriate species of mosquito, the ingested protozoans penetrated the insect's stomach wall and made their way to the mosquito's salivary glands. As the insect bit another person, the parasites were injected into the blood plasma of the next human host.[8]

In the new host the protists first invaded the liver, in which they reproduced, and then entered the red blood cells, where they fed and further multiplied. After forty-eight hours, the infected red blood cells burst, each releasing between ten and twenty new protists into the plasma. These immediately entered other red blood cells to continue the process of growing and reproducing, and so the infection kept increasing in intensity.

The human host suffered chills before and a fever following the rupturing of blood cells every forty-eight hours. These symptoms became more and more intense over a period of two weeks, and some sufferers died. When the human host survived, the periodic chills and fever could continue for several years, a period during which the parasite might be ingested by a feeding mosquito and passed to a new victim.[9]

Until the life cycle of *Plasmodium,* as described above, was outlined in 1898, the recurrent symptoms and occasional deaths were ascribed to the breathing of bad air, *mala aria.* Local names for the illness included "autumnal, bilious, intermittent, remittent, congestive, miasmatic, malarial, marsh, malignant, chill-fever, ague, fever and ague, dumb ague, and, lastly the Fever." The bad air causing the autumnal fever was thought to be miasma, the stench of rotting vegetation in wet environments. This classic theory concerning the source of malaria explained the low disease rate during dry seasons, the malariousness of bottomlands, and the spread of the disease in certain directions by the wind.[10]

According to Dr. Daniel Drake in 1810, the natural source of malaria in Cincinnati was the inundated flood plain of the Mill Creek. He noted that most of the people affected with autumnal fever lived in the area downwind from the lowlands surrounding the creek's mouth. Drake believed that the disease would be worse in Cincinnati if it were not for the efficiency of the intervening forest in intercepting the miasmata spreading from the pooled Mill Creek waters to the west of the city. He concluded that "This forest should, therefore, be considered in the light of a rampart against a perpetual enemy, and preserved in the most sacred manner."[11]

Forty years later, in 1850, Drake repeated his idea that trees arrest the spread of malaria. As evidence for this hypothesis, he pointed out that "those who first penetrate our woods, and establish themselves in cabins, closely surrounded by trees, remain comparatively exempt from autumnal fever, till the clearing is extended." This observation linking deforestation with malaria appears contradictory, since the opening of land to the influences of sun and wind should induce surface drying. However, the original forest canopy caught a great deal of precipitation, much of which evaporated before the vegetation transmitted it to the ground. The trees also transferred an enormous amount of water from the earth to the air through leaf transpiration. Removal of the forest, therefore, increased the total volume of water reaching and remaining on the ground. Over the wide floor of the Mill Creek Valley, deforestation had the effect of transforming relatively dry areas into malarious wetlands.[12]

During the mid-nineteenth century, autumnal fever was described by Cincinnati reporter Charles Cist as "an annual endemio-epidemic" for residents in the Mill Creek Valley and for "inhabitants of the neighboring bluffs." In 1857, a group of concerned citizens petitioned the Cincinnati City Council to eliminate the sources of malaria from the Mill Creek bottomland:

> Decaying vegetable or animal matter may generate malaria, which wafted eastward by the prevalent western winds, may render the whole eastern and central, as well as the western part of the city unhealthy. But if the few ponds of stagnant water should be drained, decaying animal and vegetable matter removed, and the valley covered with grass and trees, no malaria would be generated... If one would improve the health of Cincinnati, it is obvious that his first field of action should be Mill Creek valley.[13]

In response to continuing public pressure, the Cincinnati City Council Committee on Public Improvements in 1864 proposed the elimination of the creek's overflow pools, which sent a "malarious exhalation over the whole city." But an editorial in *The Cincinnati Commercial* of October 18, 1872, opposed the expenditure of public monies for reclamation of the stream's miasmatic flood plain:

> The clamor that we must improve the Mill Creek marsh lying west of the city is a false cry. There is no public necessity for its improvement. The swamps of Mill Creek, no matter how improved, will never be suitable for dwelling houses. Even if filled with clean gravel the impure subsoil will breed fevers forever... There is room for people to live on the healthy hills, and to them our population must ultimately go.[14]

The Cincinnati Board of Health Report for 1874 noted that the Mill Creek bottomland "has long been a source of malarial fever." However, most nineteenth-century Cincinnati health officers neglected to even mention malaria. The illness was so prevalent that it was not singled out for special attention any

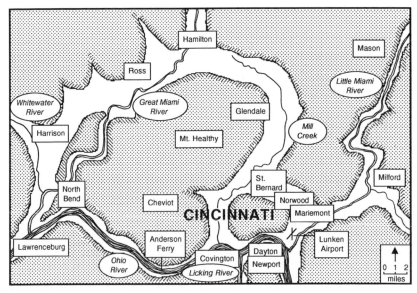

Figure 5. Southwestern Ohio in 1994 (with valleys shown in white).

more than the common cold is today. Luckily for city residents, land drainage and filling continued, virtually eradicating malaria in the Mill Creek basin by the beginning of the twentieth century. The standing-water sources of miasmata and mosquitoes (finally recognized as the real vectors of the disease) were eliminated.[15]

Malaria would have been a much less serious problem in the area if the Mill Creek bottom were not so broad and level. Its one-half to one-and-a-half mile width allowed precipitation and creek overflows to form numerous mosquito breeding pools across the valley floor, and its flatness permitted only slow drainage from these pools. The extensive bottomland of the Mill Creek is a striking exception to the much narrower bottomlands fringing similar-sized streams in Ohio and surrounding states. This peculiarity was noted by early geologists, who described the Mill Creek basin as "a deep and wide valley traversed by an insignificant stream, wholly inadequate to account for the erosion of which it has availed itself."[16]

During the nineteenth century, both glaciers and ancestral rivers were suggested as erosive agents of the broad valley. Professor Florien Giauque theorized that the basin was created by a lobe of an ice sheet. He wrote "that an immense mountain of ice and snow found its way from far northern regions to the southward, until its southern base reached to the Ohio river and perhaps beyond, and extended as far back as Glendale." Giauque postulated that the valley was formed when the movement and enormous weight of the ice ploughed out and deepened an elongated area originally filled with soft earth.

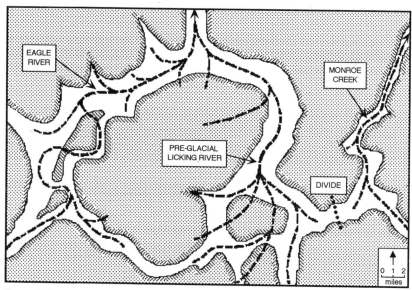

Figure 6. Pre-glacial Teays Drainage (with modern valleys shown in white).

The surrounding bluffs presumably resisted the glacial action because they are composed of stone. Finally, when the ice mountain melted, the glacial runoff supposedly deposited the alluvial gravel, sand, and soil on the valley bottom.[17]

An alternative explanation of the origin of the valley and its alluvial deposits had been developed earlier by Judge Jacob Burnet. He noted in 1837 that the Great Miami River Valley and the head of the Mill Creek Valley are connected near Hamilton by what appears to be an abandoned river trough (Fig. 5). He hypothesized that the trough and the Mill Creek Valley were carved by the original Great Miami when that river bent to the east at Hamilton. The mouth of the Great Miami at that time presumably was located on the Ohio River at Cincinnati, instead of at its present point several miles west of the city.

Judge Burnet speculated that the extensive alluvium in the Mill Creek valley was deposited by the Great Miami, but "whether suddenly or gradually, is a question for the geologist to settle." Ten years later, in 1847, Judge Burnet seemingly ruled in favor of sudden deposition:

> [I]t would not require a very great stretch of imagination, to conceive of a violent convulsion, accompanied with an unusual rise of water in the Big Miami, sufficiently powerful and irresistible to carry with it the material which filled up its original channel, and opened for itself a new one, through which it discharges itself into the Ohio river.[18]

It was Burnet's theory concerning the formation of the Mill Creek Valley that was most often recast and repeated. But near the end of the nineteenth

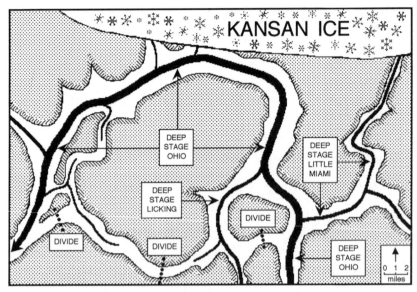

Figure 7. Deep Stage Drainage (with modern valleys shown in white).

century, the validity of a Great Miami parentage of the valley began to be chal-
lenged. In 1889, Professor Joseph James recorded that wells dug into the alluvial deposits found the Mill Creek Valley to have a greater depth to bedrock
than does the Ohio River Valley at Cincinnati. This fact led James to suggest
that the Mill Creek Valley was not created by an ancestral Great Miami running south, but by the Ohio River that once turned north at Cincinnati. This
ancestral Ohio supposedly flowed north and west to Hamilton, where it again
turned to pass southwestward along the present valley of the Great Miami until it regained its present channel at Lawrenceburg, Indiana.[19]

In 1900, physical geologist Gerard Fowke also disputed Judge Burnet's
theory. Fowke argued that the Great Miami could not have accomplished "the
improbable feat of eroding a deep channel and then, without any discoverable
reason, deserting this course and carving a new one for itself through the bordering hills." He theorized that the Mill Creek Valley had been formed instead
by the ancestral Licking River flowing northward from Kentucky past Cincinnati to its mouth at Hamilton. There its waters were supposedly received by an
ancient river that flowed northeastward from Kentucky through the Great
Miami Valley to the old Kanawha River north of Dayton. Fowke thought that
the present mouth of the Licking opposite Cincinnati was formed later when
the Ohio River cut across and intercepted the Licking's flow. Due to the Ohio's
piracy, Fowke concluded, the Licking's "ancient valley from Cincinnati to
Hamilton has been pre-empted by the insignificant Mill creek," a stream that
"seems almost lost as it meanders aimlessly back and forth" across the broad

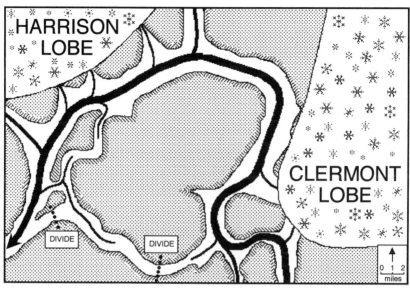

Figure 8. First modification of Ohio River channel during Illinoian Glaciation (with modern valleys shown in white).

valley floor.[20]

Present-day geologists substitute the less pejorative adjective "underfit" for "insignificant" when describing the Mill Creek as a stream too small to have carved the valley in which it lies. Otherwise, the contemporary understanding of the valley's geological history incorporates parts of many of the earlier theories recounted above. The scenario of the valley's formation that is outlined below is based largely on an account formulated by Professor Richard Durrell of the University of Cincinnati.[21]

More than two million years ago, before the beginning of the Pleistocene Epoch or "Ice Age," the pre-glacial Licking River flowed northward more or less along the current course of the southward-flowing Mill Creek (Fig. 6). (Throughout this account, present-day place names are used for reference.) At Hamilton, the pre-glacial Licking joined the Eagle River to continue north together to the large Teays River. The Teays flowed across central Ohio, Indiana, and Illinois to drain into the Mississippi in the vicinity of St. Louis.[22]

About 1,200,000 years ago, the Kansan glacier became the first of three Pleistocene ice-sheets to invade southwestern Ohio. This mass of ice pushing down from the north blocked the Teays River and caused a new westward drainage system to the Mississippi to be established south of the glacier. Because the volume and speed of glacial meltwater in this drainage caused deep channels to be formed, the major watercourse in the system is called the Deep Stage Ohio River.

The Deep Stage Ohio entered the Cincinnati area from the south through

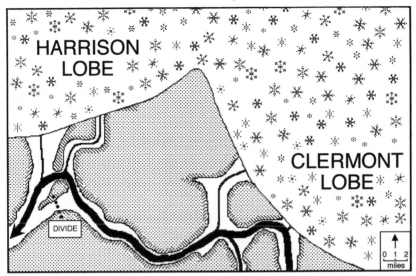

Figure 9. Second modification of Ohio River channel during Illinoian Glaciation (with modern valleys shown in white).

the still-used Ohio River Valley (Fig. 7). At the point where Lunken Airport is now situated, it turned north up the present Little Miami River Valley to Mariemont, where it again turned to continue flowing west through the Norwood Trough to St. Bernard. The Deep Stage Ohio absorbed the smaller Licking River at St. Bernard, and turned north to flow along the pre-glacial Licking River channel to Hamilton. Near Hamilton, the advancing Kansan ice sheet deflected the Deep Stage Ohio toward the southwest, past Harrison and Lawrenceburg down along the channel previously cut by the Eagle River. As the Kansan glacier melted, water continued to follow this new drainage system through the region. The erosive action of the Deep Stage Ohio greatly widened the portion of the pre-glacial Licking River channel through which it flowed, so that today the Mill Creek Valley broadens from a half-mile average width south of St. Bernard to a one-and-a-half mile average width north of that city.[23]

The present course of the Ohio River in the Cincinnati area was established about four hundred thousand years ago near the southern edge of the Illinoian glacier, the second ice sheet to invade southwestern Ohio. The Clermont Lobe of the Illinoian glacier advanced into the area from east-northeast, eventually damming the Deep Stage Ohio River in the vicinity of the Norwood Trough. The resultant lake, reaching from the ice dam upstream toward Portsmouth, rose higher and higher until it overflowed a low divide between Walnut Hills (Cincinnati) and Dayton, Kentucky. The Ohio River thereafter flowed through this channel from Lunken Airport to the downtown areas of Cincinnati, Newport, and Covington (Fig. 8). Between the latter two cities, the Ohio received the waters of the Licking River and turned north into the portion of the ancient

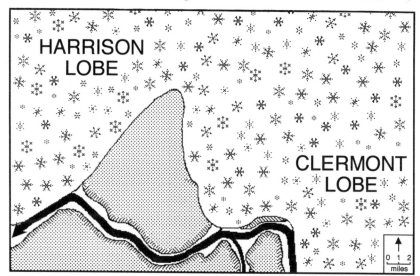

Figure 10. Third modification of Ohio River channel during Illinoian Glaciation (with modern valleys shown in white).

Licking River channel running through Cincinnati to St. Bernard. At St. Bernard the Ohio re-entered its former channel, flowing north to Hamilton and then southwest past Harrison and Lawrenceburg.[24]

The Illinoian ice continued to creep into the area, and next cut across the Deep Stage Ohio River in its valley in northern Hamilton County. A second lake formed, extending up the Ohio to the east, with an arm extending up the Licking to the south. Deposits of lake clay settled over the river gravels previously deposited by the Deep Stage Ohio. As time passed the impounded waters rose to a sufficient level to overflow a divide at Anderson Ferry, allowing the Ohio to establish a westward channel south of the Illinoian ice sheet (Fig. 9). The waters drained through this still-used Ohio River Valley from Cincinnati to the vicinity of Lawrenceburg, where the Ohio re-entered its former channel.

The new drainage of the Ohio River westward from Cincinnati allowed the first Mill Creek to form in the abandoned Ohio River Valley segment between the Illinoian ice dam and what is now downtown Cincinnati. At the same time, the Great Miami and Whitewater Rivers were born between the ice and the present site of Lawrenceburg. These three streams served to carry glacial meltwaters south to the Ohio River until they, too, were enveloped by the advancing ice (Fig. 10). Upon the Illinoian lake clays in the Mill Creek lowlands, as well as on the surrounding highlands, the Illinoian glacier deposited a blanket of glacial till—intermingled gravel, sand, and clay. As the glacier retreated from the area, the Mill Creek re-emerged from the ice to begin eroding through the till on the valley bottom.

The Wisconsinan glacier, the most recent North American ice sheet,

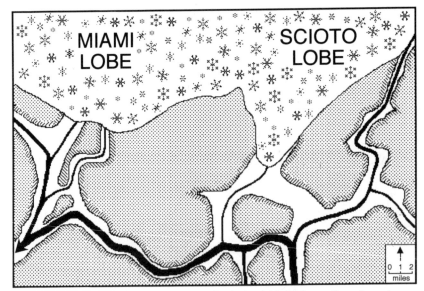

Figure 11. Maximum extent of Wisconsinan Glaciation (with modern valleys shown in white).

pushed into the area about seventy thousand years ago. Its Scioto Lobe advanced down the Mill Creek Valley to within a few miles of St. Bernard, with meltwaters discharging from the glacier's toe into the creek (Fig. 11). As the continental ice sheets of the period increased in extent, the consequent lowering of the worldwide sea level caused downcutting on the Mississippi River and its tributaries, among them the Ohio River and the Mill Creek. The stream downcutting in the Mill Creek basin left terraces of Illinoian till along the sides of the valley. Spring Grove Cemetery and Norwood are largely located on such Illinoian terraces.[25]

The Wisconsinan glacier carried large quantities of sand and gravel south to the Cincinnati area from Ohio and Ontario. When this glacier began melting back about seventeen thousand years ago, deposits of these materials known as outwash partially filled the Mill Creek Valley. Postglacial stream erosion has left a terrace of Wisconsinan outwash near the mouth of the valley. Losantiville, now downtown Cincinnati, was established on this terrace above the floodwaters of the Ohio River and the Mill Creek.

Wisconsinan outwash is also found in the Mill Creek Valley north of downtown Cincinnati, though in lesser amounts. Excavations and erosion in these outwash deposits have uncovered bones and teeth of Ice Age animals that lived in the valley: mammoth, giant beaver, giant ground sloth, and others. The English scientist Charles Lyell wrote of the creek in 1845 as "a place where several teeth of mastodons have been met with." In 1990, a Sycamore High School student and his friend from Miami University discovered an entire mastodon jawbone in the Mill Creek near the Evendale-Reading city line. The two Blue Ash residents were searching for lost golf balls when they found the seventy-pound bone resting on a pile of flood debris.[26]

After the retreat of the last glacier from the Mill Creek Valley, prehistoric Indians immigrated into the area and most of the large Ice Age mammals became extinct, perhaps a cause and effect relationship. Through the postglacial period, the Mill Creek eroded only a shallow channel into the valley floor, since the stream dissipated its flood-erosive power by quickly overflowing its channel and spreading its flood waters across the broad valley bottom. The small creek in its wide basin is definitely a "misfit," as it was labeled by Professor Durrell in a 1961 geology guidebook.[27]

Three-quarters of a century earlier, in an 1889 paper on the geological history of the Ohio River, the "misfit" Mill Creek was even more scathingly characterized by Professor Joseph James as "an unworthy descendant of the mighty river which carved out its broad and lengthy channel." James ended his paper with a passage that alluded to the Mill Creek Valley's contemporary use as a transportation corridor, the topic of the next chapter:

> Where once the stream pursued its northward course, the iron horse carries thousands daily to and from their homes in the wide and fertile Mill Creek Valley. Never would all this have been, had not the Glacial Period wrought its wondrous change... [leaving the abandoned Ohio River channel] to be utilized by man as a way for his iron servant and as a place whereon to build his cities.[28]

PART TWO

Spreading Industry, Increasing Pollution

The Glendale Station on the Cincinnati, Hamilton and Dayton Railroad. (From the collection of The Cincinnati Historical Society. B-91-134)

CHAPTER FIVE

A Route for Draft and Iron Horses

Mill Creek itself could scarcely be a factor even in canoe travel. Nevertheless this natural crossroad was followed by Indians from prehistoric times. By this route the tribes north of the Ohio made their raids on the Kentucky settlements. Later it became, in succession, the line of wagon travel, canal traffic, and finally the chief entrance for railroads into Cincinnati.

—Nevin N. Fenneman[1]

IN 1789, when General Harmar was ordered to protect the Miami Purchase and Kentucky settlers against the natives, he had Fort Washington built in Losantiville (soon to be Cincinnati), astride the Indians' Mill Creek-Licking River warpath. From 1790 to 1793, Generals Harmar, St. Clair, and Wayne launched their military campaigns against the Indians from Fort Washington or its immediate vicinity. Their armies marched up the Mill Creek Valley accompanied by wagon trains that required established roads. In some places the troops were able to widen and use pioneer traces already blazed between Cincinnati and Ludlow's, White's, and Runyan's Stations. In other areas of the valley, forward patrols had to clear and open new roads in order to reach the next bivouac.[2]

The military roads (Fig. 4 in Chapter One) were made public highways following the passage of the armies. In 1792, St. Clair's Mill Creek Valley road from White's Station to Fort Hamilton was improved and a connecting trace was opened from White's Station to Columbia. After Wayne's march over St. Clair's road, the fourteen-mile route was further improved in 1794. Another road was laid out in 1795 along the six miles of Harmar's track that ran from Fort Washington to the trace connecting White's Station and Columbia.[3]

Crossroads eventually were built in every direction from these early highways. However, the main thoroughfare for the Cincinnati region always has remained in the Mill Creek basin. Charles Cist in 1841 wrote of the valley as "the only opening through which a road can reach the city without passing over hills, and descending steep declivities." More than a century later, in the 1947

Cincinnati Metropolitan Master Plan Report, the City Planning Commission echoed Cist's observation while outlining the fitness of today's Millcreek Expressway, as the part of Interstate 75 that runs through the valley is officially known: "Easy grades can be used because it follows a water-level course down the Millcreek Valley."[4]

The curves of the valley and the meanders of the Mill Creek and its tributaries caused the valley roads to swerve and turn in marked contrast to the straight avenues of the city. The streets in central Cincinnati were laid out in a checkerboard pattern inspired by William Penn's Philadelphia plan. In addition to simplifying the problems of surveying and reducing the number of legal arguments over property boundaries, the street grid imposed an orderliness on nature that settlers associated with civilized places. As Dr. Daniel Drake declared in a speech to fellow Cincinnati physicians, "Curved lines, you know, symbolize the country, straight lines the city."[5]

An early straight line that was forced into the naturally curving Mill Creek Valley was Garrard Avenue. This road was surveyed to run due north from the mouth of the creek, with perpendicular cross streets (a remnant of Garrard Avenue survives today at the east end of the Hopple Street viaduct). Other straight lines were dug into the valley and joined together to form a canal leading northward from Cincinnati. Dr. Drake first suggested this water route in 1815 in a proposition that again demonstrated his geometrical vision for a civilized landscape:

> The transportation on this canal and the Miami above (if its navigation were somewhat improved) would, in less than half a century, be great indeed. The country on each side, for the average distance of twenty-five miles, and as far north as the navigable waters of the Maumee, about 110, would be dependent on it. In this parallelogram of 5,500 square miles, there is no spot which is not susceptible of cultivation; and by far the greater part is equal to any land in the United States. It only, therefore, requires facilities for the exportation of its surplus produce, and the importation of foreign articles, to ensure for it a very dense population; and such facilities would be afforded by the canal.[6]

A decade of economic arguments such as this one culminated on February 4, 1825, when the Ohio Assembly authorized the construction of the Miami Canal. Digging for the canal began on July 21 at Main Street in Cincinnati, the canal's southern terminus from 1829 until it was extended to the Ohio River in 1834. To the north, the Great Miami and Maumee Rivers proved unnavigable, and so the canal was extended through to Toledo by 1845. The legislature officially designated it as the Miami and Erie Canal on March 14, 1849.[7]

The entire route of the Miami and Erie Canal was almost identical to that followed years earlier by Generals St. Clair and Wayne. Beginning at the Ohio River near the site of Fort Washington, the canal rose through ten locks along the present Eggleston Avenue and out the length of the present Central Parkway

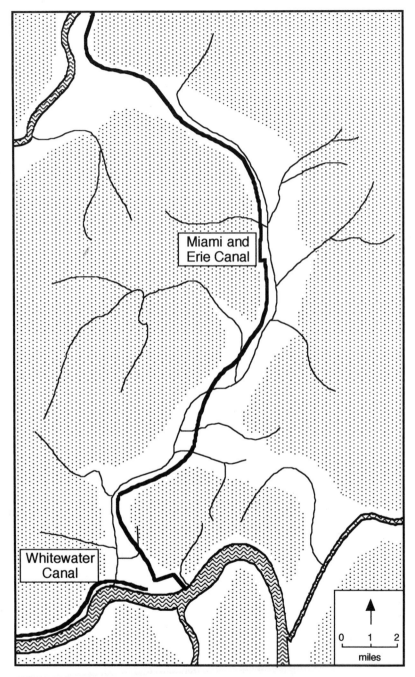

Figure 12. Canal routes in the Mill Creek region (with valleys shown in white).

(Fig. 12). It continued to parallel the Mill Creek by bending around the base of the Clifton hill and then bridging Mitchell Avenue on an aqueduct, so that one could cross the canal at that point by going under it. Farther up the valley, the canal again used aqueducts to cross the Mill Creek at White's mill between Carthage and Hartwell, and to cross the West Fork Mill Creek in Lockland. Smaller Mill Creek tributaries were diverted through culverts under the canal.[8]

The canal continued through Hamilton County, paralleling the Mill Creek from Lockland north toward the city of Hamilton. It rose through a series of four locks in Lockland, crossed Beaver Run on an aqueduct located a half-mile south of the county line, and rose again through single locks at Crescentville and Rialto in Butler County. Between Port Union and Hamilton, the canal crossed through the long-dry Deep Stage Ohio River Trough from the Mill Creek Valley into the Great Miami Valley. Approximately nine hundred laborers were involved in the construction of the canal between Cincinnati and Hamilton; for a day of working from sunrise to sunset, they each received thirty cents and four jiggers of whiskey to ward off malaria.[9]

From Hamilton, the canal paralleled the Great Miami River north past Middletown, Dayton, and Piqua. It passed from the Ohio River watershed into the Lake Erie watershed at the Loramie Summit, a hundred miles from Cincinnati and 516 feet above the Ohio River at Cincinnati. From the twenty-four mile long summit, the canal descended 374 feet over a distance of 125 miles to Lake Erie at Toledo. The waterway had a four- to six-foot depth, a forty- to sixty-foot surface width, and a twenty-six- to forty-six-foot bottom width. A total of nineteen aqueducts, 106 locks, and three water supply reservoirs were constructed along the 249-mile canal.[10]

On July 1, 1827, the first water was let into the canal ditch at a point along the Great Miami River two miles above Middletown. The water level was deep enough by the Fourth of July to enable a packet boat to carry holiday revelers on the canal segment north of Middletown. Following completion of the Mill Creek aqueduct, the first boats arrived in Cincinnati on March 17, 1828. The six vessels were greeted by a crowd of thousands and a bust of DeWitt Clinton, father of American canals.[11]

The construction of the Miami and Erie Canal represented a small portion of a national canal-building craze. Between 1790 and 1850, 4,400 miles of hand-dug artificial waterways were constructed, almost one-and-a-half times longer than the distance from New York to San Francisco. Locally, the early success of state-sponsored canals in Ohio led to the 1839 groundbreaking of the Whitewater Canal by a private company. From its eastern terminus at Third and Central Streets in Cincinnati, the canal crossed the Mill Creek on a fifty-foot aqueduct, and paralleled the Ohio River to North Bend (Fig. 12). There the canal entered a 1,900-foot tunnel in order to reach the valley of the Great Miami, a river it then bridged on another aqueduct. Once on the west side of the Great Miami, the canal paralleled the Whitewater River from its mouth into the

Winter view of the Miami and Erie Canal aqueduct over the Mill Creek at Carthage, with icicles forming from aqueduct leaks. (From the collection of The Cincinnati Historical Society. B-94-257)

farm country of southeastern Indiana. The canal opened to Brookville, Indiana, in 1843, and extended to Connersville in 1848.[12]

The canal aqueducts spanning the Mill Creek leaked large volumes of water into the stream below, increasing the creek's flowage. Along the Miami and Erie Canal, additional water entered the creek via spillways and mill races. Of the eighty-four million gallons of water brought into the Mill Creek Valley every day by the Miami and Erie Canal, only forty-eight million gallons were discharged into the Ohio River at Cincinnati. The other thirty-six million gallons found their way into the Mill Creek, causing a 35 percent increase in the average flow. Millers and some stream biota benefitted from the increased flowage. On the other hand, organisms that inhabit slackwater pools were adversely affected.[13]

The importance of the Mill Creek Valley as the area's transportation corridor to the north was confirmed on July 27, 1845, when the first canal boat from Cincinnati arrived in Toledo. During the same year, the valley's appearance was described by Rebecca Clopper following a morning climb to an overlook:

> I had no conception of such a prospect, beautiful beyond description—the feeble efforts of my pen could never do it justice, nor will I attempt it. My companion for a time seemed speechless, we both stood enjoying the lovely view, below, around, in every direction. Oh! nature, how beautiful thou art! I

at last exclaim'd, how lovely in all thy variety—the meandering Mill Creek, below, the canal with its boats gliding along, the sheep & cattle browsing on the sloping hills, the well-cultivated farms, even the turn-pike had a beauty in our eye.[14]

The Mill Creek Valley's loveliness during the mid-nineteenth century also was extolled in the ballad "Dovecote Mill" by Phoebe Cary, a resident of the Cincinnati area from 1824 to 1850. In the undated poem, Cary depicted the valley's landscape as it might be seen from a Northside hillside facing downvalley toward the Ohio River and Cincinnati:

> Ah, you might wander far and wide,
> Nor find a spot in the country side
> So fair to see as our valley's pride!
>
> How, just beyond, if it will not tire
> Your feet to climb this green knoll higher,
> We can see the pretty village spire;
>
> And, mystic haunt of the whippoorwills,
> The wood, that all the background fills,
> Crowning the tops to the mill-creek hills.
>
> There, miles away, like a faint blue line,
> Whenever the day is clear and fine
> You can see the track of a river shine.
>
> Near it a city hides unseen,
> Shut close the verdant hills between,
> As an acorn set in its cup of green.
>
> And right beneath, at the foot of the hill,
> The little creek flows swift and still,
> That turns the wheel of Dovecote Mill.[15]

Many years later, in 1922, Sherwood Anderson continued the tradition of Ohio landscape writing when he contributed an article about the state to *The Nation* magazine. In "I'll Say We've Done Well," Anderson updated the previous descriptions of the Mill Creek Valley with Cincinnati at its mouth:

...[A] poet coming there might have gone into the neighboring hills and looked down on the site of the great city; well, what I say is that such a poet might have dreamed of a white and golden city nestling there with the beautiful Ohio at its feet. And that city might, you understand, have crept off into the green

hills, that the poet might have compared to the breasts of goddesses, and in the morning when the sun came out and the men, women, and children of the city came out of their houses and looking abroad over the sweet land of Ohio—
But pshaw, let's cut that bunk.
We Ohioans tackled the job and we put the kabosh on that poet tribe for keeps. If you don't believe it, go down and look at our city of Cincinnati now. We have done something against great odds down there. First, we had to lick the poet out of our own hearts and then we had to lick nature herself, but we did it.

The article continued with a lamentation over the growth of manufacturing in Ohio and its ill effects on the state's air, land, and waters. Anderson depicted in microcosm the industrialization of the United States and the concurrent degradation of the nation's natural resources.[16]

The Industrial Revolution in the United States had begun over a century earlier at sites where manufacturers could tap large, reliable flows of water to drive their machinery. The first industries in New England and the middle Atlantic states were erected on river banks, usually near waterfalls. Fall River, Lowell, Lawrence, Paterson, and many other factory towns sprang up on swiftly flowing natural watercourses along the East Coast.[17]

Inland, where river flows are usually slower and more variable, would-be manufacturers and mayors sought alternative sources of water power. For example, as plans for the Miami Canal were being formulated in the early 1820s, manufacturing interests in Cincinnati pressed for a design that would provide water for factory use. A proposed canal route that would follow the Mill Creek all the way to its mouth was successfully opposed because it bypassed growing

The Mill Creek as it meandered through Northside. (Postcard from the collection of The Public Library of Cincinnati and Hamilton County)

The Miami and Erie Canal in Cincinnati, with Mt. Adams in the background. (From the collection of The Cincinnati Historical Society. B-88-307)

industries in the city. The route that was excavated instead carried the canal water on a level course from Lockland to the Central Parkway area of Cincinnati, about one hundred feet above the level of the Ohio River. The fall of water from this elevation could turn manufacturers' water wheels as it was directed down to the river. The volume of water involved in this scheme was estimated to be three thousand cubic feet per minute, generating an hydraulic power equivalent to the force necessary to turn sixty pairs of millstones.[18]

In the Mill Creek Valley twelve miles above Cincinnati, a series of four canal locks located along a forty-eight-foot fall provided water power to early industries in Lockland. The town was platted in 1828 by land speculators who understood the site's attractiveness to manufacturers. During the next half century, several mills and factories were founded in Lockland or drawn there from Cincinnati. By 1880, Lockland boasted four paper mills, two woolen mills, two starch factories, two flouring mills, one cotton mill, a box factory and planing mill, a baking powder factory, and some wagon factories. Most of these industries initially used canal water to drive their machinery, and boats on the canal to transport their supplies and products. The state's rental price for canal water power was inexpensive, on the principle that more industry would generate more canal trade and toll receipts.[19]

In 1880, The Friend and Fox Paper Company of Lockland also owned three mills at the Rialto Lock seven miles north of Lockland. During the following year, the firm built a new paper mill at the Crescentville Lock five miles above

Lockland, on the site first occupied by Taylor Webster's canal-powered grist mill. The Rialto and Crescentville mills were operated by workers who came by wagon and buggy from Lockland and other Mill Creek Valley settlements.[20]

The establishment of the Lockland, Crescentville, and Rialto canal industries was an extension of the earlier use of water power in the Mill Creek Valley: grist and lumber mills had existed along the Mill Creek since the 1790s. Within Cincinnati, on the other hand, the introduction of water power via the canal represented a new source of energy, an alternative to the animal and steam power that were already in use. Horse power had been harnessed in the city by 1815 for cotton spinning and the manufacture of shingles and barrels. About the same time, the running of small mills by means of oxen treading on inclined wheels was invented by Joseph Robinson of Cincinnati. After an ox saw mill was successfully put in operation by 1817, Robinson's invention soon was adopted by several other mills in the city.[21]

Other early Cincinnati mills tapped steam as a source of energy. By 1815, a steam saw mill and a steam woolen mill were joined by an eight-story general purpose steam mill built for manufacturing flour, flax seed oil, and fiber products. In 1827, the year before the opening of the canal in Cincinnati, there were about twenty-five steam engines in the city's factories.[22]

Compared with steam, the power available from canal water was limited in quantity; moreover, one had to use water power where the water ran, while a steam engine could be built anywhere. Thus, in Cincinnati, the number of

A flour mill adjacent to the Miami and Erie Canal in Lockland. (Postcard from the collection of The Public Library of Cincinnati and Hamilton County)

A canal boat in the Miami and Erie Canal north of Cincinnati. (From the collection of The Cincinnati Historical Society. B-84-059)

machines powered by canal water never exceeded the number powered by steam. In 1836, probably less than ten mills in the city were driven by canal water, while more than fifty mills and manufacturing industries derived their power from steam engines.[23]

As a series of improvements during the nineteenth century increased the power output of the steam engine in yield per unit of fuel, the engine became less cumbersome and more useful for small milling operations. Steam-driven machinery allowed small mills to be established anywhere on the Mill Creek watershed. Steam engines even replaced water wheels at mills along the Mill Creek; steam mills were powered by dependable and plentiful wood and coal instead of by a natural water supply that disappeared during droughts and froze in winter.[24]

Steam also was put to use as a source of energy for transportation. The *New Orleans*, the first steamboat on the Ohio River, anchored at Cincinnati in 1811. Steamboat building began in Cincinnati in 1816, and fifty-seven riverboats were completed by 1826. Smaller steam-powered vessels were introduced to the Miami Canal within months after it opened in 1827, but they soon were pro-hibited because their faster speeds created wakes that damaged the canal banks. The four-miles-an-hour speed generated by horses and mules continued to be the norm for the animal-drawn canal boats, even for those with galloping names such as the *Wild Horse of Mill Creek*.[25]

A faster, steam-powered horse owned by the Cincinnati, Hamilton and

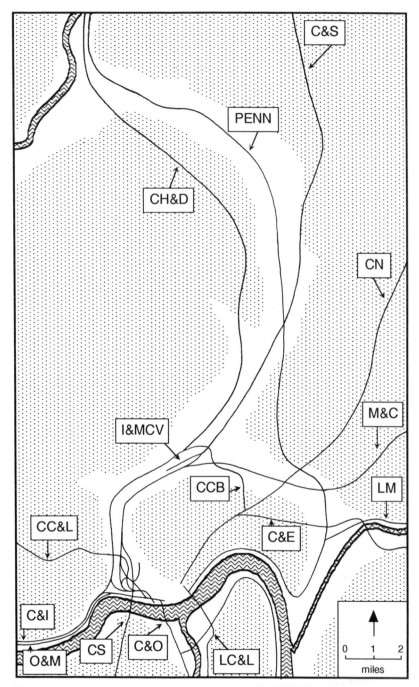

Figure 13. Railroad routes in the Mill Creek region (with valleys shown in white).

Dayton Railroad ran parallel to the canal between Cincinnati and Hamilton beginning in 1851. The company's roadbed had been built during the previous three years along the entire length of the west side of the Mill Creek Valley (Fig. 13). The coming of the iron horse quintupled the speed of freight transportation in the valley and signaled the end of a slower-paced era. When the first train from Cincinnati entered Hamilton, that city's last surviving Revolutionary War soldier announced: "I am ready to die now."[26]

Although the Cincinnati, Hamilton and Dayton was the first line in the Mill Creek Valley, it was the second railroad company to locate its southern terminus in Cincinnati. The Little Miami Railroad already had operated trains since 1842 from the city, up the Ohio and Little Miami River valleys, toward Xenia. The builders of the Little Miami and the Cincinnati, Hamilton and Dayton lines used the valleys of watercourses in order to lay out the easiest possible grades for the longest possible distances. Costs of railroad construction and operation were minimized by using valley routes, even though they required more bridges and culverts than would ridge routes.[27]

By 1852, the Cincinnati, Hamilton and Dayton operated three daily trains in each direction between Cincinnati and Dayton, at an average speed of 26.4 miles per hour. In the following year, through trains were operated from Cincinnati to Lake Erie, using the Dayton-to-Sandusky trackage of the Mad River and Lake Erie Railroad. This company already had provided a rail link between the Ohio River and Lake Erie in 1849 when the Little Miami Railroad was extended to Springfield. It was the competition presented by these railroads that eventually brought about the demise of the Miami and Erie Canal.[28]

A third railway to locate a terminal in Cincinnati was the Ohio and Mississippi Railroad. With construction beginning in 1851, this line crossed the Mill Creek Valley and paralleled the Ohio River to Aurora, Indiana, by 1854. The roadbed was extended west to East St. Louis, Illinois, in 1857. The opening of this rail route to the west was celebrated by senators, cabinet members, governors, mayors, historians, and other celebrities who were among the 1,500 passengers on the first scheduled train from Cincinnati to the Mississippi River.[29]

Also with an eye toward western traffic, the Cincinnati and Indiana Railroad was granted a charter in 1861 to construct a line to serve as the Ohio extension of the Indianapolis and Cincinnati. The company acquired the properties of the Whitewater Canal, let the water out, and laid its tracks in the bed. From an often-flooded station built in the canal's terminal basin in Cincinnati, the line crossed the Mill Creek at the site of the former aqueduct and continued into Indiana over the canal route outlined earlier in this chapter.[30]

Approaching from coal- and iron-rich eastern Ohio, the Marietta and Cincinnati in 1857 reached Loveland, from where it continued to Cincinnati along the tracks of the Little Miami Railroad. A westward extension finished in 1861 continued the line from Loveland through Madisonville and the Norwood

Procter and Gamble's Ivorydale location, the southwestern terminus of the one-and-a-half mile long Ivorydale and Mill Creek Valley Railroad. (From the collection of The Cincinnati Historical Society. B-94-247)

Trough to St. Bernard. From there, the trains entered Cincinnati through the Mill Creek Valley by using the Cincinnati, Hamilton and Dayton tracks. In 1872, the Marietta and Cincinnati had its own roadbed constructed into the city along the east side of the valley. The establishment of this new city line led to the building of the Winton Place Chester Park train station that is now preserved as part of Sharon Woods Village.[31]

To the north, the Cincinnati and Springfield began operations between the two cities in 1872. From Springfield, the line ran through Dayton and Middletown, and then came straight down along the east side of the Mill Creek Valley to St. Bernard. The close competition between the upstart "Bee Line" railroad and the valley's original railway was chronicled by Henry C. Lord, Cincinnati's first railroad historian: "the Cincinnati, Hamilton and Dayton had gotten a parallel road so near to her line that a well-drilled baseball player could have pitched his ball from one track to another almost anywhere between Dayton and Cincinnati." South of St. Bernard, the Cincinnati and Springfield used the recently completed Marietta and Cincinnati tracks in the Mill Creek Valley to reach Cincinnati.[32]

To the south, the city-owned Cincinnati Southern Railway Company began service between Cincinnati and Chattanooga, Tennessee, in 1880. The line's nearly half-mile long Ohio River bridge was built from Ludlow, Kentucky, to a point just east of the Mill Creek's mouth. The company's freight yards were constructed north of the bridge between those of all the other lines already located in the Mill Creek basin.[33]

To the east, the Cincinnati and Eastern Railroad inaugurated service in 1884 between Portsmouth and Idlewild, a small community at the southern edge of Norwood. The struggling, undercapitalized company underwent two reorganizations, finally emerging as the Cincinnati, Portsmouth and Virginia Railroad in 1891. This company extended its trackage into the industrializing Mill Creek Valley in 1901 when it acquired the tiny Cincinnati Connecting Belt Railway, a three-and-a-half-mile line between Idlewild and Ivorydale that had been completed the previous year.[34]

As small as it was, the Cincinnati Connecting Belt Railway was not the Mill Creek basin's shortest line. That distinction already belonged to the Ivorydale and Mill Creek Valley Railroad that was built in 1885 as a one-and-a-half mile long spur off the Bee Line tracks in St. Bernard. The short line, owned by Procter and Gamble, became famous for its extreme brevity and for its red locomotive sporting a boiler front covered by a brass P&G moon and stars trademark. But at its beginning, the railroad was best known for its disputed crossing of the Carthage Turnpike that separated the Ivorydale factory from the Bee Line tracks.

In the fall of 1885, the owner of the Carthage Turnpike (now known as Spring Grove Avenue) refused to accept the court-determined $2,500 payment by Procter and Gamble for a permanent right-of-way across the road. The turnpike company obtained a common pleas court order restraining track construction over the road, but before the proper papers could be served, the tracks were quickly laid across the pike on a Saturday night. On Sunday morning, "a posse of riotous, half-drunken deputy sheriffs led by the notorious attorney of the notorious avenue company" (to quote a local newspaper) ripped up the thirty feet of offending tracks and posted armed guards to see that they weren't re-

Railroad freight car yards fill much of the Mill Creek flood plain. (From the collection of The Cincinnati Historical Society. B-94-254)

placed. Only after P&G paid an additional sum to the toll road company was the Mill Creek Valley's shortest railroad line finally completed.[35]

At the other end of the scale, the giant Pennsylvania Railroad displayed a long-standing interest in using the Mill Creek Valley as a way to enter the Cincinnati market. One unsuccessful scheme had the company laying its tracks into the city on the bed of a drained Miami and Erie Canal. Finally, the railway chose to construct a line in 1888 from Hamilton to the Little Miami Valley east of Cincinnati. The roadbed ran southeast from Hamilton via the Mill Creek Valley and the Norwood Trough to the tracks of the Little Miami Railroad, a company that was by then controlled by the Pennsylvania Railroad. The new trackage allowed Pennsylvania Railroad trains from Michigan, Illinois, and Indiana to connect directly to Cincinnati.[36]

The Chicago, Cincinnati and Louisville Railroad was the last company to build a new route into the Cincinnati area. Service between Chicago and Cincinnati commenced in 1904 (the Louisville segment was never built). From Cincinnati's West End, the line went a mile and a half up the center of the Mill Creek Valley to its Lick Run tributary. There the track turned west up the Lick Run Valley to Cheviot, and then northwest toward Chicago.[37]

Thus nine railroad lines coming from all compass directions gained access to Cincinnati via the Mill Creek Valley. Only four companies did not use the valley to approach the city: the aforementioned Little Miami; the Louisville, Cincinnati and Lexington, which crossed from Newport to Cincinnati in 1872; the Cincinnati Northern, which entered the city through the Deer Creek Valley in 1882; and the Chesapeake and Ohio, which crossed from Covington to

Cincinnati in 1889. By 1889, about 220 passenger and mail trains operated to and from Cincinnati on a normal weekday, and the number of freight cars passing through the switching district in Cincinnati was exceeded only in Chicago and St. Louis. In 1889, as a sea of rolling stock filled the lower Mill Creek Valley, Cincinnati acknowledged the commercial impact of the railroads by officially switching to standard railroad time, thereby moving high noon in the city to 12:38 p.m.[38]

Also in 1889, Professor Joseph James published a paper on the geological history of the Mill Creek Valley which summarized its immense value for the railroads, the Miami and Erie Canal, and the first hundred years of Cincinnati's growth:

> While the creek scarcely exceeds in volume an ordinary canal, its valley is broad and extensive. Its usefulness is made manifest by the railroads which traverse it to enter Cincinnati.... [Several railroad lines] find modes of ingress and egress by it.
>
> The Miami Canal, too, follows its course for twenty-five miles. It is the only entrance to Cincinnati from the north, because of the hills that extend far to the eastward. Without it, tunnels, cuts or inclined planes would have been necessary, or Cincinnati would now be an insignificant village.[39]

CHAPTER SIX

Swigs and Pigs

> At this moment the four natural limits on the growth of cities were thrown off: the nutritional limit of an adequate food and water supply; the military limit of protective walls and fortifications; the traffic limit set by slow-moving agents of reliable transportation like the canal boat; and the power limit to regular production imposed by the limited number of water-power sites and the feebleness of the other prime movers—horse and wind power. In the new industrial city these limits ceased to hold.
>
> —Lewis Mumford[1]

AS MUMFORD observed in "The Natural History of Urbanization," an adequate amount of water and food was one requisite for the emergence of a nineteenth century industrial town. In the river city of Cincinnati, water and agricultural resources have never been in short supply. Visitor Edmund Dana reported in 1819, "The adjacent country, which chiefly supplies the markets of Cincinnati, lies between the two Miamies; and in point of health, good water, natural fertility of soil, and mildness of climate, combines as many means of cheap and good living, as perhaps, any considerable tract in North America." In the year of Dana's visit, farm products from the region not only provided Cincinnati residents with bountiful foodstuffs, but also made up 90 percent of the city's exports to southern and eastern markets.[2]

Many of the plant products sold in nineteenth century Cincinnati were grown on nearby Mill Creek Valley fields. A ride up the valley in 1866 by a reporter for *The Cincinnati Commercial* revealed a succession of market farms: "what beds of onions, and rows of beets and parsnips and carrots; what patches of cucumbers and melons; what multitudinous heads of cabbage and cauliflowers and lettuce, and hills of succulent young corn, one passes, are not to be reckoned by any process of mental arithmetic."[3]

Among the farm crops, unprocessed grains initially proved too bulky to be transported cheaply over unimproved roads into town. Early farmers in the Cincinnati region instead had their grain ground in nearby rural mills and brought it to market as flour. But as canal openings and road improvements

Market gardens in the Mill Creek Valley at the foot of Mt. Storm. (From the collection of The Public Library of Cincinnati and Hamilton County)

caused bulk freight costs to fall, grain was shipped directly to the larger, more efficient mills in Cincinnati and Lockland, there to be processed into flour for local consumers and distant markets.[4]

One cereal, native American corn, was so bulky to transport in either its raw or processed forms that it did not pay early farmers to raise it for market. The easily cultivated corn instead was used to supply the immediate needs of settlers and their livestock. Many farmers distilled whiskey from their corn, but by the end of the eighteenth century, government regulations that discouraged small stills were in place. As a result, several mill owners added distilleries to their operations in order to supply the local demand for alcohol.[5]

One distillery was erected in the early nineteenth century at the mouth of Whiskey Run adjacent to Jediah Hill's mill on the West Fork Mill Creek. During the same period, James Cunningham built a distillery on the Main Stem in present Evendale, sometime after James Caldwell had constructed the first Mill Creek Valley distillery in present Carthage. Caldwell's operation was destroyed in 1806 by the same Mill Creek flood that swept away his adjacent mill. Caldwell's copper still was found entangled in flood debris downstream and came, somehow, into the possession of an accused horse thief. When this man was acquitted, the victorious defense lawyer, Nicholas Longworth, took the copper still for his fee. Longworth, in turn, traded the still for a ninety-acre tract which was the beginning of the largest and richest landed estate in the history

Clifton Springs Distilling Company on the Mill Creek in Northside, with cows that fed on the spent mash. (From the collection of The Cincinnati Historical Society. B-94-232)

of Hamilton County.[6]

The loss of Caldwell's still represented only a small setback for whiskey-making in the Mill Creek Valley. Demand for the product increased both in and out of the Cincinnati region; whiskey became one of the city's major exports by 1826. Three of the major distilleries built during the next century were located along the Mill Creek above the abundant groundwater contained in the valley's glacial deposits. The distillery situated at the Mill Creek's mouth was named after the watercourse, although it made no use whatsoever of the creek's water. The ninety-five thousand gallons used daily in 1913 by the Mill Creek Distilling Company came from its own water wells and the city water supply, and all of the distillery's waste waters were discharged into the nearby Ohio River.[7]

Upstream on the Mill Creek at Northside, the much larger Clifton Springs Distilling Company backed onto the Miami and Erie Canal, on which the company operated three boats for transporting supplies and products. By 1913, this distillery daily took 1,730,000 gallons of water from the canal for use in cooling and condensing, and 25,300 gallons from the city supply for use in malting and boiling. All of the hot cooling water was discharged into the Mill Creek, but only small amounts of hot mash water escaped the factory. The distillery operated a slop evaporator that dried the spent mash for fodder; the liquid withdrawn from the mash was evaporated by machine.[8]

Still farther upstream, near the site of Caldwell's original distillery in Carthage, the Union Distilling Company used canal water for transportation only. In 1913, this distillery's daily 550,000 gallons of cooling water were drawn from the Mill Creek in the winter and from its own wells during the rest

OHIO.—THE GREAT BUSINESS INTEREST OF CINCINNATI.—ITS PRACTICAL AND ITS DISAGREEABLE PHASES.
From Sketches by a Staff Artist.—See Page 285.

Wastes from the pork industry polluted the Mill Creek throughout the nineteenth and early twentieth centuries. (From the collection of The Public Library of Cincinnati and Hamilton County) of the year. At all seasons, the company pumped about fifty thousand gallons of well water per day for use in its malting and boiling operations. Approximately 450,000 gallons per day of hot, clear cooling water were dumped into the creek, as were a hundred gallons per day of the hot, colored slop water that escaped from the evaporators. During lengthy periods when the slop evaporators were not working, an additional 150,000 gallons per day of hot water containing yellow corn mash "plainly colored the stream for several hundred feet below the point of entrance," according to a 1913 report on water pollution in Hamilton County.[9]

Downstream, the same Mill Creek waters that flowed past the corn mash whiskey distilleries were again discolored by another liquid industrial waste, one that is also, not incidentally, closely linked to corn: pig blood. The brownish-red effluent caused the lower Mill Creek in the nineteenth century to take on the same "Bloody Run" moniker that one of its tributaries had been named in the eighteenth century. It is to this earlier century that we must now return in order to understand the sequence of events that ended with the transfusion of porcine blood to the Mill Creek.[10]

Hogs were among the first livestock to be introduced into the Mill Creek Valley during the eighteenth century. Even before much agricultural land was cleared, these omnivorous animals found the valley's woodland forage so suitable that they practically raised themselves. Later, when corn was added to the hogs' diet to produce a higher quality of pork, the animals joined whiskey as conversion products of corn for consumption by farmers and their families. Surplus hogs, like excess alcohol, also became salable farm products in Cincinnati.[11]

The farmers at first brought the carcasses of their slaughtered hogs into the city's business center for packing and marketing by commissioned merchants. But farmers often butchered their hogs clumsily, and carcasses declined in freshness and cleanliness on the road from the farm to Cincinnati. Therefore, in the nineteenth century, the packers began to pay cash for live animals that they then routed to efficient slaughterhouses for butchering.[12]

The packers were located in the middle of Cincinnati, close to marketplaces, the Ohio River wharves, and the canal landings. The slaughterers, on the other hand, were grouped along Deer Creek, adjacent to the primary roads used by the farmers from the Mill Creek and Miami Valleys. The location of the slaughterhouses along a stream at the periphery of Cincinnati reduced the need to drive the hogs through the city streets, kept the smell of the holding pens away from most of the city residents, and permitted the slaughterhouse wastes to be flushed away to the Ohio River. The physical separation between slaughterhouses and packing plants gave employment to the cart drivers who transported the dressed animals to the packing district.[13]

Slaughtering in Cincinnati began in mid-November with the onset of cold weather, and usually continued until mid-February. In the winter of 1826-1827, the first season for which slaughter data is available, there were thirty thousand hogs killed and forty thousand hogs packed, ten thousand of the latter having been farm-butchered. Pork products exported from Cincinnati in 1826 were valued at $223,000. In contrast, the exports of flour and whiskey had respective values of $165,000 and $101,500 in 1826, making them Cincinnati's second and third most important exports. By 1827, Cincinnati's production of pork products surpassed that of Baltimore, the nation's previous "Porkopolis."[14]

By 1841, the annual number of hogs slaughtered in Cincinnati increased to about two hundred thousand, and the amount of pork packed yearly was calculated to be equivalent to a string of sausages long enough to encircle the entire earth at the equator. The completion of each new railroad line brought still more live hogs over longer distances into Cincinnati. By 1856, the Little Miami Railroad alone carried approximately ninety thousand hogs to the city, or about one-fifth of the 450,000 hogs slaughtered that year in Cincinnati.[15]

Cincinnati continued to kill and process about 450,000 hogs annually in the 1860s, the decade in which Chicago usurped Cincinnati's position as the nation's major pork packing center. During the 1870s, the slaughtering and packing season was extended through the warm months with the introduction of refrigerated railroad cars and storage houses. The year-around killing and processing of hogs and other animals continued to be an important industry in Cincinnati through the late nineteenth and early twentieth centuries, even as the center of livestock raising moved west to Illinois and Iowa.[16]

Several visitors to Cincinnati during its reign as Porkopolis commented on the slaughterhouses and the "torrents of blood" that poured into Deer Creek. The English author Frances Trollope described a hike from the city to the present Mt. Adams in 1828:

> ...[W]e found the brook we had to cross at its foot red with the stream from a pig slaughter-house; while our noses, instead of meeting "the thyme that loves the green Hill's breast," were greeted by odors that I will not describe, and which I heartily hope my readers cannot imagine; our feet, that on leaving the city had expected to press the flowery sod, literally got entangled in pigs' tails and jawbones...

In 1835, British author Harriet Martineau observed that below the buildings in which the hogs were killed, "Deer Creek, pretty as its name is, is little more than the channel through which their blood runs away."[17]

The number of hogs slaughtered along Deer Creek increased through the mid-nineteenth century, as did the wastes and odors produced by the slaughterhouse holding pens. In 1857, a Russian visitor "could not but express surprise at the sight of the bloody, or more accurately, the opal-like color of the water." Cincinnatians of the period failed to discern any such gem-like qualities in Deer Creek, a stream that became encircled by the city in the 1860s.[18]

Even residents living far from the hog-killing area were upset about the stream's contamination because of the proximity of the mouth of Deer Creek to the city water intake upstream on the Ohio River. A taste of the city's water "leaves us no room to doubt that the 'Deercreek eddy' does exist, and that the filthy waters of that stream are pumped into the reservoir," observed Cincinnati's mayor in 1867. But when a delegation of disgruntled citizens pressed the city to improve the conditions in the polluted Deer Creek Valley and establish a park there, at least one park commissioner defended the creek's impurities as harmless, though unpleasant, byproducts of Cincinnati's prosperous pork industry:

> Why this hurry about Deer Creek? Has that Gehenna, that Golgotha become so much worse, so much more offensive in the past ten days that it becomes important to the city of Cincinnati that it be filled up? No, sir, there is no change. It has been there since the city was organized, since your ancestors came here. The miasma arising from it may be very offensive, but it didn't kill our early ancestors. Why, they flourished and got fat on it. It didn't kill them any more than Mill Creek did my ancestors.[19]

The Mill Creek's reputation as a source of potentially lethal malaria obviously still endured. But aside from this one shortcoming, the Mill Creek generally "was a pure and beautiful stream" during the middle third of the nineteenth century, according to entomologist Charles Dury. Meanwhile, Deer Creek continued to increase "as a nuisance and a menace both to life and property." [20]

Widespread water pollution problems emerged into the consciousness of the urbanizing nation during the years following the Civil War. For example, at the 1872 meeting of the American Public Health Association, a major address on city water quality was delivered by C. A. Leas, a Baltimore physician and sanitarian. Doctor Leas decried the degradation of "streams from which others might draw a supply of water." Among the sources of stream pollution, he singled out slaughterhouses as being some of the worst offenders, asserting that "a greater outrage can hardly be perpetuated upon a people than the toleration within towns and cities of such establishments." Leas strongly suggested the banishing of the unsanitary slaughterhouses into suburbs and open country. "But it ought not to be forgotten that these open country localities for abattoirs for slaughtering purposes should be located upon streams, the waters of which are not afterwards to be used for drinking, culinary or cleansing purposes." [21]

The mounting pressure from public health advocates and local residents, combined with a desire by the livestock companies to be nearer the emerging railroad stockyards in the Mill Creek basin, impelled the removal by 1881 of the slaughterhouses originally located on Deer Creek. They relocated to the watershed of the Mill Creek, a stream that could carry off their wastes without subsequently introducing them into a town water system. An eastern municipality had much earlier established that slaughterers could dispose their offal into a non-potable city stream: beginning in 1656, Boston's Mill Creek had been designated as the only place where butchers could dump "their beasts entralls and garbidg" without penalty of a fine.[22]

The relocation of the slaughterhouses from the Deer Creek Valley was accompanied by the relocation of packing houses from the city. The packers were dislodged largely because they were polluting the Miami and Erie Canal and the Ohio riverfront with inedible grease, spent solutions from salting and curing, and unusable tank water from lard and tallow production. Most of the displaced packers merged with slaughter companies and moved to the Mill Creek basin. The consolidations improved the efficiency of the livestock industry by eliminating the need for wagon transportation of carcasses from slaughterer to packer.[23]

The first slaughterhouses in the Mill Creek Valley were opened as early as the 1830s. For purposes of water supply and waste drainage, they made use of a small stream flowing from the Ravine Street ravine southwesterly to the Mill Creek. Although this stream's waters eventually filled with slaughter wastes, it ironically came to be named Clearwater Creek after a Mr. H. Clearwater, owner of an early slaughterhouse on the stream. A more fitting title would have been "Bubbly Creek," the name Chicagoans gave to their stockyard-district stream in which gas-lifted slaughterhouse matter formed a surface scum "so thick that persons could walk upon it." Chicago's noxious Bubbly Creek eventually was encased in a sewer, as was the bloody and greasy Clearwater Creek in Cincinnati.[24]

The Clearwater Creek Sewer, completed in 1863, channeled its wastes directly into the Mill Creek. By 1871, the lowest portion of the "Mill Creek was running large quantities of bloody and offensive matter." The Clearwater Creek Sewer in 1875 was connected to the newly-built McLean Avenue Sewer that also ran to the Mill Creek. When the McLean Avenue Sewer was extended in 1882 to the Ohio River, much of Cincinnati's sewage previously entering the Mill Creek was intercepted and discharged into the river. However, the slaughterhouse offal and packing house wastes generated north of the McLean Avenue Sewer District continued to reach the Mill Creek after 1882.[25]

By January, 1913, the weekly slaughter and pack of the fifteen firms in the Mill Creek Valley north of the McLean District totalled 4,731 hogs, 1,642 cattle, 1,105 sheep, and 852 calves. These same fifteen meat companies used about 311,000 gallons per day of city water and 12,000 gallons per day of well water in their operations. They also used 425,000 gallons per day of canal water for cooling. The daily total of 748,000 gallons of heated and polluted waters carrying blood and solid livestock wastes all reached the Mill Creek through sewers and direct outflows. A sample of the Cincinnati Abbatoir Company's effluent was described as "a dark brown liquid, containing finely divided sediment and having a greasy surface. It had a very foul odor."[26]

Slaughterhouses contributed many pollutants to the Mill Creek. (From the collection of The Cincinnati Historical Society. B-81-256)

Other foul odors in the valley emanated from the stockyards where the livestock were held prior to slaughter. The earliest valley stockyards were located along Clearwater Creek in the Brighton area of Cincinnati. The encroachment of the growing city later caused the area's major stockyard to be located in Camp Washington, a couple of miles above Brighton in the Mill Creek Valley. There, in 1871, the newly-incorporated United Railroads Stockyard Company bought fifty acres of land west of Spring Grove Avenue, with two-thirds of the property located between the avenue and the Mill Creek, and one-third located across a bridge on the west side of the creek. This tract accommodated one of the largest stockyards in the United States, with fifteen miles of track and forty miles of water mains. The facility had a daily handling capacity of five thousand cattle, ten thousand sheep, and twenty-five thousand hogs for slaughter locally and for shipment to other markets for killing and packing. Wastes produced by the animals were flushed through the stockyard's eleven miles of sewers to the major drainage channel running through the property: the Mill Creek.[27]

The Union Stockyard was but one notable example of the many enterprises related to the livestock industry in Cincinnati. Other trades linked to the slaughter and packing business were wool-carding, tanning, rendering, and the manufacturing of soap, glycerine, and candles. Pollutants from these by-product industries joined the stockyard, slaughtering, and packing wastes in the Mill Creek.

Animal by-product industries discarded several types of manufacturing wastes into the creek. (From the collection of the Xavier University Biology Department)

The slaughterhouses in 1913 sent their sheep hides to the B. Steinharter & Sons Company, located on the banks of the Mill Creek in Elmwood Place. This wool-carding establishment used forty thousand gallons of well water daily, practically all of which was subsequently discharged as waste to the adjacent creek. The firm scraped and rinsed the sheep hides, soaked them in lime water, and then separated the wool from the skins. The bloody and dirty rinse water, together with spent lime water from the soaking vats and wash water from scouring the wool, constituted a foul-smelling "greenish black liquid with heavy sediment" that was poured into the Mill Creek.[28]

The six tanneries located in the Mill Creek drainage area in 1913 used 108,400 gallons per day of city, canal, and well water for processing the raw and salted hides that they bought from the wool-carder and the slaughterhouses. The tanneries prepared leather from the hides by rinsing the animal matter and brine off of them, de-hairing and de-greasing the hides in lime water, and treating them with tanning liquors. The tanners' grayish-black wash waters, alkaline lime waters, and dark brown tanning solutions were all discharged into the Mill Creek. Such tannery effluents blackened the bottom of the creek to such an extent that the watercourse became "a stream of ink." [29]

Bones, meat scraps, hide trimmings, and offal from the slaughterers and packers were rendered for the manufacture of glues, fertilizers, greases, tallows, and oils. The rendering of the raw materials used city, canal, and well waters, and produced a brownish liquid effluent that was thick with hair and other suspended organic debris. In 1913, a total of 618,300 gallons of this "very offensive wash" and eighty thousand gallons of hot cooling water were dumped into the Mill Creek each day by five rendering establishments.[30]

Greases and tallows produced at the rendering plants were sold to companies making soap, glycerin, and candles. Six of these concerns located in the Mill Creek Valley collectively discharged 4,775,700 gallons of hot and polluted waters daily to the creek in 1913. Two of the upstream establishments also took in water from the Mill Creek, but only for use as coolant; sources of production water were private wells and the municipal supplies of St. Bernard and Cincinnati. The three types of fluids discarded from the manufacturing processes were an acidic grayish liquid from the refining of greases, a white calcium carbonate sludge from the preparation of lye, and a malodorous brownish soup containing spent lye and kettle rinse waters. The removal of these wastes to the Mill Creek allowed the fabrication of nearly pure products by the soap companies.[31]

In summary, the effluent-producing industries that have been covered in this chapter were based on the conversion of cultivated plants, primarily corn, into marketable forms such as whiskey, meat, leather, glue, and soap. Thus, the early industrial pollution of the Mill Creek was due largely to the processing of farm imports from the Ohio River basin, a primary corn and pork-producing region of the United States in the nineteenth century. Later, as the center of grain and animal production moved westward in the growing nation, railroads continued to supply the needed agricultural products to the Hamilton County manufacturers who passed their wastes into the Mill Creek.

The sum of the effluent volumes recorded in this chapter discloses that each liquid gallon flowing from the Mill Creek's mouth in 1913 contained a cup of warm swill contributed by thirty-six alcohol, meat, and animal by-product firms. This industrial pollution of the Mill Creek was so apparent that the local Chamber of Commerce felt it necessary in 1914 to acknowledge and dismiss the creek's sorry plight: "the dirty fetid stream of today is the martyr of the onward progress of civilization." [32]

Large amounts of brewery wastes were released into the Mill Creek. (From the collection of The Cincinnati Historical Society. B-86-015)

CHAPTER SEVEN

The Rag City's Ruhr

In the early days its waters were pure, and swarmed with fish of many kinds; but, with the growth of a great city along its banks and about its mouth, its waters have become so defiled as scarcely to permit the existence in them of any living thing. Breweries, glue factories, distilleries, stock-yards and slaughter-houses empty their refuse into its waters; and these, with numerous city sewers, have made the name of Mill Creek synonymous with foul smells and turbid waters.

—Joseph James[1]

THAT EXCERPT from Professor James' 1889 paper on the Mill Creek mentions two water pollution sources that have not yet been addressed: brewers and sewers. Beer will be covered in this chapter, while sewage will be addressed in the next—a natural progression. In addition to breweries, the present chapter also will enumerate other polluting enterprises: a dairy, a galvanizing works, a laundry, several paper mills, a cotton batting and mattress manufacturer, and two roofing paper factories. The effluent volumes cited for the firms will be taken again from the 1913 City of Cincinnati inventory of the largest producers of liquid wastes in Hamilton County.[2]

The first brewery in Cincinnati was built in about 1810. Within a half century, Cincinnati became the third largest brewing city in the nation, a position it held as late as 1877. The city's breweries continued to produce more than a million barrels of beer annually through the early twentieth century, a quantity made possible by the ready availability of cereal grains grown in the Ohio River watershed.[3]

The Ohio Union Brewing Company, established in 1904, was the last brewery built in Cincinnati before Prohibition. Its construction in Camp Washington brought the number of Mill Creek Valley breweries to five. Three of these breweries used only city water in their operations, while the other two supplemented their municipal supplies with water drawn from the canal for cooling. In 1913, the five breweries produced a total of 470,000 barrels of beer annually and 113,000 gallons of wastewater daily. The sour-smelling "dirty white liquid containing considerable sediment" that they discharged into the Mill Creek consisted of spent hops, weak alkaline solutions used in washing bottles, hot cooling waters, and hot wash waters from the beer filtering process and from the scrubbing of empty casks. The volume of this effluent lessened considerably after Prohibition went into effect in 1920; only Bruckmann Brewery remained open through the Prohibition years, manufacturing near-beer.[4]

Unlike breweries and distilleries, dairies were unaffected by the temperance movement and continued to dump their wastes into the creek. Drainage from most of the area's dairies entered the Mill Creek north of Cincinnati; only one Mill Creek Valley dairy remained in the city by 1913. This Cincinnati dairy, the Mandery Pure Milk Company, was located in the neighborhood of Fairmount near Lick Run, a tributary of the Mill Creek. The firm used about 6,600 gallons of city water per day in its manufacture of butter and pasteurization of milk. The company's waste suds from churning and waste waters from washing bottles, cans, tanks, and floors joined the other dairy pollutants flowing down the Mill Creek from upstream operations.[5]

Across the valley from the Fairmount dairy, the Cincinnati Galvanizing Company in Camp Washington disposed about 1,200 gallons of spent sulphuric acid daily into the creek. Baths of the acid were used to free dirt and rust from metal pieces to be galvanized by the firm. The pieces then were dipped in an ammonium chloride flux and in molten zinc, neither of which were discharged from the plant because they could be sold when spent.[6]

Another establishment that freed dirt from material was located in the Walnut Hills neighborhood of Cincinnati. The Walnut Hills Laundry Company drained 20,500 gallons of soapy washwater daily into Ross Run, a Mill Creek tributary that today flows through a pipe beneath Victory Parkway, Reading Road, Tennessee Avenue, and Ross Avenue. (Ross Run often was misidentified as Bloody Run, the next Mill Creek tributary to the north; that's why Victory Parkway was called Bloody Run Parkway until it was renamed in honor of the Allies' victory in World War I.)[7]

Fabric articles eventually wear out after repeated use and laundering. From the mid-nineteenth through the early twentieth centuries, such articles often were sold to the rag paper mills in Lockland, Crescentville, and Rialto. These Mill Creek Valley mills procured their supplies of used fabrics via canal boat from "Rag City," their nickname for Cincinnati. The mills used water power available at the canal locks and abundant groundwater from the valley's glacial deposits in the process of changing paper stock into paper.

In 1913, Lockland's two paper mills together converted about two hundred tons per day of rags, old paper, and tree pulp into new products. They also released into the Mill Creek about three million gallons per day of a musty-smelling "dark brownish black liquid containing much finely divided suspended matter." This effluent contained spent bleach and hydrochloric acid as well as small fabric, wood, and paper fibers. Unmeasured amounts of paper mill wastes

The first factories in the Mill Creek Valley were built in the 1830s along the Miami and Erie Canal in Lockland. (From the collection of The Cincinnati Historical Society. B-94-242)

were discharged into the Mill Creek from the upstream mills at Crescentville and Rialto.[8]

Other Lockland industries joined in befouling the creek. A manufacturer of cotton batting and mattresses discharged approximately seventy thousand gallons daily of "a dark brown alkaline liquid containing considerable suspended matter." This waste resulted from the extraction of grease from raw cotton by boiling it in caustic soda, and from the washing of cotton goods in bleach and well water. The effluent discolored the Mill Creek "for one thousand feet or more downstream."[9]

Another Lockland plant took well water from the ground and discharged it, polluted, into the West Fork Mill Creek. This factory manufactured asbestos pipe coverings and roofing paper; the latter product was then treated with an asphalt and coal tar preparation. Liquid wastes consisted of turbid water from paper production and water from the asphalt and coal tar tanks. About one and a half million gallons of effluent was released daily into the creek as a dark liquid containing finely divided pulp and covered with an oily film.[10]

A rival roofing paper company situated in Carthage did not manufacture its own paper, but bought it instead from the canalside paper mills. The firm coated the paper with tars that it distilled by using about 545,000 gallons per day of cooling water drawn from the canal and the municipal supply. The resulting hot water carried oily wastes as it was discharged into the Mill Creek.[11]

A review of the discharge volumes enumerated above and in the previous chapter reveals that the Mill Creek in 1913 received about fourteen million gallons of effluent daily, a figure that does not even include the wastes from the dairies outside of Cincinnati, the stockyards in Camp Washington, and the paper mills in Rialto and Crescentville. About half of the effluent was launched by the distilleries, meat firms, and animal by-product establishments reviewed in the last chapter, while the other half spewed from the breweries, paper mills, and miscellaneous industries examined above. The total amount of industrial effluent meant that approximately one pint of every liquid gallon in the lower Mill Creek in 1913 consisted of wastes jettisoned by valley businesses.

The industrial discharges into the Mill Creek represented about 77 percent of the total effluent generated by Hamilton County industries in 1913. The creek would have conveyed about 93 percent of the county's total industrial liquid waste if the outfalls from the lower Mill Creek Valley firms had not been collected by the McLean Avenue Sewer and discharged directly into the Ohio River. The striking aggregation of factories in the creek basin caused local boosters to boast of the Mill Creek Valley as "the 'Ruhr' of the western world." The growth of this American Ruhr from its birth until World War I will be recapitulated in the remainder of the chapter.[12]

Whether in Germany, the United States, or elsewhere, industries tend to congregate where there are flat building sites, a reliable water supply, an adequate drainage system, an available workforce, a power source, and good transportation access to suppliers and markets. It's not surprising that the first manufactories along the Mill Creek were built in the 1830s in Lockland, a level townsite abundantly supplied with canal and well water. The Mill Creek provided a natural channel for the disposal of wastes, and the town of Reading across the creek accommodated a population of workers. The Miami and Erie Canal furnished water power and water transport, and valley roads provided overland transit throughout the year.[13]

The requirements for industrial growth also were met in the 1830s in Cincinnati, either along the canal, on the riverfront, or adjacent to Deer Creek. Deer Creek has been labeled as "Cincinnati's first Mill Creek" by the city's Engineering Department, because of the clustering of factories on its banks in the nineteenth century. By 1831, according to the distinguished visitor Alexis de Tocqueville, Cincinnati was "a picture of industry and work that strikes one at every step." Two years later, the English traveler C. D. Arfwedson marveled at the city's rapid industrialization: "On the spot where, not long since, the roaring of wild beasts and the yells of Indians were alone heard, the machines of manufactories and the hammers of workshops are now in motion." Nonindustrial buildings in "The Western Queen" also impressed Arfwedson during his 1833 visit: "Banks, University, Museum, Theatre, Athenaeum, Bazaar, and Hospitals are now seen, where, a quarter of a century ago, nothing but the primitive forest was standing untouched."[14]

By 1833, Cincinnati's population had grown to 28,000, about ten times larger than it had been twenty-five years before. Continuing growth allowed Cincinnati to become the nation's fourth largest city during the 1840s, increasing from 46,000 at the beginning of the decade to 115,000 at the end. Upon his return to New York from Cincinnati in 1850, Horace Greeley praised the city's expanding transportation facilities, nearby natural resources, and enterprising population: "It requires no keenness of observation to perceive that Cincinnati is destined to become the focus and mart for the grandest circle of manufacturing thrift on this continent." [15]

In 1853, the English visitor William Chambers found that the city's manufacturing districts were growing so impressive that they were "making Cincinnati one of the wonders of the New World." By 1860, Cincinnati's industrial production was surpassed only by that of New York and Philadelphia. The city was among the top five national producers of whiskey, pork, boots and shoes, soap and candles, ale, books, machinery, furniture, and ready-made clothing. [16]

Land speculators realized that growing companies would need new manufacturing districts in which to expand. They also saw that the most suitable locale for future factory sites was the level agricultural land along the lower Mill Creek. By 1845, a farmer was able to demand $22,000 from land investors for his sixteen-acre market garden across the Mill Creek from Cincinnati. On the city side of the stream, the owner of a three-acre lot in the Mill Creek

View from Price Hill toward Cincinnati in 1855, showing the beginning of industrialization in the agricultural lands bordering the meandering Mill Creek. (From the collection of The Cincinnati Historical Society. B-94-231)

The pre-industrial Mill Creek. (Postcard from the collection of The Public Library of Cincinnati and Hamilton County)

bottoms on Eighth Street refused $40,000 as being too small an offer for the land that he had bought for $2,100 in 1829.[17]

Farther north in the Mill Creek Valley, the Lafayette Bank foreclosed in 1842 on Charles Clarkson's 510-acre Clifton Farm, the largest landholding in the valley and the one that gave the area its present name. The farm was located across the Mill Creek from Northside, three miles north of the Cincinnati city limit. The Mill Creek formed the farm's western boundary, Clifton Avenue was its eastern boundary, and Colerain Avenue and the Miami and Erie Canal ran north-south across the tract. The bank broke the large estate into parcels for sale at prices of $320 per acre for the level land between the creek and the canal, and $65 to $135 per acre for slopes and highlands above the valley between the canal and Clifton Avenue. The price difference was accounted for by the fact that industries were beginning to locate along the Mill Creek, Colerain Avenue, and the canal. Despite its higher valuation, the valley bottomland sold much more quickly than did the valley slopes and uplands.[18]

The lesser value of sloped land was reflected in the 1845 sale price of the Garrard Farm above Northside on the western terraces of the Mill Creek Valley. The rolling 166-acre farm ascending from the Mill Creek's west bank was purchased for only $16,000 by the founders of Spring Grove Cemetery. The directors later purchased thirty-two acres of flat land on the opposite, eastern side of the creek to serve as a source of road gravel and to protect the front of the cemetery from future industrialization. Thus, the Mill Creek came to run through the edge of a cemetery that grew to become the largest in the world in the 1860s. By that time, the cemetery property also was traversed by the improved Hamilton Turnpike and the Cincinnati, Hamilton and Dayton Railroad, both of which paralleled the length of the Mill Creek.[19]

Despite the upgrading of its roads and the addition of rail access, most of the lower Mill Creek Valley remained relatively free of factories during the mid-nineteenth century. In 1857, a resident described it as "the charming valley made classic by the poet of the West in that beautiful song—'The Spotted Fawn.'" The only major valley industry between Lockland and Northside was Andrew Erkenbrecher's starch works, begun in 1859 in present St. Bernard.[20]

When the starch factory was being enlarged, the owner had several bricks left out of a large chimney in order to provide warm nesting cavities for the introduced European house sparrows that were then colonizing the Mill Creek Valley. The European house sparrow was special to Erkenbrecher, a German immigrant who later introduced four thousand individuals of twenty European birds to the Mill Creek Valley in an unsuccessful attempt to increase the number of Ohio songbirds. Notwithstanding his admiration for the house sparrow, "Mr. Erkenbrecher was at length obliged to put up wire trellises over the factory windows because these fellow-countrymen that had been received in such a friendly manner, were soon no longer satisfied to pick their living in the streets, but helped themselves to the best that was laid up in store."[21]

The industrial Mill Creek. (From the collection of The Cincinnati Historical Society. B-94-253)

Erkenbrecher's starch factory remained a Mill Creek Valley outpost of industry during the 1860s, surrounded by farms and dairies that used the company's waste slops as feed for chickens, pigs, and cows. An 1866 ride from the city boundary up the "beautiful valley" toward the factory provided a *Cincinnati Commercial* reporter with "a whiff of grass air, and a glimpse of nature with verdure clad." Other writers depicted the bucolic valley as "peaceful" in 1869, and "exceedingly picturesque" in 1870. According to an 1870 letter from a Cincinnatian to a Philadelphian, the Clifton "views overlooking the fields and orchards of Mill Creek valley are really lovely." [22]

In 1877, Henry Howe wrote "Makatewah," a poem describing a view of the stream valley from its western slope opposite Clifton. Howe's first stanza contrasts the restful valley with the fatiguing Cincinnati:

> O, Makatewah! peaceful spot,
>> Where Nature's sweetest charms are spread,
> My weary spirit finds repose,
>> To calmest thought is led.

But another stanza near the end of the poem presages the coming transformation of the basin from agricultural greenness to industrial grayness:

> The valley sounds rise on the air,
>> The tinkling bells, the rolling cars,
> While o'er the deep'ning gloom below
>> Look down the sad, mysterious stars. [23]

Factories began to sprout along the canal, the railways, and the pikes in the lower valley during the 1870s. Some 115 plants were located between Cincinnati and Northside by 1880. These early industries were spread over the cultivated fertile plain of the Mill Creek, causing the valley bottom to appear as a checkerboard with factory sites and market gardens. The lower span of the Mill Creek during this period became "exceedingly filthy, having received the noxious discharges of paper-mills, starch-factories, breweries, and distilleries." [24]

Even though there was a lull in industrial construction during the depression of the 1890s, by the early twentieth century the Mill Creek industrial belt had grown to occupy the twelve miles of valley from the creek's mouth upstream to Lockland. Precise factory locations were strongly influenced by the proximity of railways. Thus, as the Mill Creek basin became filled with industries, many businesses built their new plants along the railroad lines in the Norwood Trough running eastward from the Mill Creek Valley. By 1910, Norwood boasted forty-nine manufacturing concerns, many of which drained their wastes to the Mill Creek via Ross Run. [25]

Carl W. Condit of Northwestern University, in his 1977 book on local railroad history, suggested that the form and distribution of Cincinnati's industrial, commercial, and residential districts have been shaped by features of the physical environment to a greater degree than those of any other American city. In a 1901 work on the Queen City, George W. Engelhardt outlined how the area's topography was responsible for the industrialization of the Mill Creek Valley during the previous century:

> The principal break in the rampart of Cincinnati hills, that of the Mill Creek Valley, is well to the west end of the business quarter. Up this cleft the march of population and manufacturing interests naturally trod following the creek and canal. Many of the most important industrial establishments of the city are in this valley, in settlements lying both within and without the corporate line.[26]

Note that Engelhardt referred to the immigration of both people and factories to the Mill Creek Valley. Since human sewage polluted the Mill Creek to as great an extent as did industrial wastes, a complete account of the creek's degradation must next consider the growth of the human population in the watershed.

PART THREE

Growing Population, Overflowing Sewage

A nineteenth-century view of the lower Mill Creek Valley during a flood. The population in the valley increased throughout the century. (From the collection of The Public Library of Cincinnati and Hamilton County)

CHAPTER EIGHT

The Thames from Sharonville to Shantytown

I have never seen a country to appearance more fruitful in men, as well as corn.... I have seen no where else such hosts of children. The process of doubling population, without Malthus, and without theory, without natural or artificial wants, goes on, I am sure, on the banks of the Ohio as rapidly as anywhere in the world.

—Timothy Flint[1]

TIMOTHY FLINT was astonished by the area's rapid rate of growth when he arrived in Cincinnati in 1815. The town had about six thousand residents then, and approximately ten thousand in 1819, the year it became a city. The 1830 census totalled 24,831, reflecting a population growth rate that caused a local editor to predict that the "future destiny of Cincinnati cannot be less than the LONDON of the western country." In quantitative terms, Cincinnati never became a London, nor did the Mill Creek's flow through its mouth at Cincinnati ever match the River Thames' flow through its mouth at London. But in qualitative terms, the Mill Creek eventually became as polluted as the Thames.[2]

London's Thames in the 1830s lost its once-abundant fish life primarily due to the introduction of human wastes into its waters. This material previously had been carted away for use on London's market gardens. With the introduction of the water closet or toilet in the early nineteenth century, however, the foul vaults often overflowed onto the ground and into street sewers that served as stormwater drains to the Thames. When London outlawed over two hundred thousand of the overflowing privy vaults, the water closets were connected directly to the sewers. This caused the Thames to become a grossly polluted river with a smell so offensive in the 1850s that disinfectant-soaked sheets were hung in the Houses of Parliament on the river's bank. A worse consequence was the contamination of London's drinking water that was drawn from the river; the city experienced many epidemics of cholera and typhoid in the mid-nineteenth century.[3]

Commuters at the Cincinnati, Hamilton and Dayton Railroad station at South Cumminsville. (From the collection of The Public Library of Cincinnati and Hamilton County)

It was the fear of such epidemic illnesses that caused Cincinnati to forbid toilets from tapping into the municipal drainage sewers. Most of the city's early street sewers emptied into the Ohio River, the source of drinking water for Cincinnati's ever-growing population: 46,338 in 1840, 115,435 in 1850, 161,044 in 1860. The city lifted the ban on sewer taps in 1863, however, when council members became convinced that the air-borne miasma from overflowing privy vaults was a more likely source of sickness than was water-borne human waste diluted in river water. Cincinnati, with its seven hills, thus gained an eighth physical similarity to the Eternal City: in Rome the public toilets had long been connected to the sewers draining to the Tiber.[4]

Although sewer taps were allowed after 1863, most Cincinnatians continued to deposit their body wastes into unsewered underground vaults. The Cincinnati health officer urged council in 1867 to outlaw the privy vaults and to mandate direct connections of toilets to sewers. He estimated that most of the two million cubic feet of fecal matter annually deposited in the city's privy vaults was leaking into the ground since vault cleaners were removing less than half of that amount to the sullage boat moored in the Ohio River. It should be noted that the sullage vessel, when full, was swung into the current and its contents emptied to join the sewage that issued from the Cincinnati sewer outfalls.[5]

By 1870, the population of Cincinnati reached 216,239. This figure included the residents of several square miles of newly annexed land in the Mill

A swinging bridge connected farms on the west side of the Mill Creek with the railroad suburb of Elmwood, later renamed Elmwood Place. (From the collection of The Cincinnati Historical Society. B-94-230)

Creek Valley. In 1877, the health officer repeated the earlier suggestion that excrement storage in vaults be replaced by removal through sewers. But, until this transition was accomplished, he saw no reason to disallow the vault cleaners' "discharge of nightsoil into Millcreek.... For, below Cumminsville, its water is little used for any purpose; and, doubtless, not at all for the usual household purposes." The alternative would have been to require the vault cleaners to transport the fecal matter many miles to the sullage boat, thereby driving up the cost of the vault emptying for residents in the recently annexed Mill Creek Valley communities.[6]

Concerning a subject related to the privy problem, Cincinnati's chief engineer in 1878 complained about the return of glaciers to the area:

> In our city, it is the rule, rather than the exception, to discharge kitchen slop into the alley gutters. In winter, this causes the alleys to be filled with ice, forming miniature glaciers, which extend across the sidewalks into the street gutters. Even in the dryest summer weather, the gutters are befouled with soap suds, sediment from kitchen sinks, emptyings from dye houses and other manufacturing establishments, and with filth from the streets... such accumulations of filth are dangerous to health, by causing the fermentation of noxious gases.

To remedy this source of disease, the chief engineer proposed the following solution to the City Council:

On streets having sewers, every house should have a sewer connection, which should carry off, not only the contents of water-closets, but those of wash-basins, baths, kitchen sinks, and rainwater from the yards and the roofs. Then the gutters could be kept as dry and clean as the sidewalks; and then, if Cincinnati did not equal in many respects the gay Capital of France, the name of the "Paris of America" could not justly, as at present, be applied to her in derision.

The chief engineer's advice was followed, and the city's sewers henceforth carried not only a combination of street runoff and toilet wastes, but also a variety of additional effluents from residences, businesses, and other establishments.[7]

By 1880, Cincinnati's population had grown to 255,139, and the City Council had outlawed the construction of new privy vaults on properties having access to sewers. The city's chief engineer in 1880 determined that as city land in the Mill Creek watershed north of Harrison Avenue was sewered, the sewer outfalls should discharge into the creek. The engineer dispassionately concluded that the Mill Creek would, "in time," function as "an open sewer." Time passed quickly, for within two years, author Henry Teetor described how the sewage of Lockland, together with that of "the lower Villages, Infirmaries, Factories, etc. on its banks, converted Mill creek into little less, at times, than an open Parisian sewer—suggesting that described by Victor Hugo in which Jean Valjean found himself—'on all sides putridity and miasma...'" Note that here was yet another allusion to a European capital. London, Rome, Paris—it seems that one could complete most of the Grand Tour without ever leaving Cincinnati.[8]

Most of the creek-polluting valley villages referred to by Teetor started as commuter towns on railways running north from Cincinnati. Some of these were developed by railroad owners, and even named after them. For example, John W. Hartwell, vice president of the Cincinnati, Hamilton and Dayton Railroad, lent his name to the village established across from Carthage on the Mill Creek. The railroad company spurred home sales by offering a free one-year commuter ticket to Cincinnati to anyone purchasing a house in Hartwell. Not to be outdone, the builders of Elmwood, another Carthage neighbor, furnished home buyers with a year of free transportation on both the C.H. & D. and the Bee Line.[9]

Farther upvalley, the adjacent communities of Reading, Lockland, and Wyoming grew quickly after the railroads built nearby stations. Villages such as Sharon, Woodlawn, and Glendale blossomed along the railroad arteries in the Mill Creek Valley north of Lockland. Populations also increased markedly in the railway-served suburbs located on Mill Creek tributaries: College Hill and Mount Healthy on the College Hill Railroad ascending from Winton Place, Westwood on the Cincinnati and Westwood Railroad climbing from lower Fairmount, and Norwood on the tracks of the Cincinnati Northern Railway and

Shantytown, located at the mouth of the Mill Creek on the Ohio River. (From the collection of The Cincinnati Historical Society. B-90-060)

the Marietta and Cincinnati.[10]

Between 1870 and 1880, the population growth in Cincinnati (18 percent) was exceeded by that in Hamilton County excluding the city (24.2 percent) for the first time in the nineteenth century. Again during the 1880-1890 decade, Cincinnati's 16.4 percent growth was smaller than the 33.4 percent growth in the county outside the city. Workers in the expanding valley industries were joining the city commuters in the suburbs. By the 1890s, there were at least twenty-five flourishing Hamilton County communities in the Mill Creek watershed above Cincinnati, and raw sewage from most of them emptied into the creek or one of its tributaries. The Mill Creek, in turn, discharged the valley's sewage through "Shantytown," another suburb of sorts located at the southern end of the creek.[11]

Shantytown was sited "at the mouth of Mill Creek, the great open city sewer, foul and stifling during the warm seasons." The shantyboats that moored at the creek's mouth were joined in the mid-1880's by homeless squatters who fashioned streambank shacks from scrap wood and rubbish. This unannexed town within the boundaries of Cincinnati was led by a self-proclaimed mayor whose shanty served as city hall and whose followers formed the legislative council. Shantytown's population of about two hundred people living in approximately fifty hovels shared a single outhouse. The squalor of Shantytown in the 1890s caused the poet William H. Venable to wonder if anyone "would now think of singing the beauty of Mill creek banks once

In 1897, the Cincinnati Health Department proposed that the Mill Creek be encased in a giant masonry tube, thereby eliminating its notoriety as an open sewer. (Postcard from the collection of The Public Library of Cincinnati and Hamilton County)

celebrated in song as 'Maketewa's Flowery Marge.'"[12]

In 1890, Shantytown was surrounded by a Cincinnati population of 296,908. An Ohio Board of Health stream pollution study determined that the 1890 population of the Mill Creek watershed was 348,676, or 1,592 people per square mile. This was the highest population density found among Ohio's 125 watersheds, greatly exceeding the second-place 426 people per square mile density in the Cleveland area's Cuyahoga River watershed. The Cuyahoga had been characterized by Cleveland's mayor as "an open sewer through the center of the city" in 1881, and the river's pollution was known throughout the nation by the late nineteenth century. And yet, during this period, the less-renowned Mill Creek carried more sewage than the much larger Cuyahoga River.[13]

The increasing stench from the Mill Creek certainly was noted locally, if not nationally. A swelling volume of public complaints caused Cincinnati's Sewerage Department in 1887 to consider a plan to divert all of the Mill Creek Valley sewage into the McLean Avenue Sewer leading to the Ohio River. Steadily worsening stream conditions compelled the Cincinnati Health Department in 1892 to recommend the city's adoption of "some comprehensive engineering plan that will serve to abate the Millcreek nuisance."[14]

During the 1890s, the state Board of Health added its voice to the chorus complaining about the smell of the Mill Creek, "which is badly polluted and has for many years been a source of annoyance." Note that local and state health officers at the end of the nineteenth century considered the malodorous stream to be a "nuisance" or an "annoyance," but not a source of disease. The miasma theory of illness had been replaced by an emphasis on the microbial contamination of water. Therefore, even if a sewage-polluted stream emitted noxious vapors, it was no longer considered to be a serious threat to health unless its waters were drawn for drinking, cooking, or washing.[15]

The late nineteenth century demise of the miasma theory lessened the urgency to clean up the Mill Creek and other foul-smelling watercourses not used for water supply. Nevertheless, the Ohio Legislature in 1893 reacted to statewide complaints of stinking stream conditions by requiring state Board of Health approval of plans for new wastewater systems. Thus, Cincinnati had to gain the permission of the board in 1895 to build five new sewers to discharge into the Mill Creek and its tributaries. The board promptly authorized Cincinnati's construction plans, agreeing with the city that the additional sewers would "add very little to the contamination of the stream which already receives the sewage of Avondale, Clifton, Cumminsville, Camp Washington, Lick Run, part of Walnut Hills and numerous other places in the Mill creek basin."[16]

Two years later, the state Board of Health displayed a complete change of attitude about the Mill Creek when it disallowed a proposed sewer outfall from the growing village of Wyoming. In a report on the project, board Secretary Charles O. Probst relayed the Wyoming Village Council's conclusion "that the stream is already an open sewer, and that the small amount of sewage Wyoming would contribute will not materially change its character." But Dr. Probst himself urged the board's rejection of the project, because the Mill Creek's pollution "has been a crying evil for many years and in my opinion it is time to call a halt and take steps for its reclamation." The state board in 1897 took Dr. Probst's advice and refused to approve Wyoming's proposed discharge of untreated sewage into the creek.[17]

Downstream from Wyoming, the Cincinnati Health Department in 1897 repeated its now-annual observation that the Mill Creek was becoming increasingly objectionable "as the city extends its sewage system in the north and west." The department then advanced a proposal to abate the nuisance:

> The one feasible plan that seems to present itself for this purpose would be the construction of an immense trunk sewer, which would confine the contents of this creek and at the same time straighten its course. The improvement would be necessarily very expensive, and it would therefore probably be best to begin at the river and construct this great masonry tube, thus changing the present foul, open sewer into a closed one in such small sections annually as would not make the expense of the construction too heavy a burden upon the taxpayers. In this way the creek would be gradually enclosed and the objection to it as an open sewer removed.[18]

The Health Department's proposal was not the first time that the concept of encasing the Mill Creek had been brought to the attention of City Council. In 1870, the city's civil engineer had complained that the monies expended in building bridges over the Mill Creek between the Ohio River and Eighth Street could have been better used to enclose the creek from the river up to Gest Street north of Eighth. Such a project, according to the engineer, would have reclaimed the Mill Creek bottomland for residential and industrial use.[19]

Despite the fact that it had endorsed encasement of the lower Mill Creek twenty-seven years earlier, the Engineer Department in 1897 concluded that the Health Department's much extended enclosure plan was impracticable, "as the expense would be enormous and unwarranted." The Engineer Department instead proposed the construction of an interceptor sewer from the river up the Mill Creek Valley that would be "of sufficient size and depth to intercept all of the sewage from both sides of the creek as far north as Glendale, permitting the storm-water to flow into and down the creek as it now does." The sewage collected by the interceptor would flow south through the sewer and be discharged into the Ohio River.[20]

Cincinnati's population reached 325,902 in 1900, and a state Board of Health investigation in 1902 found that the Mill Creek was probably the most foul watercourse in Ohio. The sanitary survey revealed that the sewage and the nightsoil collections dumped into the stream were joined by large amounts of cow manure washed into the creek from 111 dairy farms. Members of the board appealed for the Ohio Legislature to pass mandatory legislation "to keep sewage and other polluting material out of Mill Creek."[21]

Mayor Samuel Hannaford of Winton Place complained to the state Board of Health in 1903 that "the water of Mill Creek is fearfully foul and is growing more so every passing year; in fact during the summer time Mill Creek is one long drawn out 'stink.'" The mayor noted that much of the stream's pollution derived from the sewage discharges of recently annexed areas of Cincinnati located adjacent to Winton Place. He urged the board to request the immediate construction of an interceptor sewer by the foot-dragging city. According to Mayor Hannaford, "For years the city of Cincinnati has talked of it, and has quieted efforts to publicly insist upon it by the statement that they are considering it and making plans for it, etc."[22]

The state Board of Health passed a resolution in 1904 requesting that the interceptor sewer be constructed, but not by Cincinnati. Rather, they asked the Hamilton County Commissioners to build and maintain the interceptor, since the creek's pollution was largely derived from seventeen cities and villages located outside of Cincinnati's jurisdiction. On April 28, 1904, the Ohio Legislature passed the necessary enabling legislation cumbersomely entitled "An act providing for the construction and maintenance of main and trunk sewers by the county commissioners, when the State Board of Health finds said trunk or main sewer to be necessary and have approved the plans and specifications thereof." No sewer construction activity resulted in Hamilton County.[23]

In 1905, Cincinnati's assistant city engineer completed surveys, plans, and estimates for an interceptor sewer from the Ohio River to Ivorydale. These specifications were forwarded to City Council, which then appropriated $5,000 to continue surveys north in the Mill Creek Valley to Glendale. These surveys were completed and plans were prepared, although they were not subsequently reported to council.[24]

In an October 9, 1908 lead editorial titled "Mill Creek," *The Cincinnati Times-Star* supported "the demand from those who live within the sphere of influence of that foul stream that the city or county do something for its reform." According to the editorial, the creek's "existence is a disgrace to Cincinnati, and a menace to the health of its people. It is little better than an open sewer, flowing through some of the thickly settled parts of the city." The editor acknowledged that "the work of carrying the evolution of Mill creek within the limits of Cincinnati to its logical conclusion, and making it a closed sewer, may present some big engineering difficulties. But something ought to be done."[25]

Also in 1908, Cincinnati published a report from its Engineer Department noting that the increasing number of city sewer outfalls into the West Fork and the Mill Creek had "materially increased the noisomeness and objectionable character of the latter stream." The department repeated its 1897 proposal for a city-built intercepting sewer along the Mill Creek. It added the stipulation that the interceptor should terminate near the northern boundary of the recently annexed Winton Place, and that all communities above this point in the Mill Creek watershed should install sewage treatment plants. Lockland subsequently constructed a septic tank plant in 1909, and Wyoming built a plain tank, intermittent sand filter plant in 1910. Also in 1910, College Hill erected a septic tank, sprinkling filter plant. This facility became the first treatment plant in Cincinnati when College Hill was annexed the following year.[26]

In 1910, Cincinnati's population was 363,561. According to an investigation sponsored by the state Board of Health, the Mill Creek was now receiving nearly half of Cincinnati's sewage. The same study also determined that the Mill Creek above Cincinnati was now so polluted by manufacturing wastes that it was not possible for sewage from the suburbs to worsen the creek's water quality. The Board of Health concurred with the study's recommendation that the suburban communities no longer be compelled "to construct and operate small disposal works, to purify sewage, while the stream into which the effluent flows is naturally as bad as the raw sewage from the villages." In light of this change in board policy, Lockland and Wyoming abandoned their treatment facilities in 1912. Cincinnati closed the College Hill plant in 1914.[27]

By 1910, Cincinnati's vault cleaners no longer were allowed to dump nightsoil into the Mill Creek, but instead were directed to discharge their collections into manholes of sewers leading to the creek! The abysmal condition of the Mill Creek in 1910 caused the state Board of Health to reiterate its support for an interceptor sewer to carry the watershed's domestic and industrial effluents south to the Ohio River. But until such a collecting sewer could be built, the board decided that factories, like cities and villages, may just as well continue to dump their untreated effluents into the grossly polluted watercourse. The board had no objection to permitting a Cincinnati company to redirect its wood pulp plant wastes into the creek, "at least so long as Mill Creek is not improved along the lines already suggested."[28]

Cincinnati's Mayor Henry T. Hunt in 1912 echoed the recurring protest about "the nuisance of Mill Creek as an open sewer." The mayor also complained of the estimated twenty thousand privy vaults that survived in city neighborhoods that had not yet been sewered. He noted that Manhattan had recently experienced a reduction in death rates when New York City eliminated every vault on that island.[29]

Mayor Hunt had given voice to a dilemma. More sewer lines had to be built to eliminate the remaining unsanitary vaults and to service the growing population, but such a construction program would increase the volume of sewage poured into the objectionable Mill Creek. The only alternative to making a bad stream worse would be to simultaneously construct the oft-proposed Mill Creek Interceptor to carry the valley sewage south to the Ohio River. According to the Sewer Division's latest recommendations, the interceptor would extend ten miles up the valley from the river to newly annexed Hartwell, and would be of sufficient capacity at Hartwell to serve future annexed lands north to the Hamilton County line.[30]

Conditions in the Mill Creek had become so odorous by 1912 that the necessity for an intercepting sewer was becoming obvious to the great majority of Cincinnatians. "In transacting the routine duties of life we are frequently compelled to travel over or along this stream, and are ready to admit that conditions have become so offensive that they need no assistance in the presentation of a persistent daily argument for remedy," according to City Engineer H. S. Morse. In February, 1912, City Council authorized an issue of bonds to the amount of $125,000 for a study of sewage conditions in Cincinnati. In April, the council authorized the chief engineer and the director of public service to expend the proceeds of the bonds in formulating a plan for the proper sewerage of the city. Finally, at the annual election in November, the citizens of Cincinnati delivered a necessary two-thirds vote for a $3,000,000 sewer construction bond issue.[31]

The sewage survey funded by City Council's bond issue included an inventory of industrial refuse being discharged into local watercourses, although much of this waste was not conveyed through city sewers. The industrial audit was undertaken because proposed trunk sewers were to divert both sanitary sewage and industrial effluents away from local streams. Data from the 1913 industrial inventory established that industrial waste constituted one pint of

One-fourth of the Mill Creek's flow into the Ohio River in 1913 consisted of sewage and industrial effluents. (From the collection of The Cincinnati Historical Society. B-86-015)

every liquid gallon in the lower Mill Creek in 1913.[32]

The sewage survey also determined the size of the sewered populations unserved by treatment plants. The total number in the Mill Creek's Hamilton County watershed was estimated to include 139,000 Cincinnati residents as well as 21,000 people outside of the city in towns and villages that might be annexed. The only community in the watershed for which annexation was not predicted was the rapidly industrializing Norwood, "the Chicago of Hamilton County." Norwood's 18,000 residents were about evenly divided between the Mill Creek watershed to the west and the Duck Creek watershed to the east.[33]

The total of the above numbers indicate that approximately 169,000 people contributed wastes to the Mill Creek in 1913. An average daily total of about 13,500,000 gallons of sewage flushed into Mill Creek. In 1913, sewage and industrial waste together made up about one quart of every liquid gallon flowing out of the mouth of the creek at Shantytown.[34]

By coincidence, the survey year 1913 was also the year that Shantytown "went out with the flood," leaving the land at the Mill Creek's mouth to be overrun by railroad tracks, engine terminals, coach yards, freight-handling facilities, warehouses, and viaducts. Shantytown's fate mirrored that of the once-living Mill Creek, a stream that died as a flood of industrialization and urbanization swept northward along the railroad lines in the valley. Already by 1908, according to Cincinnati Sanitary Engineer E. F. Layman, in:

> ...the main creek and both branches, as far north as the Butler County line... [the pollution from] house-sewerage and factory wastes, to which is added the drainage from a large number of dairies... has become so great that there is not now to be found any fish in the stream or its branches as above described.[35]

Beginning on July 1, 1919, the entire flow of the Miami and Erie Canal was directed over this spillway into the Mill Creek at Northside. (From the collection of The Cincinnati Historical Society. B-94-229)

CHAPTER NINE

Canal Closure Concentrates Creek Contaminants

No city in this country or Europe, as far as the writer's observation extends, can boast of as fine buildings for hog slaughtering purposes as Cincinnati. The larger stockyards of the city are likewise unequaled in this country, so far as regards neatness and good sanitary condition. The surplus fat and tallow of slaughter houses is disposed of to rendering establishments. The blood is fed to hogs, or used for blood pudding—being shipped for this purpose to Europe, or, when wasted, is run off through covered sewers into the waters of Millcreek.

— Cincinnati Health Department Annual Report, 1879[1]

SLAUGHTERHOUSE wastes caused the nineteenth century Mill Creek to be visited by one of the Old Testament plagues: "the water that was in the river turned to blood; and the fish that were in the river died; and the river stank." Actually, it was the decomposition of the blood that caused the fish to die and the creek to stink. Stream decomposers (bacteria and fungi) that fed on the blood utilized the dissolved oxygen in the water for their respiration. Formerly, the dissolved oxygen that these aquatic organisms used up was replaced in the water by oxygen absorbed at the surface of the creek. But when the inflow of blood became so great as to cause a population explosion of decomposers, dissolved oxygen was used up faster than it could be renewed, thereby causing the suffocation of fish and other members of the normal stream community. The organic matter left in the oxygen-poor water was then decomposed by anaerobic microbes that produced such foul-smelling gasses as ammonia and hydrogen sulfide.[2]

In addition to their consumption of animal blood, the Mill Creek's resident decomposers also fed and multiplied on discarded livestock manure, slaughterhouse offal, packing plant trimmings, soap factory greases, distillery mashes, brewery hops, dairy wastes, laundry washwaters, paper mill pulp, cotton batting oils, street runoff, and domestic sewage. The decomposition of these organic wastes was hastened by the heated discharges from slaughterers, packers, renderers, distillers, brewers, and other manufacturers. As decomposer activity was accelerated by higher creek temperatures, there was a more rapid depletion of dissolved oxygen.[3]

The combination of organic and heat pollution during the late nineteenth century eventually brought about the extermination of aerobic life in the lower Mill Creek. According to a 1902 report by Cincinnati naturalist Charles Dury, in 1878 the "Mill Creek was clean, with sandy banks and pebbly bottom. Now it has become a vile open sewer, the sand is saturated with sewage, which decays and gives off deadly gases, destroying all fish and insect life."[4]

In 1903, an article in *Engineering News,* a national publication, recounted the gross pollution of the Mill Creek and concluded with the following observations:

> From Lockland to its confluence with the Ohio, Mill Creek is an open sewer, foul smelling nearly all the time, and full of black, putrid mud which washes over everything in the way of the stream, making it unsightly as well. Only after heavy general rains does it lose its offensiveness, and then only for a short time, soon regaining it from the load of filth sent to it. Its condition is greatly improved over what it would otherwise be by the addition of water from the Miami and Erie Canal which parallels it for much of its length, crossing it twice, at Lockland and just above Carthage.[5]

Another observer of the Mill Creek in 1903, Winton Place Mayor Samuel Hannaford, likewise noted that the stream's objectionable condition would be worse without the canal's overflows:

> [The] water of Mill Creek is fearfully foul and is growing more so every passing year; in fact during the summer time Mill Creek is one long drawn out 'stink.' Fortunately there are one or two inflows from the Miami Canal that help, to a limited degree, to flush the channel. It must not be forgotten that during the summer droughts it is only this inflow that renders such a condition of affairs in any degree bearable.[6]

Ever-increasing pollution of the Mill Creek finally rendered the "condition of affairs" unbearable by the summer of 1910. In response to the numerous complaints reaching Columbus, the Ohio Board of Health urged the state Board of Public Works to discharge the entire Sunday flow of the Miami and Erie Canal "into the creek at Lockland, rather than at present over the spillway at Spring Grove and through the Eggleston Ave. sewer within the city limits." (The canal had flowed through the latter sewer into the Ohio River since 1870, when the uneconomical ten locks along the final mile of the canal had been paved over to form Eggleston Avenue.) In effect, the Board of Health was requesting a weekly flush of the Mill Creek's stranded toilet matter and other pollutants.[7]

The Board of Public Works obliged by having the canal's flow at Lockland

No. 524. Where the Canal and Millcreek meet, Cincinnati.

(Postcard from the collection of The Public Library of Cincinnati and Hamilton County)

turned into the creek "from midnight of Saturday to midnight of Sunday" during the dry summer months. The importance of the Sunday flush was highlighted in 1913 when canal repairs at Middletown prohibited any summer diversions at Lockland. The state Board of Health immediately requested the governor to "instruct the Superintendent of Public Works to waste into Mill Creek... all the water that can be spared from the canal" at Lockland. The governor transmitted the request, and the practice of flushing the creek resumed after the canal repairs were completed.[8]

The weekly flush directed eighty-four million gallons of canal water through the Mill Creek every Sunday. During the remainder of the week, a daily total of thirty-six million gallons still reached the creek through canal leaks and diversions. But even though the latter volume of relatively clean canal water contributed more than 40 percent of the creek's flow during dry weather, and although the stream was flushed religiously on summer Sundays, the lower Mill Creek took on the appearance and odor of concentrated sewage during the second decade of the twentieth century. It was only at the decade's end, when the outmoded Miami and Erie Canal was abandoned between Eggleston Avenue and Northside, that the water quality in the stream south of Northside reversed its long deterioration. The pollutants in the lower creek became less concentrated starting on July 1, 1919, the day when the canal's entire flow began to be diverted into the Mill Creek opposite Spring Grove Cemetery.[9]

The point at which the canal's flow was turned into the Mill Creek moved farther and farther upstream as more and more of the lower Miami and Erie Canal was abandoned during the early 1920s. By 1925, the canal diversion to the creek was located north of Lockland. Horace Johnson of that city was most thankful for the diverted canal water, as he explained in a typewritten note attached to the Wyoming Avenue Bridge over the Mill Creek:

> If you will take the time to stop on this bridge and look down into the water at the ripples over the rocks, of course it is mixed with brown water from the cotton factory, and from factories above, but if there weren't any canalwater running into this creek above it would be black and would smell, but as the canal water runs into this creek about four miles above this bridge, and if it wasn't for the canal water running into this creek, the water would be so thick that it could hardly be stired with a stick, and if they take the canal away which is the only clean water this valley has, it certainly will be to bad for the people around here...[10]

In another notice posted three blocks to the west on the Wyoming Avenue Bridge over the dry canal bed, Johnson expressed his opposition to the proposed abandonment of the Miami and Erie Canal south of Dayton, an increasingly popular proposition that would decrease state public works expenses.

> There is no water in the canal at this point.... All the water from the canal is going down the Reading Mill Creek, which keeps it clean and free from smelling. If you want health, sanitation, recreation, beautification then save your canal and keep it. But if you want unsanitary conditions, if you want to smell and breathe this in your lungs, then get rid of the canal, like some are trying to do.[11]

And in a third note attached to the Arlington Canal Bridge south of Lockland, Johnson repeated his assertion that the canal must be retained for the health of his community.

> Where is the man who pertends to be for civic affairs for this part of the country? I supose he is trying to clean up Mill Creek in some hall or, on paper. But he can't do it. The only way to clean it up is to have our clean canal so the clean water can flow it down stream.[12]

Finally, in a note posted on the Elliot Avenue Bridge over the undiluted, polluted West Fork Mill Creek, Johnson asked passers-by to imagine the condition of the Mill Creek's Main Stem without the mitigating influence of the canal's flow.

> To the one who wants to get rid of the canal, I want every man, woman, and child to take a good look from this bridge down into the creek, and remember how rotton it was last summer, as it will be that way next summer, and as there has been about five rains to wash it out, and it still is rotton. Now how do you

like this creek without the clean canal water running into it?? How did you like to smell it? How did you like to lay in bed at night and smell it? How do you like to inhale it?[13]

Horace Johnson's queries of his fellow Mill Creek Valley citizens are reminiscent of the question that Samuel Taylor Coleridge posed to fabled residents of the Rhine Valley:

> In Kohln, a town of monks and bones,
> And pavements fang'd with murderous stones
> And rags, and hags, and hideous wenches;
> I counted two and seventy stenches,
> All well defined, and several stinks!
> Ye Nymphs that reign o'er sewers and sinks,
> The river Rhine, it is well known,
> Doth wash your city of Cologne;
> But tell me, Nymphs, what power divine
> Shall henceforth wash the river Rhine?[14]

Questions about what "power divine" would henceforth wash the Mill Creek elicited no apparent concern in Columbus. In 1927, the Ohio Assembly voted to abandon the Miami and Erie Canal south of Dayton in order to make way for a high speed highway. The road was envisioned as eventually stretching from Toledo to Cincinnati, where it would connect to the Central Parkway that was built over the canal segment closed in 1919. The first step in abandoning the canal occurred on November 2, 1929, when the waterway's flow was shut off during a ceremony at the same Middletown site where construction of the Miami Canal had commenced in 1825. An accompanying pageant depicted the evolution of Ohio civilization from the canoe to the airplane, but no mention was made of the concomitant rise in pollution levels.[15]

After being cut off from the canal's flow of 130 cubic feet per second, the lower Mill Creek became a series of polluted pools during the dry summer of 1930. The city, county, and state health authorities were inundated with complaints about the resultant sickening odors and strong fumes. The City of Cincinnati at first secured relief from the contamination by having its Fire Department direct untold millions of gallons of water into the creek's channel in order to flush out the pools. But as the year progressed, the situation became so acute that the city joined the county in a successful project to drain the septic pools by dredging and channeling the Mill Creek from St. Bernard to Harrison Avenue.[16]

Stream sediments largely filled up the dredged and channelized section by 1932, and complaints of odors from the Mill Creek again flooded government offices. In response to the new public outcry, Cincinnati officials in 1932 were able to report that construction would soon commence on the last section of the

Construction of the interceptor sewer along the Mill Creek in 1927. (From the collection of The Cincinnati Historical Society. B-86-015)

Mill Creek Interceptor Sewer. They confidently announced that completion of the interceptor "will end the nuisance of Mill Creek." [17]

The interceptor sewer project had started nineteen years earlier in Northside. On November 1, 1913, at the intersection of Colerain and Spring Grove Avenues, Cincinnati's mayor used a pick and shovel to initiate excavation for the sewer. The festive event was witnessed by several hundred people, many of whom received small gift spades as souvenirs of the occasion.[18]

Construction of the ten-mile-long Mill Creek Interceptor proceeded slowly, at a rate of about a half-mile per year. Thus, when Cincinnati ran out of sewer funds in 1930, a two-mile section between the Ohio River and Harrison Avenue remained unbuilt, and the completed portion from Harrison Avenue to Hartwell lay landlocked and useless. Since a recently planned northward extension into the county also would be unusable without the southern connection to the Ohio River, the Hamilton County Commissioners came to the project's rescue with a promise of $500,000 to extend the interceptor to the river. The now-guaranteed finish of the sewer led *The Cincinnati Times-Star* of May 24, 1930, to announce that soon the "Mill Creek will again be in the state of sparkling purity of the times of the Indians and the pioneers." [19]

The anticipated completion of the long-awaited interceptor called forth a second celebration of the project, this one held on September 12, 1931, and attended by more than a thousand people. Women were especially invited to participate in the festivities since the interceptor was being built to improve public health, considered at that time to be the concern of mothers and nurses. The joint city-county ceremony included several speeches, a parade from the Carthage Fairgrounds to the Reading-Lockland Presbyterian Church, and the dedication of the first section of the interceptor to be laid in the Mill Creek Valley north of Cincinnati. Dignitaries included state officials, county authorities, and the mayors of Cincinnati, St. Bernard, Elmwood, Arlington, Lockland, Reading, and Wyoming. *The Cincinnati Enquirer*'s account of the event headlined that the "Millcreek Folk" turned out for the "Dedication of Sewer Representing Death of Evil Odors."[20]

The interceptor finally was completed to the Ohio River in 1934. On December 24, sewage and industrial wastes began to run through it from Lockland to the river, a distance of twelve miles. The interceptor's gift to the citizens was announced on page one of *The Cincinnati Times-Star*'s Christmas Eve edition: "This will eliminate the disagreeable odor from the open sewer, of which the Mill Creek Valley residents complained every summer."[21]

Despite its good press and great promise, the completed interceptor sadly failed to return the Mill Creek to its former "state of sparkling purity." The large quantities of factory and domestic effluents that bypassed the interceptor caused the Cincinnati city manager in 1940 to list the Mill Creek as one of the major sources of Ohio River pollution. A succinct summary of the interceptor's ineffectiveness appeared the next year in a city study of its sewer system:

> Stated more generally, the situation in Mill Creek is that, owing to industrial wastes now discharged directly into the creek, and, also, owing to overflows of more or less diluted sewage and other wastes, the creek channel is marked throughout its length by pools of putrescible matters, which occasion offense to sight and smell, and which, in certain instances, are reported to give rise to gases, which are corrosive of usual types of paint.[22]

A dry-weather overflow from a clogged sewer. (Photo by Stanley Hedeen)

CHAPTER TEN

Passing the Pipe Fulfills
an Indian Foreboding

But a study of Mill Creek is not complete without a personal visit. At Sharonville, it is almost a pretty stream. A rill is picturesque until you realize that the obstruction is a sewer pipe. At Reading you see the solids moving along in the current.... At Hartwell the turbidity is greater, and from St. Bernard on south—ugh!

—Richard L. Gordon[1]

BY 1940, the Mill Creek Interceptor had been extended northward to Sharonville, a distance of fifteen miles from its Ohio River outfall. Branches of the long pipe had been built up West Fork Mill Creek and West Fork. Construction of these large sewers during the thirties had provided hundreds of welcome jobs for depression era Works Progress Administration and Public Works Administration laborers.[2]

The interceptor in 1940 carried a dry-weather average flow of 45,300,000 gallons per day of effluent from sewers and factory pipes that otherwise would have discharged into the Mill Creek or its branches. Unfortunately, two million gallons per day of wastes from valley industries circumvented the interceptor and continued to pour directly into the waterways. Worse yet, during stormy weather, this industrial waste was joined by several million gallons of rain-swollen effluent that overflowed from the interceptor. These creek-borne pollutants, following the return of dry weather, would "result in creating pools of more or less diluted sewage and wastes and in deposits of solid materials, which putrefy and cause offense," according to a Department of Public Works report.[3]

The interceptor had been designed with a capacity large enough to carry the sanitary sewage and industrial wastes that the conduit was expected to receive during the second half of the twentieth century. At no time had the interceptor been envisioned as a conveyor of stormwater to the Ohio River. As first conceived by the Cincinnati Sewage Department in 1887, the interceptor was planned with many overflow points, so that any volume of water greater than the dry-weather flow would overrun to the Mill Creek. This design was deemed acceptable since the storm sewage causing the overflow would dilute the accompanying wastewater sewage. In addition, it was reasoned that the overflowing, watered-down effluent would be further diluted by the increased storm flow in the creek, thus minimizing the risk of stream pollution. Such logic resulted in the Mill Creek Interceptor being planned without any capacity for the conveyance of stormwater.[4]

As the interceptor was built and extended, overflow structures were constructed at each of the points where sewers connected to the interceptor. The interceptor connections included various devices known to sewer engineers as bottom drops, side outlets, grating openings, and float-type regulators. These regulators, during dry weather, transferred wastewater flow from sewer to interceptor. During wet weather the regulators transferred to the interceptor a mixture of wastewater and stormwater. However, the bulk of the mixture, the amount depending on the intensity of the rainfall, was by design discharged to the Mill Creek. When the storm passed and the stream subsided, the overflowed wastes caused an unforeseen problem when they formed into sludge-filled pools along the irregular bottom of the creek, thus perpetuating the pollution nuisance that the interceptor had been built to eliminate.[5]

In 1940, wet-weather overflows occurred about 8 percent of the time over the course of the year. Additional overflows occurred during dry weather, often because of clogging of the connections between sewers and the interceptor. Materials that would block a connection included rags, paper, sand, dirt, rocks, and other debris found in sanitary and storm sewage. The obstructing material would hamper the interception of raw wastewater from the sewer and cause the bypassing of part or all of the flow into the Mill Creek. The dry-weather overflow would continue until an inspection crew cleared out the blockage or until a large volume of storm sewage flushed the debris into the interceptor or the creek. Often, a connection would become clogged again within an hour after it was cleaned or flushed.[6]

A second reason why wastewater overflowed into the Mill Creek during dry periods was related to the interceptor's outfall into the Ohio River. The interceptor's outlet sat five feet above the river when the Ohio was at minimum pool stage. But when the Ohio was in flood because of wet weather upriver, the outlet and lower portion of the interceptor were submerged. With the flow to the river thus checked, the interceptor was forced to discharge its contents through an overflow point into the Mill Creek. The exact point of overflow was determined by the length of the interceptor that was submerged, which in turn was decided by the water level in the Ohio River.[7]

The dry-weather overruns were a minor problem when compared with wet-weather overflows, though. The 1941 study of Cincinnati's sewer system identified wet-weather overflows as second only to industrial waste outfalls in causing pollution of the stream:

Construction of a wet-weather overflow structure along the Mill Creek in 1927. (From the collection of The Cincinnati Historical Society. B-86-015)

Full correction of conditions in Mill Creek call, first, for eliminating the present discharge of wastes direct into the stream. Such wastes can and should be removed from the creek either through connection to the intercepting system or else by disposal of these wastes by Industry...

The second cause of nuisance in Mill Creek is the recurrence of overflows of sewage very slightly diluted by storm water. Irrespective of the removal of wastes which now go to the creek, and under present conditions in the channel, nuisance is bound to continue as long as the intercepting sewer overflows with any frequency.[8]

As serious as the wet-weather overflow problem was in the early forties, it became even worse as the decade continued. The interceptor, designed to transport 132 million gallons of wastewater per day, in 1940 carried an average dry-weather flow of 45.3 million gallons per day. The remaining 86.7 million gallon surplus capacity enabled the interceptor to also carry some stormwater without overflows. With the postwar growth of industry and population in the Mill Creek Valley, there was an increase in the volume of wastewater and, consequently, a decrease in the interceptor's capacity to also carry stormwater. Overflows of combined (stormwater plus wastewater) sewage into the Mill Creek rose in both number and volume, thereby worsening water quality in the stream that was already "foul" and an "offense to sight and smell" in 1941.[9]

By the fifties, the Mill Creek had become "grossly polluted by domestic and industrial wastes," according to biologists at the federal government's Robert

A. Taft Sanitary Engineering Center in Cincinnati. These researchers also reported that infectious poliomyelitis-like viruses found in human feces survived longer in water samples from the "gross" Mill Creek than in samples drawn from the "relatively clean" Little Miami River, the "moderately polluted" Ohio River, the "considerably polluted" Licking River, or even the "totally polluted" sewage from Cincinnati residences. On the other hand, viruses in the Mill Creek samples did not persist as long as those placed in samples of distilled and autoclaved water.

The investigators explained these results by theorizing that virus survival time was lessened in water with a normal microbiological content. They suggested that destruction of this natural flora by distillation or autoclaving increased survival of the virus population. (This hypothesis might also explain why viruses persisted longer in samples drawn from the Mill Creek than in samples taken from a residential sewer. Whereas both creek and sewer offered viruses a sewage-filled environment, the industrial wastes in the Mill Creek most likely destroyed the stream's normal microbiological flora, thereby enhancing survival of the human viruses.)[10]

Mill Creek Valley residents, like the government scientists, perceived that contact with the waters of the Main Stem and its branches constituted a public health hazard. Referring to the heavily polluted West Fork, a South Cumminsville resident told a *Cincinnati Post* reporter in 1957 that "anything that smells that bad can't be healthy. I worry that it might hurt the children. So many of them live around here." A neighbor added: "Living with this mess all the time is just plain sickening. There's no such thing as getting used to it."

Ninety-year-old Catherine Freese contributed an historical perspective to the creek's odor. "It smells awful. In all my long life I've never smelled anything quite like it." And a fourth South Cumminsville native was embarrassed by her guests' reaction to the stench:

> People come to visit us. They don't have anything like this where they live. We hate it when they ask what the smell is and we have to explain. It's even worse when they don't ask. You know they smell it and you wonder what they think.[11]

Ohio Department of Natural Resources scientists sampled the waters of the Mill Creek during 1959 and 1960. They found the watercourse at Cincinnati to be "extremely polluted" by wastes from overflowing combined sewers and twenty industrial establishments. The streamwater "contained objectionable amounts of phenols and cyanides, and was practically devoid of dissolved oxygen." The water was described as "black." [12]

The state investigators' report of the water's color introduces an element of *deja vu* to the history of the Mill Creek. "Maketewa," the Native American name for the stream, meant "he is black." This title for a naturally clear creek might be taken as evidence for the Indians' gift of prophecy. Or, less imaginatively, the name "Maketewa" may have referred to something other than the watercourse: heavy shadows in the stream bottomland, the rich soil in the flood plain, a memorable encounter in the valley with a runaway slave or a blackface-painted warrior or a cassock-attired Jesuit missionary. However, the initial conjecture that "Maketewa" embodies a prophetic vision of pollution is the only hypothesis that gains support from modern surveys of the dark stream.[13]

Another state agency, the Sewage and Industrial Wastes Unit of the Ohio Department of Health, investigated the Mill Creek watershed in Hamilton County during 1963 and 1964. Survey personnel found that industrial wastes and overflowed combined sewage caused the water quality of the Main Stem to change from "fair" at Reading to "poor" at Carthage, to "very poor" at St. Bernard, and to "septic" in Cincinnati from Winton Place to the Ohio River. Because of overflows along the branches of the Mill Creek Interceptor, water quality of five major tributaries entering the Main Stem was "septic" in Cooper Creek, "poor" in Ross Run, and "very poor" in West Fork, Bloody Run, and West Fork Mill Creek. The investigators observed floating fecal matter in practically every tributary in heavily populated areas, and sludge banks along the entire length of the Main Stem below its confluence with West Fork Mill Creek.[14]

As the sixties drew to a close, Cincinnati and Hamilton County sewer operations were merged to form the Metropolitan Sewer District of Greater Cincinnati. There was nothing great about the Mill Creek, though, as it still flowed inkily through the district. "If you can't drink it, you can at least write with it." This saying, originated by Philadelphians to characterize their polluted Schuylkill River, was used by local author Dick Perry in 1969 to describe "the open sewer we call Mill Creek." The Philadelphia maxim was an apt description of other U.S. urban watercourses as well.[15]

In Cleveland, the industrial waste in the Cuyahoga River caught fire on June 22, 1969. Several linear miles of that watercourse burned before the Port of Cleveland fireboat sailed upstream to put out the river. At about the same time, a couple of newsmen watched a pair of ducks land on the Detroit River, swim about for a moment, start choking, and die. Highly publicized incidents such as these ushered in the 1970 Earth Day and the beginning of the modern environmental movement.[16]

The start of the "environmental decade" in 1970 was locally chronicled in a lengthy *Cincinnati Magazine* piece titled, with irony, "Our Good Life." Author Richard L. Gordon, who traveled down the Main Stem while researching the article, related how the Mill Creek's odor, color, and turbidity made it a truly "unlovely stream." These conditions in the creek remained unchanged in 1974 when *Cincinnati Post* reporter Richard Gibeau depicted the "dismal stream" as a "brew of industrial effluent and wastewater." In the following year, *Cincinnati Enquirer* columnist Frank Weikel used the creek as the benchmark against which to judge the pollution of another area watercourse:

> Some Newtown residents are happy to see the cool weather. It permits them
> to close their windows and avoid the smell from the raw sewage that runs
> through a creek in the community. The smell rivals the stink that has often
> been found around Cincinnati's Mill Creek.[17]

During 1976, the nation's Bicentennial year, the state of Ohio disclosed that the Mill Creek failed to meet the four fundamental "freedoms" established by the Ohio Water Pollution Control Board. These minimum conditions applicable to all state waters were 1) freedom from substances that will settle to form objectionable sludge deposits, 2) freedom from floating debris, oil, scum, and other floating materials in amounts sufficient to be unsightly or deleterious, 3) freedom from materials producing color, odor, or other conditions in such degree as to create a nuisance, and 4) freedom from substances in concentrations or combinations which are toxic or harmful to terrestrial and aquatic life. State inspectors determined that even with the elimination of all direct industrial discharges into the creek, the four "freedoms" would still not be attained until combined sewer overflows were reduced in number and volume.[18]

The Ohio-Kentucky-Indiana Regional Council of Governments (OKI), the planning agency for the Cincinnati and Hamilton-Middletown Standard Metropolitan Statistical Areas, announced in 1977 that the water quality of the Mill Creek was the worst of any watercourse in the OKI area. According to the agency, the twenty-seven industrial dischargers in the Mill Creek watershed had recently reduced their effluent volumes to such a degree that they now bore little responsibility for the stream's problems. Instead, the major sources of pollution were fifty-four overflow points that bypassed a mixture of wastewater (sanitary and industrial wastes) and stormwater during 25 percent of the time over the course of the year. In the Hamilton County portion of the Main Stem, Ohio's water quality standards were violated for bacteria, dissolved oxygen, acidity, ammonia, and several heavy metals.

OKI recommended that the valley factories, except for one that was discharging too much dissolved iron into West Fork Mill Creek, be allowed to maintain their effluent flows at current 1977 levels. The Mill Creek Valley industries were generally in compliance with the effluent standards that had been mandated by the federal government since 1973. The combined sewer overflow problem, on the other hand, had not yet been solved by the Metropolitan Sewer District. Because of the high cost of overflow controls, OKI recommended a program for the district to develop, build, and monitor pilot projects in order to evaluate them for their cost effectiveness. No implementation schedule for the installation of overflow controls was proposed.[19]

The "environmental decade" in Cincinnati closed as it had begun, with a journalist voyaging down the Mill Creek. *Cincinnati Post* reporter Douglas Starr started in Butler County and canoed the length of the Main Stem in September, 1979. As he paddled downstream into Hamilton County, Starr found that the creek became "a mutation, something that wouldn't appear in the natural world." South of Evendale, he watched "bubbling sewage and oozing metals kill off all life in the stream." The poisoning peaked at the end of Starr's voyage in the pooled mouth of the creek on the Ohio River:

> Grease sits here in pools an inch thick. Debris, toilet paper and prophylactics drift into the pool. Tiny bubbles rise from bacterial action on the sewage below. An acrid smell stings the senses.[20]

Kay Brookshire, also a reporter for the *Cincinnati Post*, visited a small tributary of the Mill Creek in 1980. From its origin in Wooden Shoe Hollow above Winton Place, the unnamed run typified most Mill Creek tributaries as it conveyed combined sewage overflow effluent to the Main Stem. Wooden Shoe Hollow householders complained to Brookshire about the filth in the watercourse, the outhouse stench in the hollow, and the diseases attributed to the raw sewage. Resident Virginia Kemper showed reporter Brookshire the polluted run: "You can see toilet tissue at times. There's a piece now."[21]

During the eighties, *Cincinnati Enquirer* humorist Jim Knippenberg made frequent use of the Mill Creek's plight. He characterized sauerkraut as smelling "like the Mill Creek in August." He reported on a *Home* magazine article documenting that "a view of a river, seaside, mountains, even a golf course, adds about 25 percent to a house's value.... *Home* did not estimate the value of a view of Cincinnati's Mill Creek. We won't either."[22]

By 1977, industrial discharges into the Mill Creek had been greatly reduced. (Photo by Stanley Hedeen)

Real estate along the Mill Creek evidently interested Mr. Knippenberg, as may be seen in this excerpt from a 1983 column:

> When the Ohio General Assembly emerged from its last reapportionment, three Southwest Ohio state senators found themselves in the same district— Richard H. Finan, Stanley Aronoff and H. Cooper Snyder. None of the three relished facing the other two in a primary, so two of them moved.
>   Senator Aronoff now lives in Price Hill, where he has a view of the river, and Senator Snyder now lives near Rocky Fork State Park, where he has a view of the lake. Senator Finan laments that he is left where he's always been—with a whiff of Mill Creek.[23]

Another politician, President Millard Fillmore, had his 185th birthday celebrated in 1985 at Shuller's Wigwam Restaurant. The party was advertised as "a full evening of unique events.... The big event will be the awarding of a no-expense-paid cruise on the Mill Creek. Meanwhile, there will be a run-of-the-Mill-Creek happy hour."[24]

The belittled creek was also an object of derision by neighbors of Shuller's Wigwam. In 1986, North College Hill residents complained about the mixture of human waste and rainwater that overflowed into West Fork Mill Creek. Anxious parents worried that the combined sewage would end up on the hands and feet of children who played in the stream. Their concerns were validated by fecal coliform bacteria counts made by the Ohio Environmental Protection Agency. The number of colonies of these human and animal intestinal microbes greatly exceeded the safe water standard of 2,000 per 100 milliliters. In fact, the Mill Creek system throughout Hamilton County was identified as a considerable health hazard, with counts of up to 1.3 million per 100 milliliters occurring near the creek's mouth.[25]

The Ohio EPA in 1986 reaffirmed that the lower Mill Creek's biological, chemical, and physical degradation was due primarily to overflows from antiquated, undersized combined sewers serving an ever-growing population. Industrial discharges were again identified as relatively small contributors to the creek's pollution load, though they still were sometimes singled out by the news media. For example, *The Cincinnati Post* of Wednesday, April 29, 1987, carried the following news item:

> The Metropolitan Sewer Department is investigating the discharge Tuesday afternoon of a red liquid into Mill Creek through a storm sewer near the CSX Corp. Queensgate Yards. Authorities suspect the liquid was animal blood and checked a nearby packing plant. He said plant officials denied any knowledge of a discharge.[26]

Thus was the Mill Creek's bicentennial year of 1987 marked by the cameo appearance of an historical bloody red tint in Cincinnati (formerly Porkopolis). And then, during the 1988 Bicentennial of Cincinnati, a more contemporary red hue in the city was linked to the stream. In the August 9 *Cincinnati Enquirer,* baseball writer John Erardi characterized the Cincinnati Reds' offense as having "the same fragrance about it as the Mill Creek after a downpour." The fact that the team carried a .241 batting average should give the reader a sense of how far down the Mill Creek had slumped.[27]

Storm-generated combined sewage overflows caused the eighties to end with a serious public health incident. During much of 1989, a hepatitis-A outbreak involved school-age children from Mt. Airy and South Cumminsville. Cincinnati Health Department staff found that the youth in these communities regularly played in West Fork, the tributary that runs through the neighborhoods on its way to the Mill Creek. Overflowed sewage in West Fork was singled out as the likely source of the disease, since hepatitis-A usually is transmitted by human wastes. Early in 1990, Cincinnati's Health Commissioner reported the distressing findings to City Council:

> Investigations by health department staff indicate there are significant ecological damage and reason for public health concern....
> On-site inspection of the channel following a moderate rainfall revealed deposition of various types of waste, including needles, syringes, sanitary napkins and prophylactics....
> The potential for the spread of infectious disease...is, in our opinion, one which should concern everyone.

The Health Commissioner asked the Metropolitan Sewer District to take immediate steps to solve the health problem presented by West Fork. These included fencing the channel, posting warning signs to inform trespassers of health threats, and ending combined sewage overflows into the waterway.[28]

Later during 1990, an Army Corps of Engineers water survey team was twice forced to retreat from a sampling site along the lower Mill Creek. In both instances, chemical sheens on the stream's surface emitted organic vapor levels of 165 parts per million (ppm) and 525 ppm, respectively. These levels, measured five feet above the creek's surface, exceeded the 10 ppm safe exposure level for personnel working without respiratory protection. The survey team hastily abandoned the sampling site until the chemical slicks passed downstream.[29]

In 1991, employees of Cincinnati Butchers' Supply in Elmwood Place were treated with oxygen and taken to University Hospital after they were overcome by chemical fumes from Bloody Run, a tributary of Mill Creek. The six men were vomiting, dizzy, and short of breath. Others in the Elmwood Place neighborhood complained that chemical-laced sewage regularly overflowed the Mill Creek Interceptor and entered the small run. "It stinks so bad sometimes you feel you're going to gag your guts out," according to resident Bobbie Wesley. Such chemical-caused health problems were to be expected, since at least 20 percent of the interceptor's wastewater flow in the early nineties consisted of

The Ohio EPA in 1992 identified a marginally good fish community in the Mill Creek headwaters, but only severely degraded fish communities were found in the remainder of the stream. (Photo by Stanley Hedeen)

industrial effluent.[30]

The fact that interceptor overflows contained human as well as industrial wastes was made evident in 1991 when the Cincinnati Health Department conducted its first survey of the Mill Creek. On August 22, fecal coliform bacteria colonies per 100 milliliters of water at five sampling sites ranged from 300 at Ludlow Avenue to 2.4 million near the Western Hills Viaduct. On October 31, results from ten sites ranged from 3,300 at Mitchell Avenue to 13,000 at Gest Street. Tom Rotte, senior sanitarian, reported these results to City Council's environment committee and explained that "all diseases that you can possibly get in a sewer—everything from intestinal viruses to polio—a person can get through this water." University of Cincinnati environmental engineering professor Pasquale Scarpino added that insects, birds, and dogs that come in contact with the water can transmit disease-causing microbes to areas far beyond the immediate Mill Creek area.[31]

Overflows from undersized combined sewers leading to the interceptor were identified in 1992 as sources of human waste, toilet paper, and razor blades in Mill Creek tributaries running through Cincinnati city parks. Health Department tests of a Mt. Airy Forest stream found up to 53,000 fecal coliform colonies per 100 milliliters of water, a level far above the health department's "clean" standard of 1,000 colonies per 100 milliliters. Signs warning park users about contamination were erected at the Mt. Airy stream, as well as at other "unclean" waterways traversing McFarland Woods and the Caldwell Nature Preserve.[32]

Humans can read warning signs and choose to walk away from the Mill Creek and its tributaries, but fish are illiterate. In the event that fish could read the signs, they still would not be able to escape from their unclean aquatic homes. It came as no surprise in 1992 when an Ohio EPA survey of the Mill Creek found only pollution-tolerant fish species downstream from the Butler County headwaters. While the survey team did identify one marginally good fish community in the headwaters area, 26.4 miles above the creek's mouth, only severely degraded fish communities were found in the remainder of the length of the stream.

The Ohio EPA team also noted a high rate of gross external anomalies (deformities, fin erosion, lesions or ulcers and tumors) on fish taken from the segment of the creek impacted by combined sewer overflows. Other Ohio surveys showed that a high frequency of anomalies reflects water pollution stress. Pollution also was indicated in tissue samples taken from four species of fish found surviving in the creek. Barium, lead, mercury, zinc, phenol, and 1,2,4-trichlorobenzene were detected. The concentration of total PCB (polychlorinated biphenyl) exceeded the health standard for consumption by humans, and caused the Ohio Department of Health to warn people not to eat more than one-half pound of fish per month from the creek.

Water samples from the creek documented violations of water quality criteria for selenium, cyanide, copper, various pesticides, dissolved oxygen, and bacteria from sewage contamination. Sediment sampling revealed "highly" and "extremely" elevated concentrations of copper, cadmium, chromium, lead, zinc, DDT, and PCB 1248. Sediment from the West Fork Mill Creek contained the second-highest levels of lead concentrations ever found in an Ohio stream. Based on the Ohio EPA's biological and chemical monitoring, the Mill Creek was evaluated as the waterway with the poorest quality among all of Ohio's fifty-five principal streams and rivers.[33]

The Ohio EPA singled out combined sewer overflows as being primarily responsible for the creek's degraded water quality. However, sewage sources other than combined sewers also contributed to the Mill Creek's notoriety as Ohio's worst stream. In the early nineties, combined sewers serviced less than half of the sewered area of the Mill Creek watershed. Separate sanitary and storm sewers served most of the sewered portion of the basin in Hamilton County, and all of the sewered portion of the basin in Butler County. Separate sanitary sewers had been built in Cincinnati's newer suburban areas because combined sewers with their pollution-causing overflows had fallen out of favor earlier in the century. In theory, sanitary sewers do not overflow when they are separated from stormwater sewers. In practice, however, separate sanitary sewers often overflow because of inadvertent and sometimes deliberate inflows of stormwater.

Rain and meltwaters in the Mill Creek basin entered sanitary sewers through breaks in damaged and deteriorated pipes, and via stormwater drains that were illegally connected to the sanitary systems. A 1990 federal water study found that the West Fork Mill Creek and its branches were subjected to numerous sanitary sewage overflows caused by improper tap-ins into sanitary sewer pipes. Most of the tap-ins were traced to home builders who had illegally connected roof downspouts to sanitary sewer laterals, an expedient way to direct stormwater away from their building foundations and basements. The Metropolitan Sewer District established a program to disconnect the tap-ins, and in 1991 scheduled several future rehabilitation and replacement projects for damaged and deteriorated sections of the separate sanitary sewage collection systems. In areas where the sanitary sewers were badly overloaded by excessive stormwater, the MSD could initiate moratoriums on new development until stormwater inflow was reduced to acceptable levels.[34]

Sanitary sewage pollution occurred in even the non-sewered portions of the Mill Creek basin. A major source of effluent in these areas was the discharge of inadequately-treated sewage from private wastewater disposal aeration units whose mechanics were poorly maintained. Approximately 40 percent of the units were malfunctioning in 1993, causing the degradation of stream communities in several Mill Creek tributaries. In response to strong urging from the Ohio EPA, the Hamilton County Department of Health greatly increased its inspection and enforced remediation of private treatment systems that discharged into county streams.[35]

Other sources of sewage pollution in streams of non-sewered areas were badly sited and maintained septic tanks and drainfields. Sewage effluent from these sources did not flow directly into an adjacent stream, but was instead carried to the waterway by stormwater and snowmelt moving over and through the soil. This sewage inflow from septic systems was an example of non-point source pollution, wherein the pollutant was transported to the stream by runoff instead of being introduced into the stream from a specific outlet point. Other examples of non-point source pollutants were soil particles from construction sites and eroding areas, oil and salt from roads and parking lots, and pesticides, fertilizers, and animal wastes from farms and lawns. The total concentration of all non-point source pollutants in the Mill Creek in 1992 was matched in only two of Ohio's other fifty-four principal streams and rivers.[36]

Since non-point source pollution could not be pinpointed, it could not be completely addressed by means of traditional regulatory mechanisms. Government agencies were unable to investigate every one of the Mill Creek basin's farms, lawns, septic systems, parking lots, construction sites, and other generators of non-point source pollution. Instead, the agencies helped to reduce non-point source pollution by sponsoring public educational programs on "best management practices." These methods included operation techniques, maintenance procedures, and structural controls designed to minimize septic system sewage inflows and the many other types of non-point source pollution.[37]

In summary, programs had been initiated by 1993 to reduce inflows into the Mill Creek from overfilled separate sanitary sewers, from malfunctioning wastewater disposal aeration units, and from improperly sited and maintained septic systems. On the other hand, although the Metropolitan Sewer District in 1993 had started to design a remediation plan, there was still no implementation of a comprehensive program to reduce combined sewer system overflows, the largest cause of water pollution in the Mill Creek. In 1993, the Hamilton County Environmental Action Commission, a local advisory group established two years earlier by the Ohio EPA, issued a report that included a succinct description of the creek's greatest problem:

> During heavy rains, as much as 95 percent of the Mill Creek Valley's industrial and sanitary wastes escape interception and pour directly into the Mill Creek, there to be trapped in polluted pools following the passage of the wet weather. The sewage-borne viruses and bacteria found in these septic pools are potentially major public health hazards for the surrounding neighborhoods....The Mill Creek continues to be a long-standing civic embarrassment for the Hamilton County metropolitan area.[38]

An overflow outlet for combined sewage from the Fairmont area. (From the collection of The Cincinnati Historical Society. B-86-015)

CHAPTER ELEVEN

To Cleanse the Queen's Creek
Will Cost a King's Ransom

The same lines carry both stormwater runoff and raw sewage, because they
were built before cities required separate pipes for the two.

As a result, a hard rain can cause the pipes to overflow through regulators,
spilling both the rain water and untreated sewage into the creek.

"We do what we can to monitor the creek and keep the equipment working properly," says [Metropolitan Sewer District Director Donald] Miller. "But
you can't put ten pounds in a five-pound bag. That's what it boils down to."
— *The Cincinnati Enquirer Magazine*, April 18, 1984[1]

This [lower Mill Creek] segment will not meet Clean Water Act goals. Fur-
thermore, because of the extremely high economic impact of separating the
combined sewers, it is unlikely that this segment will ever meet the Clean
Water Act goals.
—Ohio Environmental Protection Agency, 1986[2]

THE ULTIMATE objective of the Clean Water Act, passed by Congress in 1972,
was "to restore and maintain the chemical, physical, and biological integrity of
the nation's waters." To attain its objective, the Clean Water Act established
two primary goals: l) "water quality that provides for the protection and propa-
gation of fish, shellfish, and wildlife" and for "recreation in and on the water"
by 1983, and 2) no discharge of pollutants into the nation's waterways by 1985.
Neither of these deadlines was met by the Mill Creek, and government scientists doubted that the act's goals would ever be attained in the section of stream
impacted by overflows from Hamilton County's sewer system.[3]

To review: the area's combined sewer system originated in 1863 when the
Cincinnati City Council lifted its ban on the discharge of sanitary wastes into
underground storm drains. Thereafter, storm conduits became "combined"
sewers carrying both sanitary sewage and storm sewage to the Ohio River and
Mill Creek. The city built more combined sewers after 1863 since that was
cheaper than constructing separate sewers for stormwater and for sanitary

wastes.[4]

Effluent from numerous sewer and industrial outlets caused putrefaction of the lower Mill Creek by the beginning of the twentieth century. The subsequent stink raised by both the stream and the public induced Cincinnati to construct a Mill Creek Interceptor to carry the combined sewers' contents and industrial wastes directly to the Ohio River. However, in order to reduce costs, the interceptor was completed in 1934 with a capacity only large enough to convey the anticipated 1950 dry-weather flow of the sewers and industrial discharge pipes that it intercepted. When it rained, regulatory devices admitted to the interceptor a volume of mixed stormwater and wastewater that was about equivalent to the dry-weather wastewater flow. Everything else went overboard through the old outlets into the Mill Creek.[5]

Combined sewage overflows caused by a heavy rain would often be twenty times greater than the volume going to the interceptor. During such a storm, about 95 per cent of the wastewaters would escape interception and pour into the Mill Creek. Just seven years after the completion of the interceptor, city engineers concluded that the Mill Creek's polluted condition was "bound to continue as long as the intercepting sewer overflows with any frequency."[6]

The lower Mill Creek's continued pollution was the result of Cincinnati's 1863 decision to establish a "combined" sewer system wherein wastewaters were carried through stormwater conduits. The expensive alternative would have been to provide distinct conduits for the city's sanitary wastes, thereby creating a "separate" sewer system such as had been advocated as early as 1842 by English civil engineers. If a separate system had been established in Cincinnati, relatively clean storm runoff from roof leaders, foundation drains, and catch basins in the Mill Creek Valley would have been carried by storm sewers to the Main Stem or its tributaries. Concurrently, wastewaters generated within the Mill Creek basin would have been transported via a second set of sewers. If there had been a system of separate sewers in place, the Mill Creek Interceptor would have carried only wastewater to the Ohio River, and would not have been subject to overflows caused by stormwater.[7]

Unlike Cincinnati and older Mill Creek Valley towns, newer valley suburbs have been built with separate sewer systems in order to prevent the pollution caused by overflows from combined sewers. But because these suburbs' separate sanitary sewers feed into the Mill Creek Interceptor sewer, the suburbs' wastewaters still end up in the creek as a result of interceptor overflows. A 1987 recommendation on correcting the overflow problem suggested that a separation of the stormwater and wastewater collection systems should begin upvalley where the suburban sanitary sewers connect to Cincinnati's combined system. The separation program could then proceed downvalley, coincident as much as possible with normal sewer replacement and road maintenance projects.[8]

Complete separation of the combined system in the Mill Creek Valley would be enormously expensive, given the costs associated with entering all existing properties and buildings to separate roof and footing drains from waste-water lines. Asked in 1984 for the total price of separation, Metropolitan Sewer District Director Donald Miller announced deadpan that, "The federal budget deficit would just about cover it." Miller added that he would like to see a "really good, clean" Mill Creek unpolluted by sewage overflows from a combined system. "But given the circumstances under which we live, that would be untenable."[9]

In January, 1988, new MSD Director Thomas Saygers disagreed with his predecessor by avowing that the $1 billion-plus project of complete separation could in fact be completed if spread over a fifty- to seventy-five-year period. But in July of the same year, an amendment to the Clean Water Act made combined sewer overflows illegal immediately, thereby scuttling Saygers' proposal to spend another half century to solve an overflow problem that was already more than a half century old. The new law forced the MSD to consider alternative, previously-developed solutions to its overflow nuisance.[10]

As early as 1941, Cincinnati's Department of Public Works had outlined two non-separation options that would reduce the frequency of combined sewer overflows into the Mill Creek: enlarged interception and overflow detention tanks. In reference to the first solution, the department calculated that half of the hours of overflow could be eliminated by providing for the interception of all sewer discharges that resulted from rains of four-hundredths of an inch, or less, per hour. This solution would require the replacement of the original Mill Creek Interceptor, whose diameter ranges from four feet near the Carthage Fairgrounds to eight feet at the Ohio River, with a much larger pipe. The cost of the replacement interceptor, with a diameter ranging from eleven and a half feet near the fairgrounds to sixteen feet at the river, was estimated at over ten million dollars. Even with such a costly 1941 investment in an enlarged interceptor, there would be only a 50 percent reduction in the frequency of overflows into the Mill Creek during the 1980 design year.[11]

The 1941 study did not result in the substitution of the original interceptor with another one of increased size. However, the overall interception capacity in the Mill Creek Valley was enlarged when an auxiliary interceptor was built parallel to the original Mill Creek Interceptor. Overflows to the stream decreased in frequency and volume following the installation of the second pipe, but later increased again as postwar suburbanization produced greater volumes of sanitary and storm sewage in the Mill Creek watershed.[12]

The second overflow reduction method studied by the city in 1941 was the construction of overflow detention tanks that would store flows in excess of interceptor capacity. The stored combined sewage would then be pumped back to the interceptor after the storm abated, and when the night-time and week-end flows in the interceptor would permit. The holding tanks would be constructed at a number of different sites along the Mill Creek, usually at the principal points of interception. Sufficient tank capacity to provide for storing combined sewer discharges resulting from rainfalls of four-hundredths of an inch or less and lasting up to a duration of one hour would involve a 1941 construction price of six million dollars, plus additional and substantial operating costs. The plan would eliminate half the hours of overflow projected for the 1980 design year.[13]

No detention tanks were built subsequent to the 1941 report, and the interceptor continued to overflow directly into the Mill Creek. A third of a century later, the 1973 Environmental Task Force for the City of Cincinnati recommended that the temporary storage of combined sewage again be studied as a solution to the ever-worsening overflow problem. To the previous idea of off-line storage in holding chambers, the task force added the possibility that in-line storage capacity might also be available if proper gates and flow regulation devices were installed in the existing system. Although the task force characterized both the off-line and in-line remedial measures as "within the reach of the taxpayer," no overflow storage capacity was added to the interceptor.[14]

In 1991, in anticipation of tougher federal enforcement of overflow reductions, the Metropolitan Sewer District commissioned a Stormwater/Wastewater Integration Management Plan for Hamilton County. The SWIM Plan proposed several projects that would reduce overflows from the Mill Creek basin's 158 regulator locations, including dry-weather bypasses that occurred at sixty-two of the locations when high water stages on the Ohio River caused backwater flooding of the interceptor's regulator structures. Many of the proposed improvements involved storage facilities for detaining sewage that would otherwise overflow.[15]

The largest proposed detention facility would be a ten-mile long tunnel located seven hundred feet underneath the Mill Creek Valley from Galbraith Road south to Gest Street. The three hundred-foot diameter tunnel would detain up to 612 million gallons of combined sewage, and would reduce the frequency of overflows from about seventy times a year to between ten and fifteen times a year. The overflow occurrences would be reduced to less than one a year if a $50 million cavern was added at the downstream end of the $400 million tunnel. The sewage detained in the underground facility would be pumped back to the surface as interceptor capacity became available after a wet-weather or high-water event.[16]

Because of the high construction costs for detention storage facilities, the Hamilton County Commissioners voted to not include any of them in the initial capital budget for the implementation of the SWIM Plan. In 1993, the MSD engaged a set of consultants to again examine the district's options for reducing combined sewer overflows in the county. One option considered by the consultants was the installation of sewage treatment facilities at the overflow points. Although the 1991 SWIM Plan had not recommended such facilities for the Mill Creek basin, they had been proposed earlier by the 1973 City of Cincinnati Environmental Task Force.[17]

According to the task force proposal, each treatment facility would detain the overflowing mixture of stormwater and wastewater in large sedimentation tanks, thereby allowing settling of much of the solid sewage content responsible for causing pollution. The water from near the top of each sedimentation tank would then be discharged into the Mill Creek, while the accumulating sludge on the tank's bottom would be continuously removed to an incinerator or landfill. Such flow-through sewage treatment facilities would not reduce the incidence of overflows to the creek, but the discharges would be cleaner and would result in significantly less water pollution.[18]

The task force recommendation for treatment facilities was based on evidence that such installations already had been effective in reducing sewage pollution in the upper Mill Creek. Sewage treatment works had been erected at Lockland in 1909, Wyoming and College Hill in 1910, Glendale in 1922, and Mount Healthy in 1927. All five facilities released their treated effluent into the Main Stem or one of its branches. Unfortunately, the Wyoming and Lockland plants were abandoned in 1912, after the Ohio Board of Health determined that these suburbs along the industrially-polluted Mill Creek were wasting their money "to purify sewage, while the stream into which the effluent flows is naturally as bad as the raw sewage from the villages." The College Hill plant was decommissioned in 1914 in recognition of the year-old decision to carry that suburb's untreated sewage to the Ohio River via the planned Mill Creek Interceptor. Likewise, the Mount Healthy facility was closed in 1940 upon connection of that community's sewers to the interceptor.[19]

Only the Glendale plant remained unconnected to the interceptor at the time of the Second World War. But with the post-war building boom, population and commercial growth in the upper Mill Creek Valley necessitated the construction of many new sewage works north of Glendale. A total of twenty-eight treatment plants were built in the upper portion of the Mill Creek basin during the thirty-year period following the war.[20]

Microbiological and chemical data collected during 1971-1973 by the Metropolitan Sewer District demonstrated the effectiveness of upstream treatment facilities in mitigating sewage pollution in the Mill Creek. The mean density of fecal coliform bacteria, a measure of sewage contamination, was within the safe water standard of 2,000 colonies per 100 milliliters in the upper portion of the creek. Downstream in the overflow-impacted lower basin, all mean bacterial counts violated the safe water criterion. In parallel manner, dissolved oxygen concentrations in the upper Mill Creek always exceeded 4.0 milligrams per liter, but often fell below this clean water standard in the lower Mill Creek where oxygen-demanding sewage overran the interceptor.[21]

A 1972-1974 study by a Xavier University research team verified that the creek's quality became progressively worse as it flowed from the upstream area of sewage treatment works through the downstream domain of untreated sewage overflows. Unlike the Metropolitan Sewer District's chemical and bacterial survey, the university group looked for bottom-dwelling macroinvertebrates, spineless animals visible to the unaided eye. Decades of ecological research have documented that these organisms are reliable natural monitors of water quality, since different species have different tolerances to pollution. Pollution-intolerant organisms, such as caddisfly larvae and mayfly and stonefly nymphs, have exposed, complex gills. If these organs are subjected to pollutants, they cease to function, and the animal suffocates. Species without complicated external respiratory structures, on the other hand, may survive comparatively heavy loads of pollutants. Such pollution-tolerant animals include leeches, sludgeworms, and bloodworms.

During each of the three years of the Xavier study, macroinvertebrates were collected at ten sampling stations: five on the Main Stem, three on West Fork Mill Creek, and two on Sharon Creek. Healthy populations of many animals were collected from the stations on the upper portions of the two tributaries. Likewise, a complete community of organisms was found at the station on the Main Stem where it flowed under Interstate 275 to enter Hamilton County. The Butler County treatment plants upstream were evidently effective in protecting the creek from pollution.

Southward, as Sharon Creek, West Fork Mill Creek, and the Main Stem were subjected to sewer overflows from the Mill Creek Interceptor and its branches, the macroinvertebrates were eliminated in order of their sensitivity to polluted water. Leeches and other pollution-tolerant worms became increasingly abundant as sewage increased and pollution-intolerant competitors decreased. Sludgeworms, for example, reached densities of 100,000 per square meter in the lower Mill Creek.[22]

The relative cleanliness of the creek's upper portions showed Cincinnati's 1973 Environmental Task Force that treatment of sewage prior to its release into the stream could reduce the physical and biological degradation of the creek. The obvious success of sewage treatment moved the task force to recommend the installation of primary treatment facilities at the Mill Creek Interceptor's overflow points. This recommendation was repeated in 1977 by the Ohio-Kentucky-Indiana Regional Council of Governments, based on the fact that treatment facilities would be significantly less expensive than the alternative overflow control methods of sewer separation or overflow storage.[23]

In 1980, most of the Butler County sewage works were abandoned as the new Upper Mill Creek Regional Wastewater Treatment Plant was opened at a location near the county line. Trunk sewers connected the plant to the previously existing facilities and to unsewered areas of the county. The modern plant allowed a better treatment of sewage as well as an economy of scale. Meanwhile, downstream in the interceptor-served area of Hamilton County, none of the recommended overflow treatment facilities had been built. Dry-weather wastewater flows continued to be collected by the interceptor, and wet-weather flows continued to overrun untreated into the Mill Creek.[24]

A 1972-1974 Xavier University study found only pollution-tolerant leeches, sludgeworms, and bloodworms in the lower Mill Creek. (Photo by Stanley Hedeen)

Inaction on the overflow problem was documented when a second Xavier University research team sampled the Main Stem and West Fork Mill Creek in 1984. The group soon determined that the distribution of bottom-dwelling macroinvertebrates was the same as that found in 1972-1974. The upper Mill Creek was still inhabited by pollution-intolerant organisms, indicating that the Butler County treatment plant was operating successfully. The lower Mill Creek continued to support only pollution-tolerant animals in its sludge-filled waters, showing that overflowing sewage still contaminated the creek. Among themselves, the student researchers referred to the Cincinnati reach of the stream as "the Queen's colon." This was an apt characterization of the Mill Creek's contents and location in the river city immortalized by Henry Wadsworth Longfellow as "The Queen of the West in her garlands dressed, On the banks of the beautiful river."[25]

During the sixty years following the completion of the interceptor in 1934, no facilities were built to treat sewage overflows into the Mill Creek. However, a 120-million-gallon-per-day plant was constructed near the creek's mouth to treat the sewage running through the interceptor to the Ohio River. The Mill Creek Wastewater Treatment Plant was completed in 1959 in response to concerns that interceptor-borne sewage was contaminating the Ohio River, a valuable resource for recreation and water supply. The facility, of course, was unable to treat overflowed sewage in the Mill Creek as it oozed past the plant on its way to despoil Longfellow's "beautiful river."[26]

The Southwest Ohio Water Plan, jointly developed in 1976 by Ohio's Department of Natural Resources and Environmental Protection Agency, asserted that even with the successful operation of the Mill Creek Wastewater Treatment Plant, the Ohio River below Cincinnati would remain polluted until the amount of overflowed sewage issuing from the Mill Creek's mouth was reduced by at least 73 per cent. The Water Plan repeated some methods by which combined sewer overflows could be controlled: separation, holding tanks, and treatment at overflow points. But to these it added yet another possible procedure, one revealing that even environmental watchdog agencies were starting to accept the lower Mill Creek's debased condition as permanent. The report suggested that the creek could continue to serve as an open sewer conveying its pollution load to the Ohio River. But just before the stream merged with the river, a method could be established to "detain the streamflow and provide adequate treatment" of the Mill Creek's entire contents (!)

The Southwest Ohio Water Plan even mapped out a suitable site for the required treatment works near the mouth of the creek:

> The valley floor to the west of Mill Creek is occupied by several structures, including [the] Mill Creek treatment plant, which would be expensive and impractical to relocate. Several acres of eastern shore are occupied by railroad yards. If these yards could be purchased by the city, sufficient area would be available for treating Mill Creek wastes. Approximately 61 acres of low lying, level land would be available for construction of either a retaining basin for the Mill Creek plant or for a separate waste treatment plant.[27]

In 1993, Herbert Preul, professor emeritus of engineering at the University of Cincinnati, recommended a similar proposal to have the Mill Creek carry overflowed sewage to the treatment plant. One difference in Dr. Preul's plan was the floating of several aerators in the lower mile and a half of the stream. The fountain-like devices could introduce oxygen to provide some sewage decomposition prior to treatment, and would stir the creek's contents to prevent the accumulation of bottom sludge deposits. When apprised of Dr. Preul's plan, Metropolitan Sewer District Director Thomas Quinn speculated, with extraordinary understatement, that the use of the Mill Creek as a sewage transport and pre-treatment facility might involve some environmental problems.[28]

Although these plans for the detention and treatment of the Mill Creek's entire contents might seem to be ambitious solutions to the overflow problem, the proposals pale in comparison with other grandiose engineering schemes involving the creek, as will be seen in the next chapter.

PART FOUR

The Corps of the Story

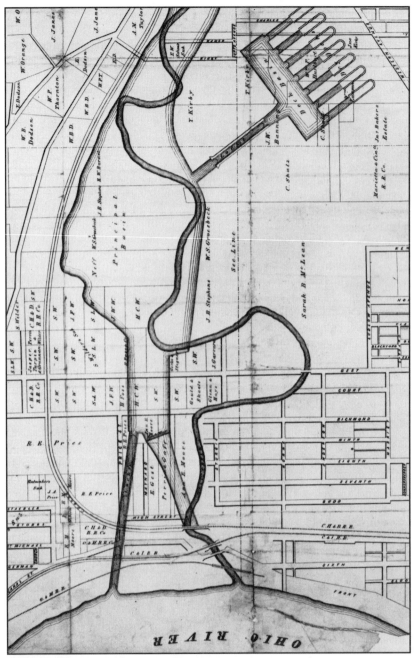

The harbor and docks proposed in 1865 for the lower Mill Creek Valley. (From the collection of The Cincinnati Historical Society. B-94-228)

CHAPTER TWELVE

Up the Creek Without a Paddle

Recommendations for Saluting Cincinnati's 200th Anniversary, an unauthorized report by the Eversole Humble Foundation, should be studied by all associated with the occasion.

Three years in the making and subtitled, "The Queen City And What You Can Do With It," the report contains easily funded, epic proposals...

THE NO-COST MILLCREEK REFURBISHMENT: Presently this watery municipal eyesore sloshes absent-mindedly toward the Ohio River doing little to earn its keep.

Properly preened... it could emerge as a key navigational artery commercially linking downtown Cincinnati with Knowlton's Corner in Northside.

Properly dredged and rigged with locks, Millcreek could accommodate the same commerce as the Ohio River.

—Dick Perry, humorist, *The Cincinnati Enquirer*, October 18, 1987[1]

It is known to most of you, that various plans have been suggested for improving Mill Creek and the grounds adjacent. A ship canal, with locks to the river, forming an immense basin, up nearly to Cumminsville, has been projected, and surveys and estimates made by very competent and scientific engineers.

—A. W. Gilbert, civil engineer, City of Cincinnati, February 21, 1854[2]

ALTHOUGH THE IMAGE of a ship channel and port stretching from the Ohio River to Northside now amuses us, the idea was given serious attention during the middle of the nineteenth century. The 1864 Cincinnati City Council Committee on Public Improvements foresaw that the Mill Creek would become either "a grand outlet for all sewerage of the northwestern portion of the city," or a source of clean water for a port linked by locks to the Ohio River. The Committee, in an encyclopedic sentence, chose to support the harbor option for the Mill Creek and its valley:

Our great commercial and manufacturing city has outgrown her river front; next to its equivalent lies at our doors—the entire western limits of the city, in its natural condition, readily favorable for development; continuously supplied by a living stream of pure water entering the river through a low bottom;

geologically and topographically well adapted to the construction of a great commercial basin and boat harbor, inviting the trade, commerce, manufactures and ship building of the future, and supplying present deficiencies of landing for supplies of lumber, coal, wood, &c.; affording also the best possible opportunity for dry docks to great extent, and probably water-power.

The committee added that the boat basin would remain uncontaminated by sewage through "the construction of a large receiving sewer along its east side, out to the river."[3]

Upon accepting the committee's report, the City Council authorized the city's civil engineer to prepare a design for a harbor and docks in the lower Mill Creek Valley. The resulting plan was submitted to council in 1865. It called for a 175-acre principal basin not less than five hundred feet in width, thirteen feet in depth, and two miles in length. An adjacent dry-docks basin would measure 350 by 13 by 1,326 feet. Locks would connect the principal basin with the Ohio River to the south, and with the Miami and Erie Canal to the east. The Mill Creek flowed into the basin from the north. The entire layout so impressed a visiting naval commission that it recommended to Congress in 1865 that a U.S. Navy shipyard and station be established in the proposed port.[4]

The $2 million cost of the harbor scheme proved too expensive to be funded by post-Civil War Cincinnati. The concept, however, was kept alive by local boosters of boat transportation. They believed that the project would rejuvenate the state-owned Miami and Erie Canal, which was faring poorly in its competition with the railroads. The editor of the *Cincinnati Daily Gazette,* in its edition of October 10, 1872, urged the Ohio Legislature to share in a joint state-city financing of the harbor proposal, since Ohio's economy would greatly benefit from a canal-river link.

With a river connection, such as would take through barges loaded at the mines, the country all along the canal line would be supplied with coal from the Ohio River. This would also be a channel for the transportation of stone from the Ohio River quarries to all parts of the country. This stone is now brought to Cincinnati by river, and shipped hence by railroad.... The exchange of iron ore and of iron and salt and lumber between the river country and the north would be greatly facilitated by this connection. It would remunerate the State in canal tolls, while it would benefit our city and a wide country by cheapening transportation.[5]

As was usual at that time, the editor of the rival *Cincinnati Commercial* quickly denounced the *Gazette*'s idea: "The sudden fury of the editor of the *Gazette* for the 'reclamation of Mill Creek valley' would be pathetic if it were not so fantastic as to suggest the lunacy of its author." The scathing editorial went on to suggest that since the harbor project would be such an obvious waste of public money, a group of conniving land speculators must have prompted the Gazette's advocacy of the scheme. Returning to the *Gazette*'s editor, the *Com-*

The frozen Ohio River. (From the collection of The Cincinnati Historical Society. B-93-253)

mercial judged that he "may be innocent of any interest, out of proportion to his share in the general welfare, in this enterprise, but if we concede the existence of his virtue, it must be at the expense of his judgment."[6]

In response, the *Gazette* portrayed the *Commercial*'s "bovine editor" as a "Cassandra," and boastfully concluded:

> We have set the editor in a rage and given him something to absorb his mind. We can not afford to give all our space to this, for it is but one of the steps in the improvement of Cincinnati.

The "step in the improvement of Cincinnati" that had inspired this sarcastic interchange, the Mill Creek Valley port, remained unfunded and unbuilt. Harbor proponents, unable to obtain either city or state backing, next would attempt to tap the federal treasury.[7]

When the Cincinnati civil engineer in 1865 had presented the initial plan for a commercial port in the Mill Creek bottoms, he had extolled its ability to also serve as a winter harbor of refuge from Ohio River ice. The undammed, shallow river of that period froze over at Cincinnati on an average of once every two years. The subsequent break-up of the ice usually occurred after it had been weakened by sun or rain, and the resultant ice floes would be too soft to cause downstream injury to boats and barges. Every few years, however, a winter flood caused the ice to break up before it had a chance to weaken, and the swift river smashed the heavy ice into the hulls of anchored rivercraft.[8]

One especially disastrous ice break-up at Cincinnati occurred on January

Ice damage to Ohio River boats docked at Cincinnati. (From the collection of The Cincinnati Historical Society. B-82-276)

12, 1877. Of thirty-seven steamboats docked along the riverfront, seven ships worth a total of $73,650 were sunk or carried away by the ice flood. In addition, 246 of the 627 coal barges moored along both shores in the vicinity of Cincinnati were destroyed or torn from their moorings. Several of the latter vessels reached the Mississippi River before they were recovered, and the cost of salvaging and returning them was very substantial. A total loss of $202,895 was incurred by the barge owners.[9]

The extraordinary ice flood disaster allowed local promoters of a Mill Creek Valley port to engage the attention of the federal government. On January 17, 1877, Ohio members of Congress were successful in having the House of Representatives pass a resolution requesting a "report upon the expediency and utility of constructing a harbor of refuge on the Ohio River at the mouth of Mill Creek, Cincinnati, Ohio." The resolution was directed through the Secretary of War to the Army Corps of Engineers, the administrative unit responsible for river and harbor improvements.[10]

The Corps of Engineers was, and still is, a military and civil engineering and construction agency. Congress established the Corps in 1802 to provide military defense works for the country. In the early 1820s, as national security policy broadened to include interior improvements as well as coastal fortifications, the Corps was assigned the additional responsibility for internal routes of communication. This involved the agency in projects to continue the Cumberland Road, build the Chesapeake and Ohio Canal, and improve navigation on the Ohio, Mississippi, and Missouri Rivers. Congress also placed harbors work under the Corps, making the engineers responsible for designing, building, and operating havens for interstate navigation. Thus, Cincinnati boosters were hopeful that the Corps would choose to construct and maintain a harbor of refuge in the Mill Creek Valley.[11]

In its cost/benefit assessment of the project, the Corps estimated that an ice harbor connected by locks to the Ohio River and supplied by water from the Miami and Erie Canal would cost $2,455,000, not including ongoing maintenance and dredging expenditures. Turning to the project's benefits, the report next addressed the question, "Would steamboat-men use this harbor if built?" The answer was negative:

> Even should the basin be constructed, there will always be boats at the [Ohio River] wharves, some of which will be caught there while loading or unloading, and others will stay there by choice, taking the chances of a safe breakup, in order to save time and get their cargoes aboard, so as to start out the moment the river is clear.

Believing that the benefits of a costly ice harbor would be slight "when business is carried on in this way," the Corps concluded that the project was "impracticable." After receiving the negative report on February 1, 1877, Congress dismissed the Cincinnatians' appeals for a Mill Creek harbor of refuge. This was just the beginning of the proposed harbor's long and frustrating association with Congress and the Corps.[12]

Undaunted by their initial defeat, the determined harbor proponents continued plumbing for federal money by having the port project tied to a renovation of the Miami and Erie Canal. Widespread concern for the deteriorating Ohio canals had produced intense lobbying since the Civil War for a federally-funded rehabilitation of the state system. Continued western Ohio agitation for a widened and updated Miami and Erie Canal finally resulted in a June 14, 1880 act of Congress authorizing a Corps of Engineers survey:

> to ascertain the practicability and cost of construction of a ship canal from Lake Erie... to the Ohio River, by way of the Miami and Erie Canal, or any variation in route to produce the most practical and least expensive ship canal..., the estimates in each case to be for a water channel and locks of the same size and capacity as those of the present enlarged Erie Canal in New York.[13]

The Corps survey for an enlarged Miami and Erie Canal suggested that its route remain unchanged except at its northern and southern ends. At Toledo, the canal's outlet would be moved from Swan Creek to Delaware Creek. At Cincinnati, where the Ohio River outlet had been closed in 1863 and since covered over by buildings and railroad tracks, the proposed canal would divert from the original course at Northside and descend through six locks into the bed of the Mill Creek. The ship canal's dimensions, and thus those of the lower creek, would equal those of the Erie Canal: seventy feet wide at water surface, fifty-two and a half feet wide at bottom, and seven feet deep. The locks would be double, with lengths of 110 feet, widths of eighteen feet, and depths of seven feet.

At the mouth of the Mill Creek the connection of the ship canal to the Ohio River would be achieved through a flight of four locks. The Corps of Engineers (strangely, considering its negative ice harbor report of 1877) advised that these final locks:

> should be constructed of a size sufficient to pass the largest vessels navigating the Ohio River, so that Mill Creek could be utilized as an ice harbor of refuge and prevent the enormous damage and loss which annually occurs when the ice in the Ohio River breaks up.

The Corps made no attempt to measure the ship canal's benefits, but did determine its cost to be $28,557,183.13 (one marvels at the estimate's detail). The Corps neither promoted nor condemned the ship canal, but only stated that its construction was "feasible." Congress accepted the Corps' neutral report on February 25, 1881, and decided against appropriating funds for the expensive project. Lobbying for a Mill Creek Valley harbor therefore continued through the eighties and into the nineties.[14]

Congress again responded to the unremitting advocacy for a Mill Creek port in 1893 when it requested the Corps to reassess the suitability of the creek's mouth as a location for a harbor of refuge. The engineers' reply this time failed to consider any possible linkage between the harbor site and the Miami and Erie Canal. The Corps' report reviewed its 1877 research on a Mill Creek ice harbor and reaffirmed its earlier conclusion that the port's construction was "impracticable within any limits of cost commensurate with the amount of benefit that would be derived from it by navigation interests." In the face of an adverse cost/benefit ratio, Congress once again refused to allocate any monies for a Mill Creek harbor.[15]

The indefatigable Mill Creek port proponents next resurrected their earlier failed attempt to secure federal funding by having the harbor project tied to an enlarged Miami and Erie Ship Canal. Mr. H. D. Burke, in a paper read before the February 15, 1894 meeting of the Engineers' Club of Cincinnati, suggested that the national treasury should bear the ship canal's estimated $28.5 million construction cost, as well as additional expenses that were overlooked in the Corps' 1881 report. The latter costs included purchases of privately-held water rights, and construction of harbor facilities in Toledo's Maumee River bottoms and in Cincinnati's Mill Creek Valley. Burke predicted that the ship canal would allow hard iron ores from the Lake Superior district to be brought together with the coal, limestone, and soft ores already reaching the industrializing Mill Creek Valley via the Ohio River and railroad lines.

Having our central position for distribution, an almost unlimited supply of fuel, of limestone for flux, and of the hematite and limonite ores, with direct water transportation from the Superior mines, would not our valley become the great manufacturing center of the iron and steel industries of the United States? Certainly no other location can offer superior advantages.[16]

Envisioning Cincinnati as the nation's hub for steel production, Ohio politicians convinced Congress to request a federal study of a ship canal route across Ohio. The Rivers and Harbors Act of August 17, 1894, directed the Corps of Engineers:

to survey the Miami and Erie Canal, the Ohio Canal and such branches thereof and such river and stream channels as may in their judgment form available portions of a continuous canal connecting the waters of Lake Erie with the Ohio River through the State of Ohio, and to report as to the feasibility and advisability of improving and widening such canal to seventy feet at the water line, and deepening the same to seven feet.

The Corps soon identified three possible routes: Cleveland-Marietta, Sandusky Bay-Portsmouth, and Toledo-Cincinnati. The latter route, although the longest, involved the fewest modifications of an already existing waterway. The major changes proposed for an enlarged Miami and Erie Canal were to relocate its northern and southern terminuses, lower the summit by fourteen feet, and increase its locks to 150 feet in length and twenty-one feet in width.

Near its southern terminus, the new Miami and Erie Ship Canal would divert from the old alignment at a point near the Colerain Avenue bridge over the Mill Creek. It would at once be locked down fifty-three feet to a boat basin 3,200 feet long and three hundred feet wide, located just east of Spring Grove Avenue. At the southern end of the basin it would be locked down an additional thirty feet to the flood plain of the Mill Creek. The canal would then parallel the creek to the Ohio River, which it would reach through a final lock-down of twenty-nine feet. The canal route purposely avoided the flow of the Mill Creek, a stream that by 1894 had become choked with sewage and industrial refuse.

The Corps' report was transmitted to Congress on March 4, 1896. The cost estimates for the three routes were $12,299,372 for Cleveland to Marietta, $18,094,165 for Sandusky Bay to Portsmouth, and $23,011,374 for Toledo to Cincinnati. The latter estimated cost for enlarging and realigning the Miami and Erie Canal was considerably less than the Corps' 1881 estimate for virtually the same project. Nevertheless, the Corps did not recommend the Toledo-Cincinnati route, or even the other two less expensive routes. Because Great Lakes ships would be unable to enter a seven-foot-deep canal, and canal boats with full draft would be unable to navigate the Ohio River during its low stages, the Corps advised against building a ship canal connecting Lake Erie and the Ohio River. Congress concurred with the Corps' recommendation.[17]

With the beginning of the twentieth century, *The Enquirer* took up the cause of a Mill Creek harbor. The paper's port proposal had the harbor connecting a canalized and deepened Ohio River with a widened and deepened Miami and Erie Canal. A June 14, 1909 editorial argued that the project's completion was necessary to ensure the future prosperity of the city:

> With nine feet of water the year around in the Ohio River and in the connecting canal between the river and the lakes there would come a grand change for the better upon the business methods of Cincinnati, upon its manufactures, with advance in its population and its whole appearance, as it would grow into a city with stone docks and quays, with its swampy Millcreek succeeded by fine basins of navigable water.[18]

By the final years of World War I, a Lake Erie-Ohio River canal again was being widely promoted as a condition for the nation's successful commercial competition with the rest of the post-war world. The canal also was envisioned as an interior route for secure transportation in the event of enemy occupation of the nation's coasts during future wars. Acknowledging these arguments, the River and Harbor Act approved by Congress on March 2, 1919, contained a request for an updated survey of:

> The Miami and Erie Canal, Ohio, including a branch canal connecting the Miami and Erie Canal with Lake Michigan, and such other routes between Lake Erie and the Ohio River as may be considered practical by the Chief of Engineers, with a view to securing a channel 12 feet in depth with suitable widths.[19]

A 1921 progress report on the survey identified four routes as worthy of further consideration: Ashtabula to Pittsburgh, Cleveland to Marietta, Sandusky to Portsmouth, and Toledo to Cincinnati (with a branch canal to Lake Michigan). The general route envisioned for a Toledo-Cincinnati canal substantially followed the Miami and Erie Canal corridor from Lake Erie to a large terminal basin above ordinary Ohio River flood stages in the Mill Creek Valley. The Corps found it would be feasible to construct a canal by any one of the four routes, but tentatively concluded that only an Ashtabula to Pittsburgh canal would generate benefits that were "somewhat near" costs. An unfavorable cost/benefit ratio of about 1/0.4 was forecast for a Toledo-Cincinnati canal, largely because projected freight transportation rates on such a waterway would not be significantly different from the rates charged on existing railroad lines.[20]

The Cincinnati City Planning Commission in 1925 thought it unlikely that the Corps' bias towards the Ashtabula-Pittsburgh route would change as the engineers' investigation proceeded. Nevertheless, according to the commission, "studies of the situation made in connection with the planning of Cincinnati, disclosed so much merit in the old Miami and Erie scheme that it is possible that future developments may result in the construction of an enlarged canal along that route." The commission's 1925 City Plan therefore included a site for a canal terminal basin on eighty acres north of Hopple Street in the Mill Creek Valley. Ironically, the alternative use for the site identified in the City Plan was as a switching yard for the region's railroad industry, the successful rival of the Miami and Erie Canal.[21]

The canal survey initially authorized by Congress in 1919 was finally completed twenty years later. By 1939, the deterioration and filling of the Miami and Erie Canal had caused the Corps to abandon their earlier schemes for a Mill Creek Valley portion of the Toledo-Cincinnati route. The southern terminus of the route was relocated to the mouth of the Great Miami River, nineteen miles below Cincinnati.

The 1939 costs of a canal from the Lake Erie bay at Toledo to the Great Miami River mouth on the Ohio were estimated as $220,655,000 for construction and $13,857,000 annually for maintenance and operation. On the benefits side, the Corps compared waterway freight rates with rail rates and projected an insignificant $296,000 annual saving in transportation costs. The alternate scheme to place the southern terminus at the mouth of the Mill Creek was also considered, but was found even "less practicable than the plan outlined." The Corps' figures were so prohibitively high that Congress never again considered building a canal or port in the Mill Creek Valley. Since the Corps' 1939 report, even the Cincinnati Chamber of Commerce has taken and maintained the position that the construction of a ship canal and harbor in the Mill Creek basin would be economically unjustifiable.[22]

The demise of all Mill Creek basin navigation schemes did not mean the end of Corps investigations in the valley. In 1937, Congress authorized the Army Engineers to develop construction programs that would decrease, rather than increase, the amount of water in the Mill Creek bottoms. The Congressional order was part of a federal response to that year's Ohio River flood, the greatest and most destructive ever recorded. On January 24, 1937, the surging river's backwaters covered most of the Mill Creek Valley floor north to Hartwell, eight miles above the creek's mouth. The resulting chaos later was memorialized by Cincinnati native John G. Mitchell:

> In the hills, frightened suburbanites prepared to defend themselves from the homeless hoards of bottomland looters said to be on their way. It was only a rumor. The Mill Creek Valley, Cincinnati's industrial Ruhr, was not a rumor. On Black Sunday it was the worst mess of all when rising waters pried fuel tanks from their moorings and slathered the valley with floating petrol. Poof. They called it the Burning Flood.[23]

The Burning Flood in the Mill Creek Valley, January 24, 1937. (From the collection of The Cincinnati Historical Society. B-94-268)

CHAPTER THIRTEEN

Waterproofing the Flood Plain

As night must follow day, after the Flood of '37 there would be flood control action. There would be dams and reservoirs, levees and floodwalls, and after that new acts to authorize even newer projects. It is hard to keep track of it all.
—John G. Mitchell[1]

THE MILL CREEK Valley has been flooded repeatedly by backwater spilling upstream from a flooding Ohio River, as well as by storm runoff from the creek's own basin. Newspaper accounts document that Mill Creek floods caused by an overflowing Ohio River occurred about every other year during the nineteenth and first half of the twentieth centuries. One year in five these backwater floods caused significant property damage as far north as Northside.[2]

James Hall described the inundation of the lower Mill Creek Valley in 1847: "the serpentine channel of Mill Creek was entirely lost in the view, and in its stead was a wide expanse of water, covering the whole plain to the base of the hill on either side." The 1847 flood stirred local memories of the larger 1832 inundation, when floodwaters in the Mill Creek Valley reached a level at least a half foot higher.[3]

The repeated flooding prohibited early residential and commercial development on the hundreds of acres of Mill Creek bottomland in Cincinnati. In 1853, City Council instructed the city's civil engineer to investigate the addition of fill to bring the elevation of the Mill Creek Valley floor to the high water line of the 1832 flood. The engineer responded that the valley could be filled "as fast as it will be actually necessary to use this portion of the city." Suggested fill materials included dirt graded from city lots, earth excavated from building cellars, and refuse cleaned off city streets. The engineer concluded by forecasting that the growing railroads "will occupy no small portion of what is now considered comparatively valueless property," and that "an immense business will be done in the southern portion of this valley, in the course of a few years."[4]

As predicted, the lower valley was gradually filled as Cincinnati expanded toward the western hills. By 1880, the Mill Creek's floodway had been

151

An Ohio River backwater flood in Camp Washington in 1880. (From the collection of The Cincinnati Historical Society. B-94-240)

considerably narrowed by "making land" for homes, industries, and railroad yards. Continued filling eventually raised the banks of the creek between the Ohio River and Ivorydale by fifteen to twenty feet. From Ivorydale northward through Carthage most of the bottomland west of the stream was raised and occupied by residential and commercial developments. Above Carthage, fill was added to flood-prone land in Reading, Lockland, and Wyoming.[5]

Unfortunately, the elevations of the filled bottomlands were generally insufficient to raise them above the higher Ohio River floods in the Mill Creek Valley. A 1907 deluge caused nearly $1 million in damages, including emergency costs of caring for flood refugees and the expense of restoring flooded areas to pre-flood conditions. Damages from a 1913 flood also totalled almost $1 million. Severe (and expensive) flooding occurred again in 1918 and 1924.[6]

When another Ohio Valley municipality guaranteed flood immunity to industries that might relocate to that city, Cincinnati's city planners were spurred to action. In 1925 they proposed building a dike to seal off all or portions of the Mill Creek Valley from the Ohio River. One version envisioned a dike across the whole width of the valley and included an expensive watergate at the mouth of the Mill Creek. A less costly alternative eliminated the gate by having the dike turn up the eastern side of the creek to Liberty Street, thus protecting the Mill Creek Valley lands adjacent to downtown Cincinnati. The 1925 City Plan suggested that the feasibility of constructing a flood control dike be studied in collaboration with the United States Army Corps of Engineers.[7]

Debris from wrecked buildings was used as fill material in the lower Mill Creek Valley. (From the collection of The Cincinnati Historical Society. B-94-256)

The Corps had become officially involved in flood control just eight years earlier, when Congress passed the first Flood Control Act in 1917. The act required the Corps to consider flood control needs and other river basin issues during its navigation surveys. However, subsequent flood control reports compiled by the Corps were general in nature and made no specific recommendations for flood protection, since there was no federal authority to undertake flood control activities across the nation.

During the Depression years of the 1930s, the Corps was ordered to furnish technical assistance to work-relief flood control projects funded by the federal government. These Depression-born activities led the public to consider flood control as a general federal obligation. Following disastrous floods in New England during the mid-1930s, Congress passed the 1936 Flood Control Act that adopted flood control as a federal responsibility where "the lives and social security of people are otherwise adversely affected." Flood control was thereafter accepted as a proper Corps activity on navigable waters and their tributaries.[8]

In December of 1936, scattered moderate to heavy rains began falling across the Ohio River's two hundred thousand-square mile drainage area. As the watershed's soils became saturated, and in many places frozen, it became impossible for the ground to absorb massive January downpours that next drenched the Ohio Valley. The fourteen inches of rain that fell in Cincinnati between December 26 and January 25 were nearly five times the normal

The 1937 flood submerged the Mill Creek Valley between the Ohio River and Carthage. (From the collection of The Cincinnati Historical Society. B-94-269)

amount for that period. The Ohio River at Cincinnati, then normally at a twelve-foot pool stage, rose above the official flood stage of fifty-two feet on January 18. Within three days the surging river topped its twentieth century high water mark of 69.9 feet, the crest of the 1913 flood.[9]

As two inches of rain fell in Cincinnati on January 24, the flood reached 77.3 feet. The rising water pried a number of Standard Oil Company storage tanks from their foundations in the Cincinnati portion of the Mill Creek basin. The upended gasoline tanks spread their contents over the water-filled valley, creating a flammable lake that was immediately declared a no-smoking area. Unfortunately, at 10:30 a.m. an electric streetcar wire snapped and dropped into the floating fuel. The resulting three and a half-square mile holocaust was witnessed and later recalled by *Cincinnati Times-Star* reporter George P. Stimson:

> Within minutes, the scene was a roaring inferno. Two hours later the dancing flames had consumed the refrigerator and storage building of the Crosley Corporation. In two hours, this building was reduced to twisted girders, fused glass and fallen brick. The fire next raced to the Standard Oil plant. The smoke and flame billowed to tremendous heights as tanks and drums of oil, gasoline, naphtha and other volatile fuels exploded in a staccato fashion. The flames swept through the Triumph Manufacturing Company and the Cincinnati Fence Company. At one time, firemen reported that thirty-two buildings were ablaze.... "Black Sunday" a *Times-Star* reporter with the appropriate name of Bob Waters called it, and so it is known to this day in local tradition.[10]

The Ohio peaked at eighty feet on Tuesday, January 26. The inundated lower Mill Creek basin appeared to be a lake, but one on which there was "no life, except that in rescue craft." Its shoreline followed the 509-foot contour line, thus putting the Cincinnati Reds' Crosley Field under twenty feet of water. This temporary lake, which had taken eight days to fill, drained back into the Ohio River during the next ten days. The 1937 flood officially ended in Cincinnati on February 5, when the river finally dropped below the fifty-two foot mark.[11]

Damages caused by the 1937 flood in Cincinnati and Hamilton County totalled $17.6 million, with losses in the Mill Creek Valley accounting for about half that figure. Twelve people died in the county, part of the toll of 137 flood-related deaths in the Ohio Valley. From the Ohio River's headwaters to the Mississippi River confluence and down to New Orleans, the flood submerged 12,700 square miles of usually dry land, destroyed thirteen thousand buildings, severely damaged sixty thousand more, and drove 1.6 million people from their homes. The Red Cross assessed the 1937 flood as the nation's second worst disaster to that point in the twentieth century, surpassed only by World War I.[12]

Numerous flood control bills were introduced in the U.S. House of Representatives during the weeks following the 1937 flood. The House Committee on Flood Control assembled these bills into a Flood Control Act that embodied the various proposals covering all of the localities that had suffered flood damage. This legislation, approved on August 28, 1937, authorized Corps of Engineers investigations of existing flood problems and of the practicality of providing corrective measures. The Corps' studies and flood protection plans resulting from the examinations were funded by $178 million in federal appropriations during 1937 and 1938.[13]

On the basis of two years of research and public hearings, the Corps in 1939 supported Cincinnati's 1925 plan to wall off the mouth of the Mill Creek Valley against Ohio River floods. To determine the necessary height of a barrier

Flooding in Northside, 1937. (From the collection of The Cincinnati Historical Society. B-88-145)

dam, the Army Engineers calculated a maximum possible river stage by super-imposing the 1913 flood upon the 1937 flood. From this theoretical stage they subtracted the height of the total flood waters that would be withheld from the Ohio River by the flood control reservoirs planned for the river's watershed above Cincinnati. These calculations resulted in the Corps' plan for a one-and-a-half mile barrier dam erected to the height of an eighty-three foot river stage.

The barrier dam would consist of earthen levees and concrete walls with openings and gates at railroad and street crossings. The gates would be closed when the Ohio River reached flood stage. The dam also would have a watergate through which the Mill Creek would pass during normal river stages. With this gate closed at flood stage, the waters of the Mill Creek would be pumped through the barrier dam. The engineers determined the maximum required pump capacity by estimating the heaviest rainfall that could occur in the Mill Creek watershed. Having provided for the greatest possible water volumes behind and in front of the barrier dam, the Corps vowed that the structure would prevent any inundation of the lower Mill Creek Valley during an Ohio River flood.[14]

The project was pronounced "economically justified" on the basis of a favorable cost/benefit ratio. The protection of the Mill Creek Valley would save an estimated $14,600,000 in flood losses within a decade, almost twice the barrier dam's estimated $7,543,000 construction expense. Cincinnati's share of the construction cost would be about $1,657,000, financed out of a $5,000,000 flood protection bond issue approved by its citizens in November, 1937. The project also would cost the city between $17,200 and $23,500 annually to operate and maintain.[15]

In 1940, the Cincinnati City Planning Commission and City Council debated and adopted the barrier dam proposal, and local supporters initiated intense lobbying for Congressional support. The editor of *The Cincinnati Post,* in an open letter soliciting federal assistance for the dam, began by assuring Congress that the request was not for any "Roll Out the Pork Barrel" appropriation. The letter pointed out that the people of Cincinnati already had voted to tax themselves to pay for the city's share of the project. The letter also outlined the local, regional, and national importance of protecting the Mill Creek basin from Ohio River floods:

> In this valley live more than 40,000 of the city's 470,000 residents. In this valley are situated factories which represent perhaps 75 percent of the city's capital investment in industry, and which employ 65 percent of its industrial workers. It is truly the city's "meal ticket."
>
> In this valley is a great network of railroads, the key to much of the rail transportation of this part of the Ohio Valley. In this valley are important machine tool, chemical and plastics factories whose products would prove invaluable to the nation in any emergency of war preparation.

The letter concluded by reiterating that Cincinnati was not begging for a

The barrier dam pumping station with the Mill Creek watergate at its right.
(From the collection of The Cincinnati Historical Society. B-94-239)

100 percent gift. Instead, the city was requesting Congress to share in "an investment which will pay rich dividends in preventing human tragedy and business paralysis resulting from the recurring floods of the Ohio River."[16]

Congress heeded the many requests for barrier dam funding and authorized the Corps to proceed with the awarding of contracts for the project. On October 16, 1941, bulldozers and steam shovels started on a construction program that was projected to last two years. But just fifty-two days after excavation had begun, the nation went to war, redirecting manpower and materials away from federal flood control projects. Work on the barrier dam proceeded fitfully, so that by 1945 the dam was completed only to a height where it could protect the Mill Creek Valley against a sixty-five foot river stage.[17]

In March, 1945, when it became obvious that a quickly-rising Ohio River flood would exceed sixty-five feet, an attempt was made to temporarily increase the Mill Creek Valley's protection to seventy feet by adding sandbags to the unfinished dam. The emergency effort failed on March 6, and the lower Mill Creek basin received its last soaking from the Ohio River. The 69.2-foot flood, the century's third highest, caused at least $3,500,000 worth of damage in the Mill Creek Valley.[18]

World War II ended a few months later, but post-war material shortages and labor unrest hindered the resumption of sustained work on the barrier dam. Construction was stopped altogether in September of 1946 when the President slashed public works spending in an attempt to balance the budget. The dam project, 90 percent completed, was left $650,000 short of the funds required to finish it.

The January 25, 1947 dedication of the pumping station with its 6,500-horsepower pumps. (From the collection of The Cincinnati Historical Society. Marsh 14219-7)

Signaling the city's determination to realize the dream of flood protection for the Mill Creek Valley, Cincinnati quickly loaned the federal government the money needed to conclude the project. The loan enabled the barrier dam to be finished by March 1, 1948. The final cost of the project was $11,146,000, of which Cincinnati contributed $1,028,000.

The heart of the dam, which is still functioning, is the pumping station located adjacent to the Mill Creek watergate. This building houses eight huge pumps. When the Mill Creek gate is closed during Ohio River floods, each unit is capable of pumping creek flows into the river at a rate of one billion gallons per day. Smaller pumps also are operated during flood periods to provide for drainage from low-lying areas behind the dam.

Within a dozen years of its completion, the barrier dam already had reduced flood damage by an amount equal to its total construction and operating costs. The dam yielded its first flood control benefits in only its sixth week of operation: the $11 million project saved over $4 million in flood losses when the Ohio River crested at 64.8 feet. Transportation arteries were not disrupted, and seven thousand people who would have otherwise had to abandon their homes were spared the hardship. An estimated two hundred industrial plants were able to continue operations, thereby saving a million hours of work by thousands of men and women. Baseball's Opening Day also was preserved: without the barrier dam Crosley Field would have been under six feet of water on April 12, 1948.[19]

After completing plans to protect the Mill Creek Valley from Ohio River floods, the Corps turned its attention to the second source of valley floods, the Mill Creek itself. The engineers investigated alternative means of flood control and determined the cost/benefit ratio of each method. A favorable ratio over the life of the project is the first criterion that must be met in any flood protection scheme proposed by the Corps. Congress will authorize an investment of federal money in a flood control program only if it provides a return in excess of investment, and thus adds to the national wealth.[20]

The first Mill Creek flood protection plan considered for the basin was the provision of levees between the stream and adjacent highly-developed areas in Cincinnati and St. Bernard. This project included the installation of several pumps to lift drainage from behind the levees up to the Mill Creek during flood periods. The Corps estimated that the lifetime cost/benefit ratio of the $2,238,000 project would be 1/0.24, making levee construction an obviously uneconomical method for controlling Mill Creek inundations.

As an alternative to building levees from the Colerain Avenue bridge through Ivorydale, the Corps next considered dredging, widening, realigning, and riprapping the creek in the same reach. The enlarged channel capacity would allow the Mill Creek to handle increased volumes of runoff without overbank flooding. Compared to the more expensive levee construction, the $1,454,000 channelization plan would produce the same $28,200 average annual flood benefit. However, the lifetime 1/0.41 cost/benefit ratio estimated for the project was still too uneconomical to elicit federal support.

The Corps also conducted a study of a much larger channelization program stretching from the barrier dam north through Reading. This $8,000,000 project would eliminate flood damage over a greater area and thus produce a greater annual benefit of $54,300. The cost/benefit ratio, on the other hand, would be a plainly unacceptable 1/0.14.

In addition to levee and channelization schemes, the Corps investigated a novel proposal to divert floodwaters from the Mill Creek's upper basin into the Great Miami River. The plan would achieve an $83,200 annual benefit, an amount substantially higher than that gained through the flood control methods outlined above. However, the $4,956,000 cost of constructing a diversion channel, numerous bridges, and other required structures also was relatively high. The resultant cost/benefit ratio of 1/0.38 caused the diversion plan to join the growing list of flood control schemes that were outside the realm of economic feasibility.

The remaining flood protection method to be examined was the construction of a flood control dam in the northern portion of the Mill Creek Valley. Of the great number of dam sites recommended to the Corps by various interest groups, the engineers chose to investigate three locations: above Sharon Road and above Windisch Road on the Main Stem, and below McKelvey Road on the West Fork Mill Creek. Dams at these locations would control 35 percent, 23 percent, and 21 percent, respectively, of the drainage area affecting major centers of flood damage.

A dam at Sharon Road would produce the same $83,200 annual benefit as that which would be achieved by the diversion scheme. On the other hand, the $3,377,000 cost of the dam project would be considerably less than the price of diversion. Consequently, the 1/0.54 cost/benefit ratio of the Sharon Road dam was better than that estimated for the diversion plan.

The alternative dam site on the Main Stem was located 2.4 miles upstream at Windisch Road. A dam at this location would furnish less flood control, but also would cost less at $2,098,000. It would provide an annual benefit of $69,100, and would have a cost/benefit ratio of 1/0.74.

The third dam project to be considered was located on the West Fork Mill Creek and carried a price tag of $1,471,000. The contemplated dam would afford complete protection from the West Fork Mill Creek flows of record and would reduce flood crests on the Main Stem below its junction with the West Fork Mill Creek. Although the dam's annual benefit would average only $64,100, it would have a desirable 1/1.01 cost/benefit ratio.

The Corps' investigation determined that the proposed West Fork Mill Creek dam was the only economically justifiable project for controlling flooding in the Mill Creek watershed. The engineers also concluded that the dam should be built to provide a recreation reservoir for use by citizens in the Cincinnati "metropolitan area where similar facilities generally are lacking." Since it proved impracticable to allocate annual recreational benefits to specific beneficiaries, the additional $65,000 construction cost for the recreation pool was justified on the basis of "the public interest."[21]

The West Fork Mill Creek Reservoir project was authorized by Congress in the Flood Control Act approved on July 24, 1946. Completed in 1952, the project primarily consists of an earthen dam 1,100 feet long and a hundred feet in maximum height. The dam forms a recreation pool with an area of 183 acres at an elevation of 675 feet above sea level. Above this pool, to the crest of the spillway at 702 feet, storage capacity is available for the temporary retention of flood runoff from the 29.5-square-mile drainage area above the dam. At full pool, elevation 702, the reservoir has an area of 557 acres.[22]

The operation of the dam began on December 20, 1952, in time to make it "quite a Christmas present for the outdoors man and boy." The Corps granted a lease to the Hamilton County Park District for the development and management of boating and fishing facilities on the reservoir, or Winton Lake as it became known locally. The one thousand acres of leased Corps property presently makes up about half the total acreage of the Park District's Winton Woods.[23]

The final project cost was $3,538,000, of which $2,967,000 came from the federal government and $571,000 was paid by Hamilton County. Within two decades of its completion, the flood control benefits attributed to the Winton

Lake dam had exceeded the total construction and operating costs allocated to flood control. The largest single benefit was realized from January 19 to 21, 1959, when about five and three-quarter inches of rain fell over the Mill Creek Valley. The dam served to greatly reduce downstream discharge from the storm, and thereby prevented an estimated $2,500,000 in damages.[24]

Winton Lake was the second large impoundment created in the Mill Creek Valley. Sharon Lake was the first, completed in 1937 when the Hamilton County Park District dammed a portion of Sharon Creek to provide a recreational reservoir in Sharon Woods. Both impoundments furnish boat fishing for largemouth bass, sunfish, crappies, and catfish, species that displaced the stream fish fauna in the creek reaches that were drowned. [25]

When a reservoir pool replaces a stream, the alteration in the fish community largely reflects the change in invertebrate forms that serve as fish prey. For example, fifty-three macroinvertebrate species were collected during 1986 from the waters and shoreline of Winton Lake, but forty-five of these were not found in or along the West Fork Mill Creek immediately above the impoundment. Conversely, of fifteen macroinvertebrate species recorded from the creek, seven were absent from the lake, including two species of aquatic flies and one species each of riffle beetle, mayfly nymph, midge larva, aquatic sowbug, and crayfish. These creek-restricted insects and crustaceans are adapted to high oxygen concentrations, since tumbling creek water becomes well mixed with air and so absorbs a great deal of oxygen. Creek animals also are greatly dependent on moving water to bring them their food and remove their wastes.[26]

The current-dependent West Fork Mill Creek species have been unable to tolerate the stilled waters where the creek's velocity has been checked by the Corps' dam. They've been replaced by animals adapted to life in a tranquil aquatic habitat with the lowered oxygen levels that exist where only a small portion of the water is in direct contact with air. Slackwater dwellers have supplanted the normal stream fauna in the two-and-a-half mile stretch of the West Fork Mill Creek that is drowned under Winton Lake, as well as in the three-quarter mile reach of Sharon Creek that is submerged beneath Sharon Lake.

The destruction of stream life in the inundated portions of two Mill Creek tributaries is consistent with observations of other impounded waterways. In a summary report on their many midwestern stream investigations, aquatic biologists J. L. Funk and C. E. Ruhr reached the following conclusion:

> From an ecological viewpoint, channelization is the second worst thing that can happen to a stream. The worst is impoundment. When a stream is impounded it ceases to exist as an ecological entity; it is dead.[27]

While only two of the Mill Creek's primary tributaries suffer from the "worst thing that can happen to a stream," much of the Main Stem of the Mill Creek must endure "the second worst thing": channelization.

The General Electric Aircraft Engine plant in Evendale, with the Mill Creek flowing from left to right through the tree corridor in the upper portion of the photograph. (From the collection of The Cincinnati Historical Society. B–94-267)

CHAPTER FOURTEEN

Ditching the Ditching, Reclaiming the Creek

> You can't go in and do what we're doing without affecting the wildlife in the creek. It's a sacrifice you make for reduced flooding.
> —James Emly, Corps of Engineers design engineer, Mill Creek channelization project[1]

IN THE YEARS following World War II, the farmland of the upper Mill Creek flood plain became the focus of industrial development in Hamilton County. The area was level, accessible to transportation, and available for purchase. The new industrial construction covered the flood-prone land with sprawling factory roofs and paved parking lots. Floodwaters that previously had soaked into the ground now rapidly drained over impervious asphalt and concrete surfaces into the Mill Creek, intensifying the stream's downstream flood peaks.

A flood in 1959 damaged the new upvalley industrial parks and the established downvalley communities as well. Forty families were forced from their homes in Reading and eight hundred people were displaced in Elmwood Place. Cincinnati's Northside neighborhood sustained an estimated $1 million in losses. The Mill Creek flood caused about $3 million in total damages.[2]

The 1959 flood convinced the affected communities that more flood protection was a necessity. In 1962, the governments of Cincinnati, St. Bernard, Elmwood Place, Arlington Heights, Reading, Lockland, Evendale, Sharonville, and Hamilton County established the Mill Creek Conservancy District to control flooding on the Main Stem. Although the district had its own bonding and tax assessment powers, its officers soon realized that federal support would be needed for an adequate flood control project. Conservancy-led lobbying resulted in a 1967 authorization for the Corps of Engineers to review its former plans for the "alleviation of urgent problems in the Mill Creek Basin." The Corps immediately set about reconsidering the flood control schemes that it had dismissed two decades earlier: dams along the Main Stem, diversion, channelization, and levee construction.[3]

163

Cribwalls and paving protect the banks from stream erosion where bridges are present. (Photo by Alan Vicory)

The Corps discovered that the sites of the large Main Stem flood control reservoirs contemplated in the forties were occupied by industrial complexes in the sixties. Smaller reservoirs could still be built on the undeveloped parcels of land that remained, but rising property values made their purchase prices prohibitively expensive. Estimated costs exceeded benefits in the case of every dam site studied.

The combination of recent construction and elevated land values also hindered the plan to divert Mill Creek floodwaters to the Great Miami River. The project would disrupt traffic in Fairfield, displace about fifty families in Butler County, and cause a $24,000 loss in yearly property taxes. The approximate cost/benefit ratio of the diversion plan was a clearly unfavorable 1/0.31.

Compared to the diversion scheme, a newly developed plan combining eighteen miles of channelization and eleven miles of levees on the Main Stem was ten times more cost efficient. The plan was confined to Hamilton County, since channelization of the creek's headwaters in the still-undeveloped southeastern Butler County was determined to be uneconomical. The channel improvement plan's 1/3.1 cost/benefit ratio persuaded Congress to authorize a Mill Creek Local Protection Project as part of the Flood Control Act of 1970. The Corps spent the next decade refining the plan, while the Conservancy District drew together the funding necessary to start construction.[4]

Finally, on April 23, 1981, Ohio Governor James Rhodes headed a groundbreaking ceremony in Sharonville to signal the beginning of construction. In his metaphor-mixing remarks, Gov. Rhodes characterized the rain-swollen Mill Creek flowing past him as "a sleeping giant" and "the little monster." The governor also boasted to local and federal officials in attendance that the state's $20 million contribution to the project had been in the bank since 1968. The project's cost was to be paid primarily by the federal government, but state and local interests were to provide a portion of the total amount.[5]

The channel improvement project widened and straightened sections of the Main Stem from the Butler County line to the barrier dam. Streambanks in the channelized sections consist of grass-seeded earth in those areas where land availability permitted side slopes of three to one (no more than one foot of vertical rise for every three feet of horizontal distance). Where constrictions are present, steeper side slopes are protected by riprap, cribwalls, or paving. Concrete paving also lines the creek bottom where high velocity channels and passages under bridges must be protected from erosion.

Smoothing and straightening of the streambed served to increase the creek's speed and allow a given storm discharge to pass through the channel at a lower water surface elevation. The channel's dimensions were designed for conveying a peak runoff that recurs at an average frequency of once each century. The theoretical hundred-year storm would still cause some minimal overbank flooding, except in the developed areas where levees would contain the high water.[6]

The project included the addition of two more pumps to the original six at the barrier dam in order to convey an increased volume of stormwater from the Mill Creek to the Ohio River. Finally, about 164 acres of land adjacent to the

Streamside trees were eliminated during the Corps of Engineers channelization project. (Photo by Graham Mitchell)

Unchannelized sections retain a range of habitat types. Note the mallard duck next to the near bank. (Photo by Robin Corathers)

creek were to be developed for recreational activity, including a trail system running from Sharonville to Northside. William Leegan, chief of planning for the Corps' Louisville District during the seventies, predicted that the Mill Creek Project's combination of flood protection and urban recreation would give the Corps unit its best opportunity to be seen as "a well-balanced resource planning and development agency."[7]

Just as the Hamilton County Park District had dammed Sharon Creek before the Corps' impounding of the West Fork Mill Creek, so had other local interests channelized portions of the Main Stem prior to the start of the engineers' channelization project in 1981. Beginning more than a century earlier, railroad companies had straightened several sections of the irregular streambed in order to permit track construction and yard expansion. Agricultural interests in southern Butler and northern Hamilton Counties had realigned and dredged a long stretch of the upper creek in order to furnish greater channel capacities for storm drainage. Sewer engineers had eliminated large "kinks" in the lower Main Stem to allow the Mill Creek Interceptor to take a more direct route directly to the Ohio River.[8]

As a result of a 1945 flood that was the fourth largest in Reading's history, the Ohio Department of Public Works had straightened and broadened the Main Stem through that city to prevent future overflows of the creek's banks—this rechannelization project caused Columbia Avenue to cross two Mill Creek bridges for many years thereafter. Downstream, Cincinnati had relocated and widened sections of the channel during the 1950s to provide flood protection

Biological diversity is absent where channelization has destroyed the natural variety of streambed and streambank habitats. (Photo by Graham Mitchell)

for low-lying commercial and residential areas. Finally, highway engineers building the Mill Creek Expressway in the 1960s had realigned and enlarged the Main Stem in the vicinity of its junction with the West Fork Mill Creek.[9]

Prior to the 1981 start of its own channelization program, the Corps divided the Main Stem in Hamilton County into nine sections in order to allow phased construction of the eighteen-mile project. The first two sections to be channelized were in Cincinnati between Northside and the southern city limit of St. Bernard, and in Sharonville between Sharon Road and Interstate 275. When a Xavier University research team surveyed the Hamilton County portion of the Main Stem in 1984, the students were able to study and record the ecological differences among areas that were not channelized, those that were newly channelized by the Corps, and those that had been channelized in previous decades by other agencies.[10]

The unchannelized stretches, with varying current velocities, water depths, and bottom types, offer the Mill Creek's fauna a diversity of habitats in which to live. There are shallow riffles with sediment-free rocks and pebbles at the bottom. Tailwaters below the riffles hold current-sifted deposits of gravel, sand, and silt. Deep pools that alternate with the riffles have bottom beds of soft mud and organic debris. The natural riffle-pool sequence allows a variety of organisms to coexist in the creek.

Along the unchannelized sections' wooded shorelines, trees hold the banks while permitting undercutting by the stream, thus providing cover among the submerged roots for many aquatic species. Trees that fall into the creek offer additional shelter. The importance of trees in a stream habitat has been verified by a study of two sections of Jordan Creek in Illinois. The sections were each divided by hardware cloth supported by steel poles. One side of each section was stripped bare of all fallen trees, logs, and limbs, while on the other side the same debris was secured along the bank. In a few months the total weight of fish caught from the tree-littered areas was 9.4 times that of the bare areas. The submerged trunks and branches had provided habitats for invertebrate animals that were eaten by small fish, that were in turn eaten by large fish hiding among those same branches.[11]

Channelized sections of the Mill Creek are similar to the featureless portions of Jordan Creek. The excavations that widened and straightened the Main Stem also eliminated streamside trees. In Northside, for example, where willows had been planted in the 1850s to reduce shoreline erosion, the Corps replaced the tree-lined banks with concrete, riprap, and grass slopes.[12]

Trees will not be welcomed back to the stream's channelized edges. The hydraulic efficiency of the Engineers' channel requires ongoing shoreline mowing and maintenance. The branches of trees would retard the desired speed of bank-full flood flows. Streamside trees would also catch debris carried downstream by floodwaters, further slowing flood flows. Finally, trees along the banks could be uprooted by a flood current, floated downstream, and hung up on a bridge abutment to catch debris and block flow. Thus trees are not tolerated along the Mill Creek's channelized stretches, and the many habitat niches provided by shoreline trees have vanished.[13]

A channelized section denuded of trees is also without riffles, tailwaters, and pools. The water flows at a nearly uniform speed and depth through a straight, wide ditch. The variety of streambed habitats, created by the varying speeds and depths of a natural waterway, have been replaced by an even bottom of unsorted gravels and stones.

In the channelized sections, the velocity of the channelized creek during high water periods exceeds what most stream animals without cover can tolerate. During low water intervals the flow in the widened channel is only inches deep, too shallow to conceal or support many types of aquatic organisms. The shallowness of the channel during the summer and the absence of shade from streambank trees allow water temperatures to reach levels that are lethal to some animals. In sum, the creek's diversity of life, already decreased by pollution, is further reduced where channelization has demolished the natural mosaic of substrate, current, depth, and temperature conditions.

There have been many proposals to reduce the Mill Creek's pollution to a level where clean water organisms could recolonize the stream. The fact is that channelization forecloses any possibility of restoring a natural stream community. In their review of stream channelization in the Midwest, J. L. Funk and C. E. Ruhr drew a sharp difference between the recoverable status of a polluted creek and the hopeless condition of a channelized one:

When a stream is polluted, its ecology is greatly changed. Like a man with a serious or acute illness, its activities and functions are altered, often drastically, but there is always the hope of recovery. When a stream is channelized, it is permanently disabled. Like a man who has suffered a paralyzing stroke, it lives on, a pitiful remnant of its former self, unable to function productively, an object of pity from those who love it and a continuing burden on them and society.[14]

By 1990, the Mill Creek was well on its way to becoming permanently disabled. Approximately 40 percent of the channelization program in Hamilton County was complete, and Butler County interests continued to press for the extension of the project upstream into rapidly-developing Union Township. But also in 1990, soil sampling in the project right-of-way unearthed a difficulty that caused the Army Engineers to reevaluate and then retreat from the unfinished channelization campaign. The problem that the Corps uncovered was a site contaminated with hazardous wastes, a pollution category for disposed chemicals that are toxic, corrosive, flammable, or explosive.

Hazardous waste sites are located throughout the industrialized Mill Creek Valley. There are at least thirty-one known or suspected sites located adjacent to the Mill Creek in Hamilton County. Most of the sites are bottomland dumps and landfills that hold wastes generated by the area's numerous manufacturers. Runoff and leachate from these sites contribute to the total non-point source pollution load carried by the Mill Creek.[15]

Runoff and leachate from abandoned landfill and dump sites contaminate the Mill Creek. (Photo by Robin Corathers)

Two of Ohio's worst hazardous waste sites are located in the Mill Creek basin. (Photo by Graham Mitchell)

One example of a hazardous waste site is the Skinner Landfill located on the East Fork Mill Creek near West Chester in Butler County. Originally a sand and gravel operation, the site became a landfill in the mid-fifties and accepted all types of wastes until its state-ordered closure in 1990. More than 160 contaminants have been identified in the landfill, representing essentially all classes of chemicals. The site may hold up to seven thousand buried fifty-five gallon drums of hazardous wastes. Ohio Environmental Protection Agency officials plan to use a variety of methods to clean up the site before the materials contaminate the East Fork Mill Creek.[16]

The Skinner Landfill is considered by the United States EPA as one of the nation's worst hazardous waste sites, a designation that it shares with thirty-three other locations in Ohio. Among these other Superfund sites is the failed Pristine Inc. hazardous waste disposal plant in Hamilton County. In 1974, Pristine Inc. began its operations in the city of Reading at the location of a former sulfuric acid manufacturing plant, six hundred feet from the Mill Creek. Wastes from more than a hundred companies were sent to the facility, where they were supposed to be incinerated or neutralized and disposed of at the site. Responding in 1979 to numerous complaints, the Ohio EPA inspected the facility and found two tanks of polychlorinated biphenyls (PCBs), eight thousand drums of plating sludges, thirty thousand gallons of acid, one hundred thousand gallons of chlorinated solvents, and large amounts of other untreated wastes. Following an eight thousand gallon spill of acid into the Mill Creek, the State of Ohio in 1981 closed Pristine Inc. for failure to comply with waste control regulations. Cleanup of the site began in 1990, and will continue into the next century.[17]

Skinner Landfill and Pristine Inc. are but two recent examples of the many firms that have disposed hazardous wastes along the Mill Creek and its tributaries. Many of these companies ceased operations years ago, and their existence and location have long since been forgotten. In 1974, the U.S. EPA apparently suspected that hazardous wastes from some of these sites might be uncovered as the Corps straightened and widened the Mill Creek in Hamilton County. A U.S. EPA letter reminded the Corps of its responsibility to properly dispose of contaminated materials that might be unearthed by channelization activities. In reply, the Corps promised that the excavation and disposal of polluted materials would adhere to state and federal regulations. The Corps did not anticipate that these government guidelines would become increasingly stringent, that compliance expenses would significantly inflate, or that several contaminated waste sites would be found within or adjacent to the project right-of-way.[18]

On July 13, 1990, the Corps received a set of chemical analyses that identified buried wastes in the channelization project alignment between Gest Street and the Western Hills Viaduct. Since many of the chemical contaminants exceeded the state criteria for reporting regulated hazardous substances, the Ohio EPA was immediately notified about the findings. The Ohio EPA responded by reiterating the Corps' responsibility for the remedial cleanup of any hazardous wastes uncovered by channelization activities. According to Ohio EPA Southwest District Chief Tom Winston, "It is their waste when they dig it out. They would be subject to the handling requirements even though they're not responsible for putting it there."[19]

The Corps calculated that hazardous waste cleanups would join underestimated costs and inflation in driving the price of channelization far beyond its original $30 million estimate. Consequently, the Corps in 1991 placed a moratorium on the start of new construction while it investigated whether the increasingly-expensive flood control project should be abandoned. The investigation focused on the ability of the Mill Creek Conservancy District to pay its share of the project's total construction cost, to raise money for the remediation of waste contamination, and to cover all future expenses for maintenance and operation of the completed project. The Corps estimated that the district would be responsible for $44 million of a total $313 million project cost, not counting additional expenses for unbudgeted waste cleanups. The district's upkeep costs were forecast at $800,000 annually beginning in 2000, the estimated project completion date.[20]

In response to the Corps' financial concerns, the conservancy district pointed out that it already had paid about half of its share of the estimated final construction cost. The district proposed to raise most of the money needed to meet its remaining obligations through assessments on fifteen thousand pieces of property that would benefit from the flood control project. In 1992, after reviewing the district's funding proposal, the Corps decided that the district had failed to develop a credible plan for meeting the non-federal costs of construction, waste remediation, and upkeep. Consequently, the Corps initiated a study on how to close the project down in an efficient and environmentally sound manner.[21]

When the last major construction work ended in 1992, four portions of the Mill Creek had been channelized: Western Hills Viaduct to Center Hill Road, Sharon Road to Interstate 275, and two small sections near Arlington Heights. Only 42 percent of the project had been completed, but at a cost of about $110 million. Using these figures along with post-1970 Mill Creek flood damage reports, Glendale resident Mike Fremont concluded that the original cost/benefit calculation had been badly flawed. Mr. Fremont, speaking as president of the Ohio stream conservation group Rivers Unlimited, characterized the flood control project as "the worst boondoggle we have ever seen," and shared a vision for a restored Mill Creek: "It could be beautiful." *Cincinnati Enquirer* columnist Tony Lang lumped the Mill Creek project with other public works "megamillion-dollar turkeys," and found it ironic that the supporters of channelization "still yearn to spend another $240 million plus upkeep on this concrete ditch when Los Angeles groups are crusading to tear up their concrete and restore the Los Angeles River to a natural stream."[22]

With restoration, much of the Main Stem and its tributaries may again look like this area of the West Fork Mill Creek in Winton Woods. (Photo by Stanley Hedeen)

Urban stream reclamation programs had been launched in many American cities during the seventies and eighties. Leaders and residents together found better, cheaper, and environmentally sound ways to live with city streams. By 1990, there were more than three hundred programs aimed at preserving or restoring urban waterways. With the Mill Creek in mind, elements of the nation's most successful restoration efforts were compiled and studied by the Hamilton County Environmental Action Commission, an Ohio EPA advisory committee formed in 1991 with a membership drawn from industry, government, academia, and conservation groups. The fifteen-member commission unanimously concluded that a long-term local effort could change the status of the Mill Creek from "civic embarrassment" to "community asset."[23]

The commission's report, *Creating a New Vision for the Mill Creek*, was released on April 9, 1993, by chair Alan Vicory, executive director of the Ohio River Valley Water Sanitation Commission, and vice-chair Robin Corathers, executive director of The Hillside Trust and primary author of the forty-four page report. The document began by having the reader imagine the Mill Creek "as it once was, and as it could be again."

> If its waters were pure and its banks forested, the Mill Creek could be a seventeen-mile greenway, a park that would link our communities, our east and west, extending downtown to the Ohio River. It could offer fishing (and the fish would be edible) and other forms of recreation. It would in many spots be a refuge of quiet beauty in the urban environment, not unlike Rock Creek Park

or the C&O Canal in Washington, D.C. It would increase land values in the communities through which it flows. It would buffer and mitigate the transportation corridor's noise and exhaust gas pollution and enhance the quality of life in Hamilton and Butler Counties. It could be a source of pride.[24]

The commission report next reviewed the degraded condition of the Mill Creek, provided several examples of successful stream reclamation projects elsewhere, and presented a strategy "to reclaim what can be again a valuable natural resource for present and future generations." The first step in the recommended strategy would have the political jurisdictions along the Mill Creek enter into an intergovernmental agreement, a binding pledge to restore the stream. The signatories also would jointly establish and fund a Mill Creek Restoration Committee to oversee the intergovernmental agreement. The committee would be assisted by the Ohio-Kentucky-Indiana Regional Council of Governments or some other appropriate organization that could provide staff support in the areas of research, planning, implementation, and administration. The restoration committee would identify sources of local, state, federal, and private funding for the reclamation effort. The committee would not compete with existing agencies such as the Mill Creek Conservancy District or the Metropolitan Sewer District, but would rather "work cooperatively with all interested parties to ensure that future decisions are environmentally sound and in the public interest." [25]

The Hamilton County Environmental Action Commission's vision and strategy to restore the creek were applauded and encouraged by community representatives. According to an editorial in *The Cincinnati Post,* the commission had made "the moral case for restoring the Mill Creek to its original, pristine condition." A supportive editorial in *The Cincinnati Enquirer* ended by challenging the political jurisdictions "that border the Mill Creek to get busy and show that they can work together for common benefit." Using Ohio EPA funds, the commission and OKI established a task force to enlist support for the restoration plan from the counties, cities, villages, and townships in the Mill Creek watershed.[26]

In 1993, about two hundred years had passed since the building of the first mill on the stream legitimized the name "Mill Creek." During its first century, the Mill Creek served valley residents as a source of power, fish, beauty, turtles, water, frogs, recreation, and ducks. It provided stones for fences, scenes for paintings, clay for bricks, inspiration for poems, gravel for roads, and drainage for all but the largest storm runoffs. With the urbanization of the Mill Creek Valley, many of the stream's early uses were eliminated as the creek became a waste receptacle and storm sewer for an increasingly populated, industrialized, roofed, and paved watershed.

Two centuries after its debut as a mill stream, the creek in 1993 was an ill stream. Eliminating the causes of its sickness, while curing and rehabilitating the creek, was predicted to be a difficult and expensive process. In an April 13,

1993 editorial entitled "Restoring the Mill Creek," *The Cincinnati Post* warned its readers about the scope of the project:

> Anyone who's even remotely familiar with Cincinnati's history knows how ambitious such a proposal is. It's been more than a century now since the Mill Creek ran red from the slaughter houses along its banks, but since then pollution has gotten worse, not better. Today much of the Mill Creek is fouled with industrial pollutants. Abandoned dumps line its shores. Too often it carries raw sewage.[27]

Healing the damage to the creek will be a lengthy undertaking, but it's a project we owe to the stream, to our children, and to ourselves. The Mill Creek serves as an indicator of our own well-being, in addition to all of its other uses. The history and health of the society along its banks have always been reflected in the water of the Indians' Maketewa and the current residents' Mill Creek. From its mouth in Hamilton County to its headwaters in Butler County, in the words of an August 31, 1993 editorial in *The Cincinnati Enquirer,* the condition of the stream is "a 28-mile measure of local character, responsibility and good sense." There's more than environment at stake in the creek's restoration.[28]

Notes

If I seek...the information of a thousand books,...the insights of my own city past, I do so only, solely, and entirely that I might look well at the creek.

—Annie Dillard, *Pilgrim at Tinker Creek*

1   John G. Olden, "An Apostrophe to Millcreek," *The Miami Valley News*, n.d., n.p., reprinted in *The Millcreek Valley News Diamond Anniversary Edition*, April 27, 1961, section 2, p. 15, and section 4, p. l4.

CHAPTER ONE

1   Debbie Wietmarschen, quoted in Sue MacDonald, "Down by the Old (M)Ill Creek," *The Cincinnati Enquirer Magazine*, April 8, 1984, p. 4.
2   Henry B. Teetor, *The Past and Present of Mill Creek Valley* (Cincinnati, 1882), p. 78; John G. Olden, *Historical Sketches and Early Reminiscences of Hamilton County, Ohio* (Cincinnati, 1882), p. 134; Charles T. Greve, *Centennial History of Cincinnati* (Chicago, 1904), I, p. 255.
3   W. H. Perrin, J. H. Battle and G. C. Kniffen, *Kentucky: A History of the State* (Louisville, 1887), pp. 114-115; C. P. Eling, *Reading, Ohio's Double Anniversary Souvenir Book for 1976* (Reading, 1976), p. 15.
4   Olden, *Sketches*, p. 135; A. E. Jones, *Extracts from the History of Cincinnati and the Territory of Ohio* (Cincinnati, 1888), p. 31; Perrin *et al.*, pp. 172, 188; Eling, p. 17.
5   Christopher Gist, "First Journal of 1750-51" (1751), reprinted in William M. Darlington, ed., *Christopher Gist's Journals* (Pittsburgh, 1893), p. 47; John Mitchell, *Map of the British and French Dominians in North America* (London, 1755), reproduced in Stanley E. Hedeen, "Return of the Beaver, *Castor canadensis*, to the Cincinnati Region," *The Ohio Journal of Science* 85(1985), p. 202; Thomas Hutchins, *New Map of the Western Parts* (London, 1778), reproduced in Thomas H. Smith, *The Mapping of Ohio* (Kent, 1977), pp. 22-23.

6   Gist, p. 47; Beverley W. Bond, Jr., ed., *The Correspondence of John Cleves Symmes* (New York, 1926), p. 26.

7   *Ibid.*, pp. 7-8.

8   *Jonathan Dayton to John Cleves Symmes, October 22, 1788*, reprinted in Bond, p. 204.

9   *Contract between John C. Symmes and Benjamin Stites, December 17, 1787*, reprinted in Greve, pp. 147-148; *Supplement to Contract between John C. Symmes and Benjamin Stites*, n.d., reprinted in Greve, p. 148.

10 "Miami Lands for Sale," *Brunswick Gazette and Weekly Monitor*, Jan. 8, 1788, reprinted in Bond, p. 282.

11 *John Cleves Symmes to Jonathan Dayton, May 18 to June 15, 1789*, reprinted in Bond, pp. 53-95.

12 Edgar Erskine Hume, "The Naming of Cincinnati," *Queen City Heritage* 41, No. 2(1983), p. 13; *John Cleves Symmes to Jonathan Dayton, May 18 to June 15, 1789*, reprinted in Bond, pp. 53-95.

13 *Ibid.*, pp. 61-65.

14 J. Matson, "Mill Creek Bridges" (1845), reprinted in Charles Cist, *Cincinnati Miscellany* (Cincinnati, 1844-1846), II, p. 56; *John Cleves Symmes to Jonathan Dayton, May 18 to June 15, 1789*, reprinted in Bond, pp. 83-84; *Jonathan Dayton to John Cleves Symmes, September 26, 1789*, reprinted in Bond, p. 236; Cist, *Miscellany*, II, p. 26.

15 Greve, I, p. 310; *John Cleves Symmes to Jonathan Dayton, January 9, 1790*, reprinted in Bond, p. 123; Hume, pp. 10-11, 13-14; Olden, *Sketches*, pp. 95-97.

16 *John Cleves Symmes to Jonathan Dayton, April 30, 1790*, reprinted in Bond, p. 126.

17 Henry A. Ford and Kate B. Ford, *History of Hamilton County, Ohio* (Cleveland, 1881), p. 58; Richard Scamyhorn and John Steinle, *Stockades in the Wilderness* (Dayton, 1986), pp. 90-91, 105-110, 112, 136-139, 141-142, 146-147, 149-155; D. A. Hutslar, "The Log Architecture of Ohio," *Ohio History* 80(1971), p. 241; Olden, *Sketches*, p. 82.

18 *Ibid.*, pp. 136-137; Daniel Hurley, *Cincinnati: The Queen City* (Cincinnati, 1982), p. 16; Marge Niesen, *St. Bernard, Ohio, 1878-1978* (St. Bernard, 1978), p. 140.

19 *John Cleves Symmes to Jonathan Dayton, June 19, 1791*, reprinted in Bond, pp. 143-144.

20 *John Cleves Symmes to Jonathan Dayton, August 15, 1791*, reprinted in Bond, p. 150; Olden, *Sketches*, p. 137; Hurley, p. 16; Milo M. Quaife, ed., "A Picture of the First United States Army: The Journal of Captain Samuel Newman," *The Wisconsin Magazine of History* 2(1918-1919), pp. 40-73; William Wiseman, quoted in Charles Cist, *Sketches and Statistics of Cincinnati in 1859* (Cincinnati, 1859), p. 102; *John Cleves Symmes to Jonathan Dayton, January 17, 1792*, reprinted in Bond, p. 158.

21 Jacob Burnet, *Notes on the Early Settlement of the North-western Territory* (Cincinnati, 1847), p. 435; Olden, *Sketches*, pp. 137-138; Ford and Ford, *Hamilton County*, p. 80.

22 Scamyhorn and Steinle, pp. 151-153; Teetor, *Mill Creek Valley*, pp. 33-39; William D. Ludlow, quoted in Ford and Ford, *Hamilton County*, p. 335.

23 *Ibid.*, p. 335; Ford and Ford, *Hamilton County*, pp. 63-64.

24 Scamyhorn and Steinle, p. 15; *John Cleves Symmes to Jonathan Dayton, August 6, 1795*, reprinted in Bond, p. 172; William Davis Gallagher, "The Spotted Fawn" (1844), reprinted in Teetor, *Mill Creek Valley*, p. 79.

CHAPTER TWO

1 Lewis J. Cist, "The Spotted Frog" (1845), in Teetor, *Mill Creek Valley*, p. 81.

2 Albert H. Wright and Anna A. Wright, *Handbook of Frogs and Toads of the United States and Canada* (Ithaca, 1949), p. 481; Joseph T. Collins and George T. McDuffie, "Frogs and Toads of the Cincinnati Region," *The Explorer* 12, No. 2(1970), pp. 13, 15; Mildred Schulze, *Elm Tree Days* (Lockland, 1946), p. 71.

3 *Ibid.*, pp. 70-71; Joseph T. Collins and George T. McDuffie, "Turtles and Lizards of the Cincinnati Area," *The Explorer* 13, No. 3(1971), pp. 26, 28; R. B. McLain, *Notes on a Collection of Reptiles, Made by Mr. C. J. Pierson, at Fort Smith, Arkansas, with Remarks on Other Eastern Reptiles* (Wheeling, 1899), pp. 1-5.

4 Stanley E. Hedeen, "Feeding Behavior of the Great Blue Heron in Itasca State Park, Minnesota," *The Loon* 39(1967), pp. 116-120; Edward N. Clopper, *An American Family* (Cincinnati, 1950), p. 360; Emerson Kemsies and Worth Randle, *Birds of Southwestern Ohio* (Cincinnati, 1953), pp. 4, 60; Stanley E. Hedeen, "Escape Behavior and Causes of Death of the Mink Frog," *Herpetologica* 28(1972), p. 262; John G. Olden, "To Mill Creek," in Teetor, *Mill Creek Valley*, p. 84; Milton B. Trautman, *The Fishes of Ohio* (Columbus, 1981), p. 561.

5 Joseph T. Collins and George T. McDuffie, "Salamanders of the Cincinnati Region," *The Explorer* 11, No. 1(1969), pp. 23-24; Charles Dury, "Notes on Ohio Birds," *Journal of the Cincinnati Society of Natural History* 13(1890), p. 98.

6 J. R. Geckler, W. B. Horning, T. M. Neiheisel, Q. H. Pickering, E. L. Robinson and C. E. Stephan, "Validity of Laboratory Tests for Predicting Copper Toxicity in Streams," *Environmental Protection Agency Ecological Research Series* 600/3-76-116(1976), pp. 64-65.

7 Stanley E. Hedeen, "The Mill Creek," *Quarterly of the Cincinnati Museum*

of Natural History 13, No. 3(1976), pp. l4-16; Minute Books of the Western Academy of Natural Sciences, June 7, 1842, Cincinnati Historical Society Library; Minutes, April 12, 1846; Charles Lyell, *A Second Visit to the United States of North America* (London, 1855), II, p. 292; Minutes, February 14, 1848.

8   Charles Dury, "Zoological Miscellany: Entomology," *Journal of the Cincinnati Society of Natural History* 5(1882), p. 61; Kevina Vulinec and R. A. Davis, "Coleoptera Types in the Charles Dury Collection of the Cincinnati Museum of Natural History," *The Coleopterists Bulletin* 38(1984), p. 232.

9   Edward Mansfield, *Personal Memories* (Cincinnati, 1879), p. 27; Greve, I, p. 281; Dury, "Ohio Birds," p. 98; Hedeen, "Beaver," p. 202; Daniel Drake, "Memoir of the Miami Country, 1779-1794," Beverley W. Bond, Jr., ed., *Quarterly Publication of the Historical and Philosophical Society of Ohio* 18(1923), p. 86.

10   K. W. Cummins, "Structure and Function of Stream Ecosystems," *Bioscience* 24(1974), pp. 631-641.

11   S. G. Fisher and G. E. Likens, "Energy Flow in Bear Brook, New Hampshire: An Integrated Approach to Stream Ecosystem Metabolism," *Ecological Monographs* 43(1973), pp. 421-439.

12   B. L. Redd and A. Benson, "Utilization of Bottom Fauna by Brook Trout in a Northern West Virginia Stream," *Proceedings of the West Virginia Academy of Sciences* 34(1962), pp. 21-26.

13   William S. Bryant, "Structure and Composition of the Old-Growth Forests of Hamilton County, Ohio and Environs," *Proceedings of the Central Hardwoods Forest Conference VI* (Knoxville, 1987), p. 319; Robert B. Gordon, *Natural Vegetation Map of Ohio at the Time of the Earliest Land Surveys* (Columbus, 1966), available from The Ohio Biological Survey; *John Cleves Symmes to Jonathon Dayton, November 4, 1790*, reprinted in Bond, p. 134; Winthrop Sargent, *Diary* (1791), reprinted in Bart S. Bartlow *et al.*, *Centennial History of Butler County, Ohio* (Indianapolis, 1905), pp. 59, 352.

14   *John Cleves Symmes to Jonathon Dayton, November 4, 1790*, reprinted in Bond, pp. 134-135; Ford and Ford, *Hamilton County*, p. 236; Mansfield, p. 29; Samuel F. Cary, *History of College Hill and Vicinity* (Cincinnati, 1886), p. 8.

15   Jacob Fowler, quoted in Cist, *1859*, p. 76; C. E. Cabot, "The Carters in Early Ohio. A Glimpse of Cincinnati in its First Quarter Century," *New England Magazine* 20(1899), pp. 347-348; S. Cary, p. 9.

16   Timothy Flint, *Recollections of the Last Ten Years* (Boston, 1826), p. 40; Edwin James, *Account of an Expedition from Pittsburgh to the Rocky Mountains, Performed in the Years 1819, 1820* (London, 1823), I, p. 23; Mansfield, p. 16; Mary Howitt, *Cousins in Ohio* (New York, 1849), p. 39.

17 Gorham A. Worth, *Recollections of Cincinnati, from a Residence of Five Years, 1817 to 1821* (Albany, 1851), reprinted in *Quarterly Publication of the Historical and Philosophical Society of Ohio* 11(1916), p. 45.

18 Francis Baily, *Journal of a Tour in Unsettled Parts of North America in 1796 and 1797*, Jack D. L. Holmes, ed. (Carbondale, 1969), pp. 104-105.

19 Olden, *Sketches*, pp. 94-96; Scamyhorn and Steinle, pp. 63-64; Chris McHenry, ed., *Symmes Purchase Records* (Lawrenceburg, 1979), p. 17.

20 Olden, *Sketches*, p. 121; Teetor, *Mill Creek Valley*, pp. 59-60, 88-89.

21 Arthur G. King, "Some Cincinnati Streets. II. The Ludlow Mill Tract and Clifton Avenue," *Quarterly Bulletin of the Historical and Philosophical Society of Ohio* 10(1952), pp. 291-293, 297, 301; *Contract between John C. Symmes and Benjamin Stites, December 17, 1787*, reprinted in Greve, I, pp. 147-148.

22 James McCash, quoted in Cist, *1859*, pp. 130-131.

23 E. N. Clopper, "The Waters of Discord," *Quarterly Bulletin of the Historical and Philosophical Society of Ohio* 7(1949), p. 214; S. B. Nelson and J. M. Runk, *History of Cincinnati and Hamilton County, Ohio* (Cincinnati, 1894), p. 433; Carolyn Kettell, "Flours and a Handsome Homestead," *The Cincinnati Enquirer*, Oct. 2, 1988, Supplement p. 7.

24 Robert Stubbs, *Browne's Cincinnati Almanac, for the Year of Our Lord, 1811* (Cincinnati, 1810), p. 20; Ohio-Kentucky-Indiana Regional Council of Governments, *Regional Water Quality Management Plan* (Cincinnati, 1977), p. II-22.

25 John Palmer, *Journal of Travels in the United States* (London, 1818), p. 89.

26 William Newnham Blaney, *An Excursion through the United States and Canada during the Years 1822-23* (London, 1824), p. 181.

27 D. A. Hutslar, "Ohio Waterpowered Sawmills," *Ohio History* 84(1975), p. 10; Moses King, *King's Pocket-book of Cincinnati* (Cambridge, Massachusetts, 1879), p. 53; Palmer, p. 95.

28 Flint, pp. 52-53.

CHAPTER THREE

1 Lillian H. Shuey, "The Death of the Forest," *Forestry and Irrigation* 14(1908), p. 369.

2 Blaney, p. 125; Charles Dickens, *American Notes* (London, 1873), p. 90; Teetor, *Mill Creek Valley*, p. 98.

3 *A History and Biographical Cyclopedia of Butler County, Ohio* (Cincinnati, 1882), p. 472; Alta H. Heiser, *Hamilton in the Making* (Oxford, 1941), p. 106; *History of Butler County*, p. 470; E. Lucy Braun, "The Physiographic Ecology of the Cincinnati Region," *Ohio Biological Survey*

Bulletin 2, No. 7(1916), p. 182.

4   Arthur G. King, "Clarkson's Clifton Farm and Pioneer Neighbors," *Quarterly Bulletin of the Historical and Philosophical Society of Ohio* 11(1953), p. 293; S. Cary, p. 7; A. B. Plowman, "The Work of the Spoilers," *Forestry and Irrigation* 14(1908), pp. 365-366.

5   Hutslar, "Log Architecture," pp. 240-241; Plowman, p. 365; Ford and Ford, *Hamilton County*, p. 333.

6   H. G. Smith, R. K. Burnard, E. E. Good and J. M. Keener, "Rare and Endangered Vertebrates of Ohio," *The Ohio Journal of Science* 73(1973), pp. 259-260, 270; Kemsies and Randle, pp. 15-16, 26; Charles Dury, "The Passenger Pigeon," *Journal of the Cincinnati Society of Natural History* 21(1910), p. 11.

7   Edward J. Maruska, *Cincinnati Zoo Official Guide Book* (Cincinnati, 1969), pp. 6, 46-47; David Quammen, *Natural Acts* (New York, 1985), p. 143.

8   Smith *et al.*, pp. 268-269; Trautman, pp. 274, 649.

9   David R. Dawdy, "Knowledge of Sedimentation in Urban Environments," *Proceedings of the American Society of Civil Engineers* 93, No. HY6(1967), pp. 236-238, 241.

10   Smith *et al.*, pp. 268-269; United States Environmental Protection Agency, *Report to Congress: Nonpoint Source Pollution in the United States* (Washington, D.C., 1984), pp. 1-10; H. A. Gangmark and R. D. Broad, "Experimental Hatching of King Salmon in Mill Creek, a Tributary of the Sacramento River," *California Fish and Game* 41(1955), pp. 233-242.

11   D. R. Lenat, D. L. Penrose and K. W. Eagleson, "Variable Effects of Sediment Addition on Stream Benthos," *Hydrobiologia* 79(1981), pp. 187-194.

12   E. Lucy Braun, "The Lea Herbarium and the Flora of Cincinnati," *The American Midland Naturalist* 15(1934), pp. 1-75; William Cronon, *Changes in the Land* (New York, 1983), p. 148.

13   Teetor, *Mill Creek Valley*, p. 77; A. W. Knight and R. L. Bottorff, "The Importance of Riparian Vegetation to Stream Ecosystems," in R. E. Warner and K. M. Hendrix, eds., *California Riparian Systems* (Berkeley, 1984), p. 165; J. R. Karr and I. J. Schlosser, "Water Resources and the Land-Water Interface," *Science* 201(1978), p. 231; J. W. Gibbons and R. R. Sharitz, "Thermal Alteration of Aquatic Ecosystems," *American Scientist* 62(1974), p. 663.

14   OKI Regional Council, *Management Plan*, p. III-3; Schulze, pp. 79-80; Thomas Low Nichols, *Forty Years of American Life* (London, 1864), I, p. 152.

15   Braun, "The Lea Herbarium," pp. 1-75.

16   J. R. Karr and D. R. Dudley, "Ecological Perspective on Water Quality Goals," *Environmental Management* 5(1981), pp. 63-64; G. W. Minshall,

"Community Dynamics of the Benthic Fauna in a Woodland Springbrook," *Hydrobiologia* 32(1968), pp. 305-339; M. L. Murphy, C. P. Hawkins and N. H. Anderson, "Effects of Canopy Modification and Accumulated Sediment on Stream Communities," *Transactions of the American Fisheries Society* 110(1981), pp. 469-478,

17   James A. Henshall, "Contributions to the Ichthyology of Ohio, No. 1," *Journal of the Cincinnati Society of Natural History* 11(1888), pp. 78-79; Trautman, pp. 328-329, 534-535.

18   F. H. Borman, G. E. Likens and J. S. Eaton, "Biotic Regulation of Particulate and Solution Losses from a Forest Ecosystem," *Bioscience* 19(1969), pp. 600-610; Noah Webster, *A Collection of Essays and Fugitive Writings on Moral, Historical, Political and Literary Subjects* (Boston, 1790), pp. 371-372.

19   Plowman, p. 366; *History of Butler County*, p. 476; Vogt, Ivers, Seaman and Associates, *Report on Mill Creek Channel Improvement, Hamilton and Butler Counties, Ohio* (Cincinnati, 1948), p. 5; Edward Orton, "The Geography and Geology of Ohio," in Henry Howe, ed., *Historical Collections of Ohio* (Columbus, 1896), I, p. 89.

20   Karr and Dudley, p. 58.

21   Vogt, Ivers, Seaman and Associates, p. 5; Teetor, *Mill Creek Valley*, p. 321.

22   Matson, in Cist, *Miscellany*, II, p. 56; John Cleves Symmes, *Mill Creek Bridge Subscription Paper, April 10, 1798*, reprinted in Cist, *Miscellany*, II, p. 37.

23   Matson, in Cist, *Miscellany*, II, p. 56; Cist, *Miscellany*, II, p. 27.

24   Daniel Drake, *Natural and Statistical View, or Picture of Cincinnati and the Miami Country* (Cincinnati, 1815), p. 219; Matson, in Cist, *Miscellany*, II, p. 56; Samuel P. Hildreth, *Pioneer History* (Cincinnati, 1848), pp. 319-320; John C. Fisher, John H. Klippart and Robert Cummings, *Second Annual Report of the Ohio State Fish Commission* (Columbus, 1878), pp. 66-68.

25   Matson, in Cist, *Miscellany*, II, p. 56; Cist, *Miscellany*, II, p. 27; Samuel P. Hildreth, "A Brief History of Floods in the Ohio River," *Journal of the Philosophical and Historical Society of Ohio* 1, part 1(1838), p. 61.

26   James Morris, "Walter Haller, 'The Disturbing Element,'" *The Cincinnati Historical Society Bulletin* 28(1970), p. 283; Howitt, p. 39.

27   Matson, in Cist, *Miscellany*, II, p. 56; Ford and Ford, *Hamilton County*, p. 340.

CHAPTER FOUR

1 Henry David Thoreau, *A Week on the Concord and Merrimack Rivers* (Princeton, 1983), p. 11.

2 L. Nelson Nichols, "Cliff Swallow," in T. Gilbert Pearson, ed., *Birds of America* (Garden City, 1936), III, pp. 84-85.

3 Henry B. Teetor, *Sketch of the Life and Times of Col. Israel Ludlow* (Cincinnati, 1885), p. 25; John James Audubon, *Ornithological Biography* (Edinburgh, 1831), I, p. 353.

4 Kemsies and Randle, p. 49; A. Zipperlein, quoted in Henry A. Ford and Kate B. Ford, *History of Cincinnati, Ohio* (Cleveland, 1881), p. 234.

5 Frank W. Langdon, "Ornithological Field Notes, with Five Additions to the Cincinnati Avian Fauna," *Journal of the Cincinnati Society of Natural History* 3(1880), p. 124; George F. Dieterle, quoted in Charles Ludwig, *Playmates of the Towpath* (Cincinnati, 1929), p. 104; Kemsies and Randle, p. 33.

6 Zipperlein, quoted in Ford and Ford, pp. 234-235.

7 Schulze, p. 96; United States Army Corps of Engineers Louisville District, *Final Environmental Impact Statement, Mill Creek Local Protection Project* (Louisville, 1974), Exhibit C, p. 15; Trautman, p. 263; Henshall, p. 79.

8 Donald J. Borror, Dwight M. DeLong and Charles A. Triplehorn, *An Introduction to the Study of Insects* (New York, 1976), p. 570.

9 *Ibid.*, pp. 713-714; O. Wilford Olsen, *Animal Parasites* (Minneapolis, 1967), pp. 92-94.

10 Daniel Drake, *Systematic Treatise on the Principal Diseases of the Interior Valley of North America* (Cincinnati, 1850), reprinted in Henry D. Shapiro and Zane L. Miller, eds., *Physician to the West* (Lexington, 1970), p. 355; N. D. Levine, *Malaria in the Interior Valley of North America* (Urbana, Illinois, 1964), p. xvi.

11 Daniel Drake, *Notices concerning Cincinnati* (Cincinnati, 1810), reprinted in Shapiro and Miller, pp. 29-30.

12 Daniel Drake, *Systematic Treatise*, in Shapiro and Miller, p. 359; Samuel Williams, *The Natural and Civil History of Vermont* (Burlington, 1809), pp. 70-76; Cronon, p. 125.

13 Charles Cist, *Sketches and Statistics of Cincinnati in 1851* (Cincinnati, 1851), p. 32; "Petition for a Park in Mill Creek Valley," in *Annual and Special Reports of the Several Departments of the City of Cincinnati during the Year 1857* (Cincinnati, 1858), pp. 1-2.

14 City of Cincinnati Council Committee on Public Improvements, *Improvement of Millcreek Valley* (Cincinnati, 1864), p. 2; *The Cincinnati Commercial*, Oct. 18, 1872, p. 4.

15 City of Cincinnati Board of Health, in *Annual Reports of the City Depart-*

ments, 1874 (Cincinnati, 1875), p. 428; City of Cincinnati Health Department, in *Annual Reports of the City Departments, 1880* (Cincinnati, 1881), p. 751; Levine, pp. xix-xx.

16   City of Cincinnati Health Department, in *Annual Reports of the City Departments, 1879* (Cincinnati, 1880), p. 520; Teetor, *Mill Creek Valley*, p. 74.

17   *Ibid.*, pp. 75-76.

18   *Jacob Burnet to J. Delafield, October, 1837*, reprinted in *Transactions of the Historical and Philosophical Society of Ohio* 1, part 2(1838), p. 39; Burnet, *Early Settlement*, p. 444.

19   Teetor, *Mill Creek Valley*, p. 74; *History of Butler County*, p. 278; Bartlow *et al.*, p. 10; Joseph F. James, "An Ancient Channel of the Ohio River at Cincinnati," *Journal of the Cincinnati Society of Natural History* 11(1889), pp. 96-101.

20   Gerard Fowke, "Introduction" and "Preglacial Drainage Conditions in the Vicinity of Cincinnati," in *The Preglacial Drainage of Ohio*, Ohio State Academy of Science Special Paper No. 3 (Columbus, 1900), pp. 5, 68-75.

21   Richard H. Durrell, "Geomorphology of the Cincinnati Area," in The Geological Society of America, *Guidebook for Field Trips, Cincinnati Meeting, 1961* (New York, 1961), p. 221; Richard H. Durrell, "A Recycled Landscape," *Quarterly of the Cincinnati Museum of Natural History* 14, No. 2(1977), pp. 8-15.

22   Richard P. Goldthwait, "Ice over Ohio," in Michael B. Lafferty, ed., *Ohio's Natural Heritage* (Columbus, 1979), pp. 41-42.

23   Vogt, Ivers, Seaman and Associates, p. 3.

24   Eva Tucker, Jr., "Mechanical and Compositional Analysis of Sands in the Lower Portion of the Mill Creek Valley, Cincinnati, Ohio" (M. S. dissertation, University of Cincinnati, 1962), pp. 47-48.

25   R. A. Davis, "Land Fit for a Queen: The Geology of Cincinnati," in Joyce V. B. Cauffield and Carolyn E. Banfield, eds., *The River Book: Cincinnati and the Ohio* (Cincinnati, 1981), p. 134.

26   Jane L. Forsyth, "Wisconsin Glacial Deposits," in The Geological Society of America, p. 61; Charles Lyell, *Travels in North America* (New York, 1845), II, p. 51; Scott Burgins, "Youths Find Jawbone of Ancient Mastodon," *The Cincinnati Enquirer*, July 25, 1990, p. A-1.

27   R. A. Davis, "'Mastodon's in de cold, cold ground,'" *Quarterly of the Cincinnati Museum of Natural History* 15, No. 3(1978), p. 3; Vogt, Ivers, Seaman and Associates, p. 3; Richard H. Durrell, "Road Log: Pleistocene Geology of the Cincinnati Region (Kentucky, Ohio, and Indiana)," in *The Geological Society of America*, pp. 77, 81.

28   J. James, pp. 98, 101.

CHAPTER FIVE

1   Nevin M. Fenneman, "Geology of Cincinnati and Vicinity," *Geological Survey of Ohio, Fourth Series, Bulletin* 19(1916), p. 192.

2   Frazer E. Wilson, *Journal of Capt. Daniel Bradley* (Greenville, 1935), p. 51; Arthur G. King, "Origins of Some Cincinnati Streets—A Street in Clifton," *Quarterly Bulletin of the Historical and Philosophical Society of Ohio* 10(1952), p. 146.

3   Ford and Ford, *Hamilton County*, p. 223.

4   Charles Cist, *Cincinnati in 1841* (Cincinnati, 1841), p. 76; City of Cincinnati Planning Commission, *The Cincinnati Metropolitan Master Plan Report 6. Motorways* (Cincinnati, 1947), p. 48.

5   Baily, p. 110; Richard C. Wade, *The Urban Frontier* (Chicago, 1964), p. 27; John R. Stilgoe, *Common Landscape of America, 1580 to 1845* (New Haven, 1982), p. 98; Daniel Drake, *Address to the Cincinnati Medical Association, January 9, 1852*, reprinted in Greve, I, p. 349.

6   William S. Wabnitz, "The Bates Papers and Early Cincinnati," *Quarterly Bulletin of the Historical and Philosophical Society of Ohio* 11(1953), p. 26; Drake, *Natural and Statistical View*, p. 225; Elizabeth Faries, "The Miami Country, 1750-1815, as Described in Journals and Letters," *The Ohio State Archaeological and Historical Quarterly* 57(1948), p. 63.

7   Ohio State Archaeological and Historical Society, *History of the Ohio Canals* (Columbus, 1905), pp. 18, 37; Frank Wilcox, *The Ohio Canals* (Kent, 1969), pp. 66, 68; Jack Gieck, *A Photo Album of Ohio's Canal Era, 1825-1913* (Kent, 1988), p. 125.

8   Wilcox, p. 72; Ludwig, p. 19; A. G. King, "Origins," p. 155; Herbert F. Verity, "Canals," in Cauffield and Banfield, pp. 185-186.

9   Frank W. Trevorrow, *Ohio Canals* (1973), p. 150; The Canal Society of Ohio, *The Miami Canal between Dayton and Cincinnati and the Warren County Canal* (Oberlin, 1977), pp. 5-6; William E. Smith, *The History of Southwestern Ohio* (New York, 1964), p. 256.

10 *History of the Ohio Canals*, pp. 37, 41; Trevorrow, p. 151; Latham Anderson, *Suggestions concerning the Proposed Miami and Erie Ship Canal, a Paper Read before the Engineers Club of Cincinnati, November 17, 1892* (Cincinnati, 1892), p. 5.

11 Verity, p. 188; Gieck, p. 124.

12 H. C. Drago, *Canal Days in America* (New York, 1972), p. 7; Carl W. Condit, *The Railroad and the City* (Columbus, 1977), p. 6; Verity, p. 191; J. Bonsall, *Report of the President to the Stockholders in the Cincinnati and White-Water Canal Company* (Cincinnati, 1840), p. 15.

13 Ludwig, pp. 81-83; Clopper, *Family*, p. 277; City of Cincinnati Department of Public Service, *Progress Report on a Plan of Sewerage* (Cincinnati, 1912-1913), p. 723; Ohio Department of Natural Resources, "Wa-

ter Inventory of the Little Miami River and Mill Creek Basins," *Ohio Water Plan Inventory Report* No. 18 (1964), p. 31; F. H. Klaer, Jr., and D. G. Thompson, "Ground-water Resources of the Cincinnati Area," *United States Geological Survey Water Supply Paper* 999(1948), p. 98.

14 Wilcox, p. 69; *Rebecca Clopper to Members of the Cumminsville Ladies' Correspondence Association, January, 1845*, reprinted in Clopper, *Family*, pp. 354-355.

15 Phoebe Cary, "Dovecote Mill," *The Last Poems of Alice and Phoebe Cary* (Boston, 1880), p. 162.

16 Sherwood Anderson, "I'll Say We've Done Well," *The Nation* 115(1922), p. 146.

17 Carroll D. Wright, *The Industrial Evolution of the United States* (New York, 1901), p. 133.

18 Verity, p. 185; Condit, p. 42; Cist, *1841*, p. 78.

19 Howe, I, p. 365; Sherry O. Hessler, "Patterns of Transport and Urban Growth in the Miami Valley, Ohio, 1820-1880" (M. A. dissertation, Johns Hopkins University, 1961), p. 154; Ford and Ford, *Hamilton County*, p. 379; Hessler, p. 195.

20 *History of Butler County*, p. 580; Hessler, p. 193.

21 Drake, *Natural and Statistical View*, pp. 144-145; Ford and Ford, *Cincinnati*, p. 326; Greve, I, p. 523; Charles F. Goss, *Cincinnati, The Queen City* (Cincinnati, 1912), II, pp. 329-330.

22 Drake, *Natural and Statistical View*, pp. 137-138, 144-145; Lee Shepard, "Cincinnati's First Tall Building," *Quarterly Bulletin of the Historical and Philosophical Society of Ohio* 3, No. 2(1945), p. 9; Isaac Lippincott, *Economic Development of the United States* (New York, 1921), p. 192.

23 *The Cincinnati Directory for the Years 1836-37* (Cincinnati, 1836), p. 220; James Hall, *Statistics of the West* (Cincinnati, 1836), p. 269.

24 Gilbert C. Fite and Jim E. Reese, *An Economic History of the United States* (Boston, 1965), p. 214; Teetor, *Mill Creek Valley*, p. 321; Isaac Lippincott, "A History of Manufactures in the Ohio Valley to the Year 1860" (Ph.D. dissertation, University of Chicago, 1914), pp. 86-87.

25 Carolyn E. Banfield, "One-way Street to Settlement: Two-way Street to Commerce," in Cauffield and Banfield, pp. 147-148; Verity, pp. 183-184, 189; Francis P. Weisenburger, *The Passing of the Frontier* (Columbus, 1941), p. 141.

26 Heiser, pp. 164-165, 171-172; Pierson Sayre, quoted in Heiser, p. 172.

27 Robert L. Black, *The Little Miami Railroad* (Cincinnati, n.d.), pp. 76-80; Gilbert F. White, *Human Adjustment to Floods* (Chicago, 1945), pp. 116-117.

28 Condit, p. 17; Black, p. 72.

29 Condit, p. 23; Black, pp. 124-126.

30 Condit, pp. 27-31; Black, pp. 153-154.

31 Condit, pp. 20-21, 44; Black, pp. 99-100; Clopper, *Family*, p. 548.

32 Henry C. Lord, "The Cincinnati, Indianapolis, St. Louis and Chicago,"
    Railway Age 8, No. 34(1883), p. 518; Condit, p. 31.

33 *Ibid.*, pp. 61-68.

34 *Ibid.*, pp. 95-96.

35 Alfred Lief, *"It Floats"* (New York, 1958), pp. 58-65; Oscar Schisgall,
    Eyes on Tomorrow (Chicago, 1981), pp. 39-40.

36 "Our Breeders of Pestilence," *Cincinnati Daily Gazette*, Oct. 21, 1872, p.
    2; Condit, p. 99; George H. Burgess and Miles C. Kennedy, *Centennial
    History of the Pennsylvania Railroad Company* (Philadelphia, 1949), p.
    425; "Cincinnati, Richmond & Chicago," *Railroad Gazette* 22(1890), p.
    119.

37 Condit, pp. 110-113.

38 *Ibid.*, pp. 59-61, 78, 95, 99-101, 109, 117; John W. Hauck, *Narrow Gauge
    in Ohio* (Boulder, 1986), p. 64.

39 J. James, p. 98.

Chapter Six

1 Lewis Mumford, "The Natural History of Urbanization," in William L.
   Thomas, Jr., ed., *Man's Role in Changing the Face of the Earth* (Chicago,
   1956), I, p. 390.

2 Edmund Dana, *Geographical Sketches on the Western Country* (Cincinnati, 1819), p. 82; Steven J. Ross, *Workers on the Edge: Work, Leisure,
   and Politics in Industrializing Cincinnati, 1788-1890* (New York, 1985),
   pp. 10-11.

3 "On the Avenue," *The Cincinnati Commercial*, July 29, 1866, reprinted in
   The Cincinnati Historical Society Bulletin 30(1972), p. 185.

4 Lippincott, *Manufactures*, pp. 86-88.

5 *Ibid.*, p. 88; R. A. Clemen, *American Livestock and Meat Industry* (New
   York, 1923), p. 3.

6 Nelson and Runk, p. 433; Olden, *Sketches*, p. 97; *John W. Caldwell to
   Robert H. Bishop, October 11, 1887*, reprinted in *Quarterly Bulletin of the
   Historical and Philosophical Society of Ohio* 16(1958), p. 257; Teetor,
   Mill Creek Valley, p. 89; Patricia Gallagher, "Longworth Had Sweet Suc-
   cess," *The Cincinnati Enquirer*, Feb. 28, 1988, p. A-2.

7 Ralph H. Brown, *Historical Geography of the United States* (New York,
   1948), p. 235; Teetor, *Mill Creek Valley*, p. 322; Department of Public
   Service, pp. 673-674.

8 Ludwig, p. 108; Department of Public Service, p. 672.

9 Ludwig, pp. 108-109; Department of Public Service, pp. 672, 674, 684-
   685.

10 John A. Jakle, *Images of the Ohio Valley* (New York, 1977), p. 152; L. L. Tucker, *Cincinnati's Citizen Crusaders* (Cincinnati, 1967), p. 177.

11 Henry P. Homenuck, "Historical Geography of the Cincinnati Pork Industry, 1810-1883" (M. A. dissertation, University of Cincinnati, 1965), pp. 16-17, 24-25.

12 Edward C. Kirkland, *A History of American Economic Life* (New York, 1940), p. 298.

13 Drake, *Notices*, p. 28; Alvin Harlow, *The Serene Cincinnatians* (New York, 1950), p. 80; Stephen C. Gordon, "The City as Porkopolis" (M. A. dissertation, Miami University, 1981), p. 147; R. Douglas Hurt, "Pork and Porkopolis," *Cincinnati Historical Society Bulletin* 40(1982), p. 199.

14 *Ibid.*, p. 196; R. Brown, p. 235.

15 J. S. Buckingham, *The Eastern and Western States of America* (London, 1842), II, p. 394; Hurt, pp. 202-205.

16 *Ibid.*, pp. 208, 211; Department of Public Service, p. 661.

17 Frederick L. Olmsted, *A Journey through Texas* (New York, 1857), p. 9; Alexander Lakier, *A Journey through the North American States, Canada and Cuba* (St. Petersburg, 1859), translated and excerpted in Arnold Schrier, "A Russian Observer's Visit to 'Porkopolis'—1857," *Cincinnati Historical Society Bulletin* 29(1971), p. 37; Frances Trollope, *Domestic Manners of the Americans* (New York, 1832), pp. 72-73; Harriet Martineau, *Retrospect of Western Travel* (London, 1838), II, p. 45.

18 Lakier, p. 37; Department of Public Service, p. 44.

19 City of Cincinnati Mayor, in *Annual Reports of the City Department, 1866-1867* (Cincinnati, 1867), p. 12; Commissioner Carson, quoted in Harlow, pp. 89-90.

20 Dury, "Ohio Birds," p. 98; Department of Public Service, p. 36.

21 C. A. Leas, "On the Sanitary Care and Utilization of Refuse in Cities," reprinted in Donald Worster, ed., *American Environmentalism: The Formative Period, 1860-1915* (New York, 1973), pp. 152-153.

22 Homenuck, p. 59; Walter M. Whitehill, *Boston: A Topographical History* (Cambridge, 1968), p. 12.

23 Hessler, p. 129; Department of Public Service, p. 659; Hurt, pp. 200, 202.

24 "A Cincinnati Slaughter House," *Cincinnati Daily Gazette,* March 3, 1843, p. 3; M. Mosler, J. Hoffman and J. D. Smith, eds., *Historic Brighton* (Cincinnati, 1902), p. 17; G. W. Fuller and J. R. McClintock, *Solving Sewage Problems* (New York, 1926), p. 5; Harry Hansen, *The Chicago* (New York, 1942), p. 156; Department of Public Service, p. 38.

25 City of Cincinnati Sewerage Department, in *Annual Reports of the City Departments, 1871-1872* (Cincinnati, 1872), pp. 551-552; Department of Public Service, pp. 38, 45.

26 *Ibid.*, pp. 661, 688.

27 S. Gordon, p. 149; Mosler, Hoffman and Smith, p. 29; M. King, pp. 14,

81; F. W. Brown, *Cincinnati and Vicinity* (Cincinnati, 1898), p. 174; Ohio State Board of Health, *Annual Report, 1902* (Springfield, 1904), p. 189.

28 Department of Public Service, pp. 679-680, 691-692.

29 *Ibid.*, pp. 645-651, 658, 692-694; W. C. Purdy, "Limnological Aspects of Sewage Disposal," in L. Pearse, ed., *Modern Sewage Disposal* (New York, 1938), p. 177.

30 Department of Public Service, pp. 675-677, 680, 688-690.

31 *Ibid.*, pp. 659-660, 662-668, 694-698; Lief, pp. 10-11.

32 Department of Public Service, p. 723; Ohio Department of Natural Resources, p. 31; Northside Business Club, *History of Cumminsville* (Cincinnati, 1914), n. p.

Chapter Seven

1   J. James, pp. 97-98.

2   City of Cincinnati Department of Public Works, in *Annual Reports of Officers, Boards and Departments, 1913* (Cincinnati, 1914), p. 66; Department of Public Service, p. 189.

3   William L. Downard, *The Cincinnati Brewing Industry: A Social and Economic History* (Athens, Ohio, 1973), pp. 8, 82; Susan K. Appel, "Buildings and Beer: Brewery Architecture of Cincinnati," *Queen City Heritage* 44, No. 2(1986), p. 3; Department of Public Service, p. 658.

4   Appel, p. 14; Department of Public Service, pp. 652-653, 658, 686-687; Downard, p. 133.

5   City of Cincinnati Engineer Department, in *Annual Reports of the City Departments, 1907* (Cincinnati, 1908), p. 874; Department of Public Service, p. 671.

6   *Ibid.*, p. 669.

7   *Ibid.*, p. 681; Ohio State Board of Health, *Annual Report for the Year Ending October 31, 1901* (Columbus, 1892), pp. 166-167; *Titus' Atlas of Hamilton County, Ohio* (Philadelphia, 1869), p. 50; George Maessinger and Frederick Bertsch, *Map of Hamilton County, Ohio* (Cincinnati, 1884); Department of Public Service, p. 44; James A. Green, "The Map of Hamilton County," *Ohio State Archaeological and Historical Quarterly* 35(1926), pp. 306-307; Edith K. Magrish, "Buried Treasures," *Queen City Heritage* 45, No. 2(1987), p. 46; Cincinnati Board of Park Commissioners, *Cincinnati Parks* (Cincinnati, 1988), p. 50.

8   *Millcreek Valley News Lockland Centennial Edition,* May 28, 1949, p. 25; Hessler, pp. 173-178; Department of Public Service, pp. 680-681, 687, 722; State Board of Health, *Annual Report, 1902*, p. 186.

9   Department of Public Service, pp. 679, 690-691.

10 *Ibid.*, pp. 677-678, 681.

11   *Ibid.*, p. 678.

12   *Ibid.*, p. 682; Ohio Water Commission, *Proceedings of a Special Hearing, March 24, 1961* (Columbus, 1961), p. 10.

13   Lockland Board of Trade, *The Town of Lockland* (Lockland, 1895), pp. 1-40; *Lockland Centennial*, p. 9.

14   William J. Reardon, "A Little Known Tunnel," *Quarterly Bulletin of the Historical and Philosophical Society of Ohio* 9(1951), p. 232; Alexis de Tocqueville (translated by George Lawrence), *Journey to America* (Garden City, 1971), p. 280; C. D. Arfwedson, *The United States and Canada in 1832, 1833, and 1834* (London, 1834), II, p. 127.

15   Hessler, p. 257; Blanche Linden-Ward and David L. Sloane, "Spring Grove: The Founding of Cincinnati's Rural Cemetery, 1845-1855," *Queen City Heritage* 43, No. 1(1985), p. 17; Horace Greeley, quoted in Cist, *1851*, p. 257.

16   William Chambers, *Things as They Are in America* (London, 1854), p. 151; Steven J. Ross, "Industrialization and the Changing Images of Progress in Nineteenth-century Cincinnati," *Queen City Heritage* 43, No. 2(1985), p. 4.

17   Wilfrid Gladstone Richards, "The Settlement of the Miami Valley of Southwestern Ohio" (Ph.D. dissertation, The University of Chicago, 1948), p. 83; Cist, *Miscellany*, II, p. 60.

18   King, "Clifton Farm," pp. 301-302.

19   Linden-Ward and Sloane, pp. 22, 26, 31; King, "Ludlow Mill Tract," p. 300.

20   *William Henry Brisbane to Lyman Copeland Draper, January 5, 1857*, reprinted in William B. Hasseltine and Larry Gara, "Andrew H. Ernst, Pioneer Horticulturist," *Quarterly Bulletin of the Historical and Philosophical Society of Ohio* 11(1953), p. 39; St. Bernard, Ohio, *Fifty Years of Progress* (St. Bernard, 1928), p. 93.

21   Frank W. Langdon, "Introduction of European Birds," *Journal of the Cincinnati Society of Natural History* 4(1881), p. 342; George Laycock, *The Alien Animals* (New York, 1970), p. 65; Zipperlein, quoted in Ford and Ford, *History of Cincinnati*, p. 235.

22   St. Bernard, p. 93; *The Cincinnati Historical Society Bulletin* 30(1972), p. 183; George E. Stevens, *The City of Cincinnati* (Cincinnati, 1869), p. 30; Sidney D. Maxwell, *The Suburbs of Cincinnati: Sketches, Historical and Descriptive* (Cincinnati, 1870), p. 173; *Fanny to Julia, November 1, 1870*, reprinted in Owen Findsen, "Letters Become History Lessons," *The Cincinnati Enquirer*, May 1, 1994, p. H4.

23   Howe, I, pp. 788-789.

24   Zane Miller, *Boss Cox's Cincinnati* (New York, 1968), p. 25; M. King, pp. 52-53.

25   Miller, p. 25; Department of Public Service, Plate II; J. Beaujeu-Garnier

and G. Chabot, *Urban Geography* (New York, 1967), pp. 230, 294; Hurley, p. 84.

26   Condit, p. 4; George W. Engelhardt, *Cincinnati, the Queen City* (Cincinnati, 1901), pp. 13-14.

CHAPTER EIGHT

1   Flint, p. 29.

2   Hessler, p. 257; Ross, *Workers*, p. 6; C. Hammond, "Cincinnati," *The Daily Cincinnati Gazette*, March 23, 1830, p. 2.

3   Alwyne Wheeler, "Fish-life and Pollution in the Lower Thames: A Review and Preliminary Report," *Biological Conservation* 2, No. 1(1969), p. 25; Trever Holloway, "Back from the Dead," *Environment* 20, No. 5(1978), p. 8; Alwyne Wheeler, "Fish in an Urban Environment," in I. C. Laurie, ed., *Nature in Cities* (New York, 1979), p. 162.

4   City of Cincinnati Civil Engineer, *First Annual Report* (Cincinnati, 1858), p. 32; J. P. Kirkwood, *A Special Report on the Pollution of River Waters*, (original edition 1876, New York, 1970), pp. 404-405; Geoffrey Giglierano, "The City and the System: Developing a Municipal Service 1800-1915," *Cincinnati Historical Society Bulletin* 35(1977), pp. 229-230; Mumford, p. 388.

5   City of Cincinnati Health Officer, in *Annual Reports, 1866-1867*, p. 8; City of Cincinnati Health Department, in *Annual Reports of the City Departments, 1879* (Cincinnati, 1880), pp. 560-561.

6   Department of Public Service, Plate I; City of Cincinnati Health Department, in *Annual Reports of the City Departments, 1877* (Cincinnati, 1878), pp. 974-975.

7   City of Cincinnati Chief Engineer, in *Annual Reports of the City Departments, 1878* (Cincinnati, 1879), pp. 324-325.

8   Health Department, in *Annual Reports, 1879*, p. 560; City of Cincinnati Chief Engineer, in *Annual Reports of the City Departments, 1880* (Cincinnati, 1881), p. 838; Teetor, *Mill Creek Valley*, p. 78.

9   Hessler, p. 92; "Hartwell Area Grateful for Railroad," *The Cincinnati Post*, April 23, 1986, p. 2B; Schulze, p. 16.

10   Condit, pp. 20, 78, 92-93.

11   Engineer Department, in *Annual Reports, 1907*, pp. 873-874.

12   "How Shantytown Went Out with the Flood," *The Survey* 30(1913), p. 558; "Lose Homes as Shantytown is Planning 'War,'" *The Cincinnati Post*, June 27, 1911, p. 1; Nelson and Runk, p. 71.

13   Ohio State Board of Health, *Preliminary Report of an Investigation of Rivers and Deep Ground Waters of Ohio as Sources of Public Water Supplies* (Columbus, 1897-1898), pp. 22-24; Mayor of Cleveland, quoted in Wil-

liam G. Rose, *Cleveland: The Making of a City* (Cleveland, 1950), p. 447; C. Staley and G. S. Pierson, *The Separate System of Sewage* (New York, 1899), p. 297; Ohio State Board of Health, *Preliminary Report*, pp. 22, 24.

14 City of Cincinnati Sewerage Department, in *Annual Reports of the City Departments, 1887* (Cincinnati, 1888), p. 499; Department of Public Service, p. 47; City of Cincinnati Health Department, in *Annual Reports of the City Departments, 1892* (Cincinnati, 1893), p. 773.

15 Ohio State Board of Health, *Second Report of an Investigation of the Rivers of Ohio as Sources of Public Water Supplies* (Columbus, 1899), p. 182; Ohio State Board of Health, *Preliminary Report*, p. 34; Giglierano, p. 238.

16 Ohio Department of Natural Resources, *Southwest Ohio Water Plan* (Columbus, 1976), pp. 104-105; Ohio State Board of Health, *Annual Report for the Year Ending October 31, 1895* (Columbus, 1896), pp. 101-102.

17 Ohio State Board of Health, *Annual Report for the Year Ending October 31, 1897* (Norwalk, 1898), pp. 126-127.

18 City of Cincinnati Health Department, in *Annual Reports of the City Departments, 1897* (Cincinnati, 1898), p. 1536.

19 City of Cincinnati Civil Engineer, in *Annual Reports of the City Departments, 1869-1870* (Cincinnati, 1870), p. 51.

20 Engineer Department, in *Annual Reports, 1897*, pp. 1437-1438.

21 "A Sanitary Survey of Mill Creek Valley, at and near Cincinnati, O.," *Engineering News* 49(1903), p. 154; State Board of Health, *Annual Report, 1902*, pp. 20, 181-190.

22 Ohio State Board of Health, *Annual Report, 1903* (Springfield, 1904), pp. 159-160.

23 Ohio State Board of Health, *Annual Report, 1904* (Springfield, 1905), p. 38.

24 Department of Public Service, p. 47.

25 "Mill Creek," *The Cincinnati Times-Star*, Oct. 9, 1908, p. 4.

26 City of Cincinnati Engineer Department, in *Annual Reports of the City Departments, 1906* (Cincinnati, 1907), p. 948; Engineer Department, in *Annual Reports, 1907*, pp. 874-875; F. H. Waring, "Development of Sewage Treatment in Ohio," in *Ohio Conference on Sewage Treatment Annual Report, 1941* (Columbus, 1942), p. 25; Giglierano, p. 239.

27 Ohio State Board of Health, *Annual Report, 1910, Supplement: Report of a Study of the Collection and Disposal of City Wastes in Ohio* (Columbus, 1911), p. 103; Ohio State Board of Health, *Annual Report, 1910* (Columbus, 1911), pp. 29, 48, 114, 354-361; Waring, p. 25.

28 State Board of Health, *Annual Report, 1910*, pp. 127-128, 361.

29 City of Cincinnati Mayor, in *Annual Reports of the Officers, Boards and Departments, 1912* (Cincinnati, 1913), pp. 6-7.

30 Department of Public Works, in *Annual Reports, 1913*, p. 65.

31 H. S. Morse, in *Annual Reports, 1912*, pp. 67-68.

32 Department of Public Service, pp. 645-698.

33 *Ibid.*, p. 727; Graham R. Taylor, "Satellite Cities. III. Norwood and Oakley," *The Survey* 29(1912), pp. 287-288; Ohio State Board of Health, *Annual Report, 1905* (Springfield, 1906), pp. 157-158.

34 Department of Public Service, p. 218; Ohio State Board of Health, *Annual Report, 1913* (Columbus, 1914), p. 454.

35 "How Shantytown Went Out with the Flood," pp. 558-559; Condit, p. 116; Engineer Department, in *Annual Reports, 1907*, p. 874.

CHAPTER NINE

1 Health Department, in *Annual Reports, 1879*, p. 582.

2 *Exodus* 7:20-21; T. T. Macan and E. B. Worthington, *Life in Lakes and Rivers* (London, 1972), p. 266.

3 Clarence J. Velz, *Applied Stream Sanitation* (New York, 1984), p. 355.

4 Charles Dury, "A Revised List of the Coleoptera Observed near Cincinnati, Ohio, with Notes on Localities, Bibliographical References, and Description of New Species," *Journal of the Cincinnati Society of Natural History* 20, No. 3(1902), p. 109.

5 "A Sanitary Survey of Mill Creek Valley," p. 154.

6 State Board of Health, *Annual Report, 1903*, p. 159.

7 State Board of Health, *Annual Report, 1910*, pp. 48, 355; "River Extension Canal Was a Flop," *The Cincinnati Post*, June 27, 1986, p. 2B; "Canal Extension Paved Over in 1870," *The Cincinnati Post*, June 30, 1986, p. 2B.

8 State Board of Health, *Annual Report, 1910*, p. 355; State Board of Health, *Annual Report, 1913*, pp. 149, 287.

9 Department of Public Service, pp. 532, 723; State Board of Health, *Annual Report, 1913*, p. 454; "Canal to Be Drained July 1; Million Is to Start Subway," *The Cincinnati Enquirer,* May 17, 1919, p. 9.

10 Horace Johnson, "Notice to the East Fork Mill Creek, Wyoming Ave. Bridge," 1925, carbon copy in the Public Library of Cincinnati and Hamilton County.

11 Johnson, "Notice to the Lockland Wyoming Ave. Canal Bridge," 1925, Cincinnati Public Library.

12 Johnson, "Notice to the Arlington Canal Bridge," 1925, Cincinnati Public Library.

13 Johnson, "Notice to the Elliot Ave. Bridge Mill Creek," 1925, Cincinnati Public Library.

14 Samuel Taylor Coleridge, "Cologne," *The Poems of Samuel Taylor Coleridge* (London, 1912), p. 477.

15 "Passage of Canal Bill Near; Cincinnati to Benefit Greatly," *The Cincinnati Enquirer*, April 8, 1927, p. 24; "Should Be Vetoed," *The Cincinnati*

Enquirer, April 29, 1927, p. 4; "Ceremony to Mark Passing of Erie Canal at Middletown," *The Cincinnati Enquirer*, Oct. 28, 1929, p. 1; "Historic Event Is Recalled; Old Canal Abolished in 1911," *The Cincinnati Enquirer*, April 27, 1931, p. 24.

16 Department of Public Service, p. 721; "Turbulent Millcreek Finally Mastered; Now Flows into a Sewer," *The Cincinnati Times-Star*, May 24, 1930, p. 2; "Mill Creek Channel Being Cut," *The Cincinnati Times-Star*, Oct. 24, 1930, p. 16; City of Cincinnati, *Municipal Activities, 1930* (Cincinnati, 1931), pp. 74-75.

17 "Seek to Eliminate Mill Creek Odors," *The Cincinnati Times-Star*, May 17, 1932, p. 28; City of Cincinnati, *Municipal Activities, 1931* (Cincinnati, 1932), p. 27.

18 State Board of Health, *Annual Report, 1913*, p. 458; "Mayor Used Pick and Shovel," *The Cincinnati Enquirer*, Nov. 2, 1913, Sec. 2, p. 16.

19 "County Bond Issue to Build Creek Interceptor Sewer," *The Commercial Tribune*, Sept. 27, 1930, p. l; "Sewer Extension Assured," *The Cincinnati Enquirer*, June 27, 1931, p. 24; *The Cincinnati Times-Star*, May 24, 1930, p. 2.

20 "Millcreek Folk," *The Cincinnati Enquirer*, Sept. 11, 1931, p. 10; "Parade," *The Cincinnati Enquirer*, Sept. 13, 1931, Sec. 2, p. 2.

21 "Sewer, Started in 1913, Finished," *The Cincinnati Times-Star*, Dec. 24, 1934, p. 1.

22 City of Cincinnati Manager, *Cincinnati Yearbook, 1940* (Cincinnati, 1941), p. 3; City of Cincinnati Department of Public Works, *Report upon a Plan for the Disposal of Sewage* (Cincinnati, 1941), p. 7.

CHAPTER TEN

1 Richard L. Gordon, "Our Good Life," *Cincinnati Magazine* 3, No. 10(1970), p. 40.

2 Department of Public Works, Disposal of Sewage, p. 6; "Sewer to Allow Reclamation of Acres of Productive Land," *The Cincinnati Times-Star*, May 8, 1930, p. 15; "WPA Projects Being Speeded," *The Cincinnati Post*, Dec. 2, 1936, p. 5; Hurley, p. 127.

3 Department of Public Works, *Disposal of Sewage*, pp. 6, 47-48.

4 Department of Public Service, p. 20; Sewerage Department, in *Annual Reports, 1887*, p. 499; City of Cincinnati Chief Engineer, in *Annual Report of the City Departments, 1889* (Cincinnati, 1890), p. 692; L. Metcalf and H. P. Eddy, *American Sewerage Practice, Vol. l, Design of Sewers* (New York, 1914), pp. 205-206.

5 A. D. Caster, "Monitoring Stormwater Overflows," *Journal of the Water Pollution Control Federation* 37(1965), p. 1275; Department of Public

Works, *Disposal of Sewage*, p. 7.

6 *Ibid.*, pp. 7, 48;   Caster, pp. 1275-1276.

7 Department of Public Service, pp. 236, 727-728;   J. E. Root, "Sewerage and Sewer Disposal at Cincinnati," in *Ohio Conference on Sewage Treatment Annual Report, 1937* (Columbus, 1938), p. 44;   Department of Public Works, *Disposal of Sewage*, p. 7.

8 *Ibid.*, pp. g, 49.

9 *Ibid.*, pp. 7-8, 33;   City of Cincinnati Planning Commission, *The Cincinnati Metropolitan Master Plan and the Official City Plan of the City of Cincinnati* (Cincinnati, 1948), p. 29;   Condit, p. 116.

10 N. A. Clarke, R. E. Stevenson and P. W. Kabler, "Survival of Coxsackie Virus in Water and Sewage," *Journal of the American Water Works Association* 48(1956), pp. 677-682.

11 "Herron Avenue Residents 'Overcome' by Open Sewer," *The Cincinnati Post*, July 27, 1957, p. 4.

12 Ohio Department of Natural Resources, *Inventory Report*, pp. 39, 46.

13 C. F. Voegelin, "Shawnee Stems and the Jacob P. Dunn Miami Dictionary," *Indiana Historical Society Prehistory Research Series* No. 9(1940), p. 359.

14 Ohio Department of Health, *Report on Survey of Water Pollution Problems, Hamilton County and Cincinnati, 1963-1964* (Columbus, 1964), pp. 3-4, 33, 37, 39-44, 47-48.

15 "City, County Sewer Units Join Forces," *The Cincinnati Enquirer*, April 11, 1968, p. 17;   Dick Perry, *Vas You Ever in Zinzinnati?* (Garden City, New York, 1969), p. 123.

16 William Ashworth, *The Late, Great Lakes* (New York, 1986), p. 143; "Millions Join Earth Day Observances across the Nation," *The New York Times*, April 23, 1970, p. 1.

17 Gordon, p. 40;   Richard Gibeau, "New Hope for Mill Creek," *The Cincinnati Post*, Feb. 2, 1974, p. 1;   Frank Weikel, *The Cincinnati Enquirer*, Sept. 18, 1975, p. 43.

18 Ohio Department of Natural Resources, *Southwest Ohio Water Plan*, pp. 41, 356-357, 372.

19 Ohio-Kentucky-Indiana Regional Council of Governments, *Regional Water Quality Management Plan Summary Report* (Cincinnati, 1977), pp. 2, 7-8, 10-11, 25, 28-31.

20 Douglas Starr, "Mill Creek: Clogged Artery Where Water is Laid Waste," *The Cincinnati Post*, Oct. 3, 1979, pp. 1, 4.

21 Kay Brookshire, "A Stench Now Fills the Hollow," *The Cincinnati Post*, June 25, 1980, p. 1B.

22 Jim Knippenberg, *The Cincinnati Enquirer*, Sept. 24, 1985, p. F-1;   May 20, 1983, p. D-1.

23 Knippenberg, *The Cincinnati Enquirer*, Nov. 22, 1983, p. A-6.

24 Dale Stevens, *The Cincinnati Post*, Dec. 5, 1984, p. 12c.

25 James McCarty, "Plan to End Sewer Spills Gets Cheers," *The Cincinnati Enquirer*, April 24, 1986, p. B-1; David Ivanovich and Al Salvato, "Troubled Waters," *The Cincinnati Post*, Jan. 31, 1986, p. 1B.

26 Ohio Environmental Protection Agency, *Water Quality Inventory 1986 305(b) Report* (Columbus, 1986), II, p. 225-227; "Mill Creek Discharge Investigated," *The Cincinnati Post*, April 29, 1987, p. 2B.

27 John Erardi, "Pitchers' Pleas for Bat Support Not Unfounded," *The Cincinnati Enquirer*, Aug. 9, 1988, p. C-4.

28 John Eckberg, "Raw Sewage in West Fork Called a Threat," *The Cincinnati Enquirer*, March 15, 1990, pp. C-1, C-2; Nick Miller, "Waterway Spews Disease," *The Cincinnati Post*, March 15, 1990, pp. 1A, 5A.

29 United States Army Corps of Engineers, *Contamination Assessment Mill Creek Section 8* (Louisville, 1990), p. 9.

30 Richard Green and Mickey Higginbotham, "Sewers Brim with Toxins," *The Cincinnati Enquirer*, July 26, 1991, p. A-16; Greater Cincinnati Chamber of Commerce, *MSD: What's the Story?* (Cincinnati, 1992), p. 4.

31 Nancy Firor and Richard Green, "Agency Seeks Monitoring of Mill Creek," *The Cincinnati Enquirer*, Nov. 13, 1991, pp. B1, B6; David Holthaus, "Don't Touch Creek Water, Fish," *The Cincinnati Post*, Nov. 13, 1991, p. 9A.

32 Molly Kavanaugh, "Foul Creek Worries Park Visitors," *The Cincinnati Post*, June 26, 1992, pp. 1A, 7A; "More Debris Found in Mt. Airy Creek," *The Cincinnati Post*, June 30, 1992, p. 5A; Sarah Sturmon, "Warning Signs Go Up at Park Streams," *The Cincinnati Post*, Aug.22, 1992, p. 1A; Sarah Sturmon, "Signs Up at Filthy Creeks in Parks," *The Cincinnati Post*, Aug. 25, 1992, p. 4A.

33 Ohio Environmental Protection Agency, *1992 Biological and Water Quality of the Mill Creek Executive Summary* (Columbus, 1993), pp. 2-3; France Griggs, "GE Strips Tainted Soil from Mill Creek Feeder," *The Cincinnati Post*, April 28, 1994, p. 13A; Nick Miller and France Griggs, "Mill Creek Study Holds Some Hope," *The Cincinnati Post*, April 27, 1994, p. 6A; *Ohio EPA, Ohio Water Resource Inventory Executive Summary* (Columbus, 1992), pp. 5-6.

34 Metropolitan Sewer District, *Proposed Wastewater Management Plan Summary Report* (Cincinnati, 1991), pp. 8, 15; Sue Kiesewetter, "Tap-ins Will Be Disconnected," *The Cincinnati Enquirer,* July 21, 1990, pp. D-1, D-2.

35 Sarah Sturmon, "Source of Creek Filth a Mystery," *The Cincinnati Post*, Aug. 26, 1992, p. 7A; Nancy Firor, "Sewage Systems Flawed," *The Cincinnati Post*, Nov. 10, 1993, p. 1A.

36 Ray Schaefer, "OKI Says Water Is Polluted," *The Cincinnati Enquirer*, Aug. 14, 1992, p. D-1; Ohio EPA, *Ohio Water Resource Inventory*, pp.

5-6.

37 Ohio Kentucky Indiana Regional Council of Governments, *Reducing Nonpoint Source Pollution* (Cincinnati, 1992), pp. 1-4.

38 Hamilton County Environmental Action Commission, *Creating a New Vision for the Mill Creek* (Columbus, 1993), pp. 9-10.

CHAPTER ELEVEN

1 MacDonald, p. 13.

2 Ohio EPA, *Water Quality*, p. 227.

3 OKI Regional Council, *Summary Report*, p. 2; Ohio EPA, *Water Quality*, p. 227.

4 Department of Public Service, pp. 35, 181.

5 *Ibid.*, pp. 208, 272; Metcalf and Eddy, pp. 205-206.

6 Department of Public Works, *Disposal of Sewage*, pp. 7, 49.

7 Metcalf and Eddy, pp. 23-24.

8 City of Cincinnati Infrastructure Commission, *Report on Sewers. Executive Discussion* (Cincinnati, 1987), p. 2.

9 Donald Miller, quoted in MacDonald, p. 13.

10 Sharon Moloney, "City Sewers Virtually beyond Repair," *The Cincinnati Post*, Jan. 2, 1988, p. 2B; Infrastructure Commission, p. 2; France Griggs, "10-mile Tunnel Could Reduce City's Storm Water Problems," *The Cincinnati Post*, March 29, 1990, p. 8A.

11 Department of Public Works, *Disposal of Sewage*, pp. 50-51.

12 OKI Regional Council, *Management Plan*, p. VIII-26.

13 Department of Public Works, *Disposal of Sewage*, pp. 51-52.

14 City of Cincinnati Environmental Task Force, *Report* (Cincinnati, 1973), pp. 117-119.

15 Metropolitan Sewer District, pp. 15-24.

16 Frances Griggs, "Mining Cannot Cut Sewer Repair Costs," *The Cincinnati Post*, Nov. 29, 1991, p. 8A.

17 Sharon Moloney, "Sewer Work May Be Scaled Back," *The Cincinnati Post*, May 19, 1992, p. 4A; Richard Green, "Sewer District Studies Overflow Discharges," *The Cincinnati Enquirer*, Sept. 2, 1993, p. B1.

18 City of Cincinnati Environmental Task Force, p. 119.

19 Waring, pp. 23, 25; State Board of Health, *Annual Report, 1910*, p. 360.

20 OKI Regional Council, *Management Plan*, p. VIII-12.

21 *Ibid.*, p. VIII-11.

22 Hedeen, "The Mill Creek," pp. 14-16.

23 OKI Regional Council, *Management Plan*, pp. VIII-56, 64.

24 Ohio EPA, *Water Quality*, p. 225; "Union Twp. Sewer Ban Discussed," *The Cincinnati Enquirer*, July 2, 1992, p. C-2; John Clark, "No Surprise:

Butler Avoids Sewer Ban," *The Cincinnati Enquirer*, July 10, 1992, p. B-3.

25 Stanley E. Hedeen, "Sewage and the Mill Creek's Benthic Macroinvertebrates," in Ohio River Basin Consortium for Research and Education, *Multimedia Interactions of Environmental Pollutants* (Cincinnati, 1985), p. 55.

26 Edward J. Cleary, *The ORSANCO Story* (Baltimore, 1976), pp. 28-37, 109; OKI Regional Council, *Management Plan*, pp. X-17, 21, 22.

27 Ohio Department of Natural Resources, *Southwest Ohio Water Plan*, pp. 602-604.

28 Herbert C. Preul, *Mill Creek Reclamation Plan* (Cincinnati, 1993), pp. 1, 8; Rick Van Sant, "New Mill Creek Plan Cheaper," *The Cincinnati Post*, July 20, 1993, p. 7A.

CHAPTER TWELVE

1 Dick Perry, "Happy 200th, Cincinnati!," *The Cincinnati Enquirer Tristate Magazine*, Oct. 18, 1987, p. 20.

2 City of Cincinnati Civil Engineer, *Grades and Improvements in the Valley of Mill Creek* (Cincinnati, 1854), p. 5.

3 Council Committee on Public Improvements, pp. 1-2.

4 City of Cincinnati Civil Engineer, *Improvement of Millcreek Valley by Means of a Harbor and Docks* (Cincinnati, 1865), pp. 3-7.

5 "The Canal and Millcreek Improvements," *Cincinnati Daily Gazette*, Oct. 10, 1872, p. 2.

6 "The Gazette's Great Western Job," *The Cincinnati Commercial*, Oct. 19, 1872, p. 4.

7 "Our Breeders of Pestilence," *Cincinnati Daily Gazette*, Oct. 21, 1872, p. 2.

8 Civil Engineer, *Improvement of Millcreek Valley*, p. 4; William E. Merrill, "Harbor of Refuge at Mouth of Mill Creek, Cincinnati, Ohio," in *Ex. Doc. No. 34, House of Representatives, 44th Congress, 2d Session* (Washington, D.C., 1877), p. 4.

9 William E. Merrill, "Protection of the Commerce of Cincinnati from Damage by Ice-floods in the Ohio River," in *Annual Report of the Chief of Engineers, Appendix U* (Washington, D.C., 1878), pp. 814-817.

10 Merrill, "Harbor of Refuge," p. 1.

11 Arthur Maass, *Muddy Waters* (Cambridge, 1951), p. 21; Forest Hill, *Roads, Rails, and Waterways* (Norman, 1957), pp. 5, 37.

12 Merrill, "Harbor of Refuge," p. 4; William C. Langfitt, "Report of a Preliminary Examination of the Mouth of Crawfish Creek in the First Ward and the Mouth of Mill Creek in the Twenty-first Ward of the City of Cin-

cinnati, Ohio, as to Availability of Either or Both Said Locations for an Ice Harbor," in *Annual Report of the Chief of Engineers, Appendix DD* (Washington, D.C., 1894), pp. 1892-1893.

13   "Resolution of the Legislature of Ohio, Relative to a Survey of the Miami and Erie Canal," *Misc. Doc. No. 137, House of Representatives, 40th Congress, 2d Session* (Washington, D.C., 1868), p. 1; John M. Wilson, "Proposed Ship Canals from Toledo, Ohio, to the Navigable Waters of the Wabash River, and to the Ohio River at Cincinnati," in *Ex. Doc. No. 55, Senate, 46th Congress, 3d Session* (Washington, D.C., 1881), p. 2.

14   *Ibid.*, pp. 2, 10-11, 49-50.

15   Langfitt, pp. 1891-1893.

16   L. Anderson, pp. 1-12; M. D. Burke, *A Ship Canal from Cincinnati to Toledo, a Paper Read before the Engineers Club of Cincinnati, February 15, 1894* (Cincinnati, 1894), pp. 11-13.

17   "Survey of the Miami and Erie Canal, the Ohio Canal, etc.," *Document No. 278, House of Representatives, 54th Congress, 1st Session* (Washington, D.C., 1896), pp. 1-2, 16, 22-23, 60-61.

18   "Lakes to Rivers," *The Enquirer*, June 14, 1909, p. 6.

19   Sherman L. Frost and Wayne S. Nichols, *Ohio Water Firsts, Volume 1* (Columbus, 1985), p. 49; "Author of Bill Tells Plans," *The Enquirer*, Nov. 6, 1919, p. 20; "Foundation for Favorable Report," *The Enquirer*, April 4, 1918, p. 16; "Prosperity for Queen City Seen," *The Enquirer*, May 13, 1919, p. 9; "Canal Connecting Lake Erie with the Ohio River," *Document No. 188, House of Representatives, 67th Congress, 2d Session* (Washington, D.C., 1922), p. 2.

20   *Ibid.*, pp. 2, 19, 43-45.

21   City of Cincinnati Planning Commission, *The Official City Plan of Cincinnati, Ohio 1925* (Cincinnati, 1925), pp. 133, 145-146.

22   "Lake Erie and Ohio River Canal," *House Document No. 178, 76th Congress, 1st Session* (Washington, D.C., 1939), pp. 5, 27; "Ohio River-Lake Erie Canal Plan Revival Meets Instant Opposition," *The Cincinnati Times-Star*, April 25, 1940, p. 54.

23   "Mill Creek Valley and Flood Control at Cincinnati, Ohio," *House Document No. 198, 80th Congress, 1st Session* (Washington, D.C., 1948), p. 2; L. L. Tucker, p. 169; John G. Mitchell, "Will the River Stay 'Way from Their Door?" *Audubon* 89, No.3(1987), p. 31.

CHAPTER THIRTEEN

1   Mitchell, pp. 32, 34.

2   Vogt, Ivers, Seaman and Associates, pp. 5, 10.

3   James Hall, *The West: Its Commerce and Navigation* (Cincinnati, 1848),

p. 55; Civil Engineer, *Grades and Improvements,* p. 3.

4   *Ibid.,* pp. 3-7.

5   Ford and Ford, *Cincinnati,* p. 12; Vogt, Ivers, Seaman and Associates, pp. 3-4.

6   Ohio Department of Natural Resources, *Inventory Report,* pp.78-79; L. L. Tucker, p. 167.

7   Cincinnati Planning Commission, *Plan of 1925,* pp. 151-153.

8   L. B. Leopold and T. Maddock, Jr., *The Flood Control Controversy* (New York, 1954), pp. 99-101; John Maescher, *Flood Control, a Paper Read before the Cincinnatus Association, January 25, 1938,* CA Collection, Cincinnati Historical Society, p. 2.

9   Mitchell, p. 31; David Ivanovich, "The Day the River Ran Wild," *The Cincinnati Post,* Jan. 17, 1987, p. 1A, 4A.

10   George P. Stimson, "River on a Rampage: An Account of the Ohio River Flood of 1937," *The Cincinnati Historical Society Bulletin* 22(1964), pp. 101-102, 105.

11   *Ibid.,* pp. 105-108; Richard Miller and Gregory L. Rhodes, "The Life and Times of the Old Cincinnati Ballparks," *Queen City Heritage* 46, No. 2(1988), p. 36.

12   Ohio Department of Natural Resources, *Inventory Report,* p. 79; Ivanovich, p. 1A; Mitchell, pp. 28-30.

13   John Maescher, *Report on Flood Control, a Paper Read before the Cincinnatus Association, March 14, 1939,* CA Collection, Cincinnati Historical Society, pp. 2-5.

14   *Ibid.,* pp. 5-7; Edward Mitchell, "Engineers Plan for Biggest Flood," *The Cincinnati Post,* Aug. 26, 1946, p. 17.

15   "U.S. OK's Plan for Barrier Dam Here," *The Cincinnati Times-Star,* April 25, 1940, pp. 1, 55; Maescher, *Report on Flood Control,* p. 8.

16   Carl D. Groat, "We Ask Congress," *The Cincinnati Post,* March 4, 1940, p. 7.

17   Cincinnati Chamber of Commerce, mailed announcement of Barrier Dam Dedication, January 24, 1937, n.p.

18   City of Cincinnati Manager, *Annual Report, 1944* (Cincinnati, 1945), pp. 2-3; "Real Protection," *The Cincinnati Enquirer,* April 28, 1948, p. 4-A.

19   Glenn Thompson, "City in Luck," *The Cincinnati Enquirer,* June 8, 1951, p. 30; L. L. Tucker, p. 176; Ohio Department of Natural Resources, *Inventory Report,* p. 70; *The Cincinnati Enquirer,* April 28, 1948, p. 4-A; Curtis Lovely, "5000 Snug in Homes—Thanks to Dam," *The Cincinnati Post,* April 16, 1948, p. 8.

20   Leopold and Maddock, Jr., pp. 134-135.

21   "Mill Creek Valley and Flood Control," pp. 1-58.

22   United States Army Engineer Division, Ohio River, *Water Resources Development by the U. S. Army Corps of Engineers in Ohio* (Cincinnati,

1971), p. 29.

23   United States Geological Survey, *Water Resources Data: Ohio, 1983* (Washington, D.C., 1984), p. 196; "West Fork Reservoir Project Begins to Take Form," *The Cincinnati Times-Star*, Feb. 3, 1951, p. 11; Hamilton County Park District, *With Your Help It is Possible to Save Winton Lake* (Cincinnati, 1988), p. 2.

24   Ohio Department of Natural Resources, *Inventory Report*, pp. 70, 72, 78; Army Engineer Division, Ohio River, *1971 Water Resources Development in Ohio*, p. 29.

25   Nadine Louthan, "Sharon Woods Lake Cleanup OK'd," *The Cincinnati Post*, May 1, 1987, p. 3B.

26   D. L. Deonier, *Composition, Distribution, and Abundance of the Macroinvertebrates and Macrophytes of Winton Lake, Hamilton County Park District Project Report* (Cincinnati, 1987), pp. 4-17.

27   J. L. Funk and C. E. Ruhr, "Stream Channelization in the Midwest," in E. Schneberger and L. F. Funk, eds., *Stream Channelization: A Symposium* (Omaha, 1971), p. 9.

CHAPTER FOURTEEN

1   James Emly, quoted in MacDonald, p. 13.

2   Ohio Department of Natural Resources, *Inventory Report*, p. 78; *The Cincinnati Enquirer,* Jan. 22, 1959, p. 1A; "Elmwood Place," *The Cincinnati Post and Times-Star*, Jan. 23, 1959, p. 2.

3   MacDonald, p. 8; Gibeau, p. 1; United States Army Engineer Division, Ohio River, *Water Resources Development by the U.S. Army Corps of Engineers in Ohio* (Cincinnati, 1969), p. 83.

4   Army Corps Louisville District, pp. 1-4, 31-39.

5   William Weathers, "Dignitaries Acknowledge Opening of Mill Creek Construction Work," *The Cincinnati Enquirer*, April 24, 1981, p. C-2; "Mill Creek Project Gets Funding," *The Cincinnati Post*, Aug. 3, 1990, p. 5A.

6   "$10.7 Million in Budget Plan for Mill Creek," *The Cincinnati Post*, Jan. 9, 1989, p. 2B; Army Corps Louisville District, p. 3.

7   Karen Garloch, "City to Meet with Sponsors of Flood Control Project," *The Cincinnati Enquirer*, May 3, 1982, p. D-1; Lynda Houston, "Wheels Turn Slowly for Mill Creek Trail," *The Cincinnati Enquirer*, Dec. 6, 1988, p. Extra-15; William Leegan, quoted in Leland Johnson, *The Falls City Engineers* (Louisville, 1984), p. 218.

8   Henry Waite, *Transportation History of Cincinnati, a Paper Read before the Cincinnati Literary Club*, n.d., p. 16; "Channel," *The Cincinnati Enquirer*, Dec. 1, 1926, p. 13; Vogt, Ivers, Seaman and Associates, pp. 33, 47; "Interceptor Sewer to Replace Mill Creek," *The Cincinnati Times-Star*,

June 27, 1931, p. 2.

9   Eling, p. 95; Ohio Department of Natural Resources, *Inventory Report*, pp. 70-71.

10   MacDonald, p. 11.

11   Karr and Dudley, p. 60.

12   Linden-Ward and Sloane, p. 30.

13   Council on Environmental Quality, *Report on Channel Modifications, Vol. 1* (Washington, D.C., 1973), p. 339.

14   Funk and Ruhr, p. 10.

15   Miller and Griggs, p. 6A; Allen Howard, "Residents Worry Residue Will Cause Illness," *The Cincinnati Enquirer,* Sept. 25, 1987, pp. A-1, A-12; Scott Burgins, "Concern Over Former Dump Continues to Nag City," *The Cincinnati Enquirer*, May 30, 1989, p. A-1; Griggs, p. 13A.

16   Irene Wright, "On-site Skinner Cleanup Proposed," *The Cincinnati Enquirer*, May 24, 1992, p. B-8; Alison Grant, "EPA Announces Landfill Cleanup," *The Cincinnati Post*, May 26, 1992, p. East Central Neighbors-4.

17   Mickey Higginbotham, "Toxic-site List Stirs Demand for Action," *The Cincinnati Enquirer*, July 19, 1991, p. D-1; Scott Burgins, "EPA Offers New Plan for Pristine Cleanup," *The Cincinnati Enquirer*, Dec. 1, 1989, p. B-2; Robert Berger, "$200,000 to be Spent on Restoration of Natural Resources," *Environment Ohio* 6, No. 1(1992), p. 6.

18   Army Corps Louisville District, pp. 72, A-58.

19   Army Corps, *Contamination Assessment*, p. iii; Mickey Higginbotham, "Contamination Stops Mill Creek Dredging," *The Cincinnati Enquirer*, Aug. 21, 1991, p. G-1.

20   Sarah Sturmon, "Mill Creek Project in Jeopardy," *The Cincinnati Post*, Jan. 15, 1992, pp. 1A, 8A; Nancy Firor, "District Hoping for Army OK," *The Cincinnati Enquirer*, March 19, 1992, p. B-4.

21   Sarah Sturmon and Patrick Crowley, "Suburbs Object to Mill Creek Halt," *The Cincinnati Post*, May 12, 1992, p. East Central Neighbors-6; Sharon Moloney, "Corps Study May Spell End for Mill Creek Dredging," *The Cincinnati Post*, Sept. 4, 1992, p. 9A.

22   Leonard H. Fremont, "The Future of the Mill Creek," *The Cincinnati Enquirer*, May 24, 1992, p. H-2; Camilla Warrick, "Enthusiast Spies Trouble at Mill Creek," *The Cincinnati Enquirer*, April 26, 1992, p. B-1; Tony Lang, "A Flood-control Boondoggle," *The Cincinnati Enquirer*, March 31, 1992, p. A-5.

23   Sarah Pollock, "The Charge of the Brook Brigades," *Sierra* 74, No. 6(1989), pp. 24-25; Hamilton County Environmental Action Commission, p. 1.

24   Sarah Sturmon, "Living Future Seen for Mill Creek," *The Cincinnati Post*, April 6, 1993, p. 8A; Hamilton County Environmental Action Commis-

sion, p. 1.

25   *Ibid.*, pp. 1-16.

26   "Restoring the Mill Creek," *The Cincinnati Post*, April 13, 1993, p. 10A; "Mill Creek," *The Cincinnati Enquirer*, April 10, 1993, p. A-6; Richard Green, "Mill Creek Fate Discussed," *The Cincinnati Enquirer*, Aug. 26, 1993, p. C4.

27   "Restoring the Mill Creek," *The Cincinnati Post*, April 13, 1993, p. 10A.

28   "Mill Creek," *The Cincinnati Enquirer*, Aug. 31, 1993, p. A6.

Index

205

(Photo by Gregory E. Rust)

About the Author

STANLEY HEDEEN is a professor of biology and former dean of Arts and Sciences at Xavier University. He received his Ph.D. in zoology and botany from the University of Minnesota, where he studied as a Woodrow Wilson Fellow. He has authored several papers on animal behavior, population ecology, water pollution, and the teaching of biology. He is a member of the Hamilton County Environmental Action Commission and the Ohio Biological Survey Steering Committee and serves on scientific advisory committees for Oxbow, Inc., The Hillside Trust, and the Cincinnati Zoo and Botanical Garden. Dr. Hedeen is chair of the Ohio Department of Natural Resources Little Miami River Advisory Council and is former vice president of the Cincinnati Nature Center. He has received the United States Environmental Protection Agency's Environmental Quality Award for "professional and community activities which serve to improve the quality of the environment." He is a founding member, and currently serves as vice president, of the board of the Rivers Unlimited Mill Creek Restoration Project.

About the Publisher

THE GOALS of the Rivers Unlimited Mill Creek Restoration Project (RUMCRP) are to organize an interdisciplinary environmental educational program for students who attend junior and senior high schools in the watershed; to provide leadership and vision for the comprehensive, long-term restoration of the Mill Creek ecosystem; and to link school and community education and restoration efforts together.

Founding members of the board of Rivers Unlimited Mill Creek Restoration Project are Leonard ("Mike") Fremont, Marilyn Wall, Stanley Hedeen, Drew Diehl, Brewster Rhoads, Don Newman, and Jerald Robertson.

RUMCRP's school program features physical, chemical and biological water quality monitoring by teachers, students, and adult volunteers. Participants will use a local telecommunications network to share data, observations and recommendations among the multiple school districts in the watershed. Each spring, a student congress will provide an opportunity for students to report their findings and recommendations to each other, the media, school and elected officials, and the general public. The student conference will also offer skill-building and problem-solving workshops for participants.

In 1994-95, RUMCRP's first year of operation, thirty teachers and forty adult volunteers are assisting the organization in its educational work. The Metropolitan Sewer District and General Electric Aircraft Engines are partners in the school program. In this pilot year, about five hundred students attending twelve watershed schools in six school districts are participating in our environmental education program: St. Bernard/Elmwood Place High School; Wyoming High School; Reading High School; Lockland High School; Princeton High School; and in the Cincinnati Public School District, Porter and Bloom Junior Highs, and Aiken, Walnut Hills, Hughes, Withrow and Woodward High Schools.

The students, teachers and volunteers associated with this school program are urban environmental pioneers and the Mill Creek Restoration Project salutes their efforts.

Copies of *The Mill Creek: An Unnatural History Of An Urban Stream* will be donated to Mill Creek watershed junior and senior high school libraries as part of RUMCRP's interdisciplinary approach to teaching environmental education. Proceeds from the sale of this history book will be reinvested in RUMCRP's school program.

For more information about the Rivers Unlimited Mill Creek Restoration Project, contact:

Rivers Unlimited Mill Creek Restoration Project
Suite 610, Two Centennial Plaza
805 Central Avenue
Cincinnati, Ohio 45202
(513) 352-1588